HORSES NEVER LIE
ABOUT LOVE

The Heartwarming Story of a Remarkable Horse
Who Changed the World Around Her

JANA HARRIS

FREE PRESS

New York   London   Toronto   Sydney   New Delhi

FREE PRESS
A Division of Simon & Schuster, Inc.
1230 Avenue of the Americas
New York, NY 10020

First Free Press hardcover edition November 2011

FREE PRESS and colophon are trademarks of Simon & Schuster, Inc.

For information about special discounts for bulk purchases,
please contact Simon & Schuster Special Sales at 1-866-506-1949
or business@simonandschuster.com.

The Simon & Schuster Speakers Bureau can bring authors to your live event.
For more information or to book an event contact the Simon & Schuster Speakers Bureau
at 1-866-248-3049 or visit our website at www.simonspeakers.com.

Manufactured in the United States of America

1   3   5   7   9   10   8   6   4   2

Library of Congress Cataloging-in-Publication Data
Harris, Jana.
Horses never lie about love: the heartwarming story of a remarkable horse
who changed the world around her / Jana Harris.
p.   cm.
1. Harris, Jana.   2. Horses—Psychological aspects.
3. Human-animal relationships.   I. Title.
PS3558.A6462Z46 2011
818'.5403—dc23   2011020658

ISBN 978-1-4516-0584-6
ISBN 978-1-4516-0586-0 (ebook)

For Mary Nell Harris:
Long may you ride, neighbor and friend,
you are so sorely missed.

Horses Never Lie About Love

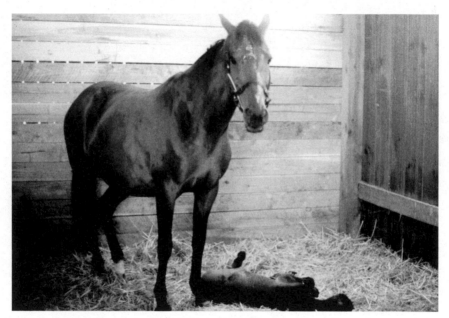

True Colors. *Mark Bothwell*

ONE

I've always had a hard time making decisions, especially decisions that involve spending money. I waffle, obsessively weighing the pros and cons, and eventually exhaust myself, in the end deciding nothing. But on this particular spring day over two decades ago, at a horse ranch in eastern Washington, I saw and knew exactly what I wanted.

It was May 1986. She was a deep red mare known as a blood bay, standing about sixteen hands—sixty-four inches at the withers, where the neck meets the back. Her arched neck flowed gently into her chest; her pretty head had a white star and a narrow stripe dripping down her face into two black nostrils. Something about the way she guarded her foal, an ebony two-month-old two-hundred-pound colt, spoke to me.

The rest of the Rocking D's herd of twenty Thoroughbred mares and their foals stood placidly in the intense noon sun. The mares—bays and chestnuts mostly, one gray—raised little puffs of smoke whenever one of them stomped a heart-shaped hoof in the dust. All the foals looked black, though they had a few white hairs like frost around their eyes and furry ears. It was hard to tell; my husband and I couldn't get closer to them than the corral fence. The mares had just been driven in from the range adjacent to the Rocking D, owned by Duke and Patsy, and weren't used to being handled; foals are timid by nature. How had these mares survived the hard winters in the rugged Okanogan? They were thin-skinned and fine-boned, their legs as narrow as my forearm.

As I was about to ask Patsy, who was standing next to me, the mares suddenly pricked their ears, all looking in the same direction at once. Behind an eight-foot-high barricade of telephone poles stacked next to a barn with a sagging roof, a gray stallion trumpeted, then furiously plowed the ground with a foreleg. Fine dust engulfed him, a Percheron from champion work-horse bloodlines. The massive crest on his neck foamed with sweat; his thick white tail cascaded to the ground, the ends

1

caked with manure. I couldn't see his expression because a white forelock covered his face, but his anger was palpable. Again my eye scanned his herd of mares.

"That one," I said to Patsy, pointing at the blood bay. "How old is she? Could we see her and her baby move around a little?" My words crackled in the clear dry air.

At that moment, the mare and her baby sauntered away from the rest of the herd, where they were all corralled in a barbwire enclosure built below a granite outcropping mottled with sage and tarweed. The foal stopped, dropped his head, then crooked his neck to nurse, taking shelter from the high desert sun in his dam's shadow. The mare's tail whisked rhythmically across the foal's sturdy back, sweeping it of flies. Not a hint of unhappiness in her expression; they were the perfect architecture of mare and foal.

Mark and I had just driven our Honda Civic six hours east from the coast to the Rocking D. Leaving the black-green rain forest and gloomy skies of the Puget Sound, we'd traveled an open-in-fair-weather-only highway over a treacherous mountain pass. Emerging from the countless white peaks that disappeared into a fog of clouds, we plunged around hairpin turns into the desert side of the state, the change in altitude making my ears pop. I squinted in the light from a different sun, a disc the color of the already dry grass it overlooked as it hung in an endless sweep of amethyst sky.

At the eastern foot of the Cascades, we turned north up a narrow valley heading for Duke and Patsy's ranch, which—according to the directions I held in my hand—was located on land leased from an Indian reservation near the Canadian border. I saw almost no houses and could count the trees, spindly pines, on one hand. The only shadows were cast by angular moonscape rocks jutting out from the benchlands. The air tasted as dry as ash, the visibility so clear I could believe that we were seeing all the way to the Northwest Territory.

I'd found Patsy's ad for a herd dispersal in a flea-market newspaper: *Thoroughbred mares with half-draft foals, sold together or separate.* The price: too good to be true—an incentive to drive halfway across the state into the middle of nowhere.

I'd lived and breathed horses as a child and felt lucky when I'd been given one as a teenager. During college and graduate school, and the next decade of being a poet in Berkeley, I'd hardly seen a horse, my lust for them going dormant. Then, when Mark, my research-scientist husband, landed a university position, we found ourselves living in rural New Jersey's horse country. We were so isolated that if I hadn't taken up riding again, I don't know how I would have found even one new friend. Now in our late thirties, we were back in the West with new teaching jobs, two riding horses, and some acreage we'd just purchased. Our new barn and covered riding arena (a costly affair but a necessity in Rain-land) left only a tiny budget, if that, for breeding stock, should we decide to breed horses. Did I say *decide*? It had been my childhood dream. I had to pinch myself to make sure it was actually me living this life: horses, a farm, and now maybe a mare-in-foal with this year's foal at her side.

As our car approached a smudge of a town, I rechecked the directions that Patsy had given me and looked at the map. We drove past a row of clapboard houses with pole beans growing in the front yards. Neat stacks of cordwood reached to the top of the eaves of cottages on either side of the state highway. Across a swift narrow river, rows of apple trees frothing with white blooms stretched toward bald hills dotted with brown-and-white cattle. We drove slowly past a row of brick two-story storefronts built in the 1920s; a grain elevator rose up to the west.

"When we come to a traffic light, turn right. Drive five miles, then start to look for a gravel road heading north," I told Mark.

He squirmed in the Civic's utilitarian bucket seat, his long back fatigued by our journey. "*This* traffic light?" he asked as he pulled up at a gas station.

"According to Patsy, it's the only one in the county."

"What're the chances of getting a triple espresso macchiato?" he asked, looking out the car window and scratching his high forehead. He yawned, running his long fingers through his pale blond mop.

"With an organic biscotti?" I joked. "I'll get us a Coke. After we find the gravel road, it's seven more miles." Clearly, we were headed to the end of the galaxy.

"Is there some way we could see her trot? And the foal?" I asked Patsy. It was a balmy day the temperature of bathwater; the sun warmed my back.

A short, sturdy woman in her sixties with a lined face the same color as the brown hills, Patsy shaded her gray eyes with her hand, a thin gold band on her ring finger her only adornment. She turned to Duke, who had been standing laconically behind us, the heel of his cowboy boot dug into the dirt. He was lean, silver-haired, and stood six feet, taller if not for the stoop in his back. Stubble the color of the granite outcroppings shadowed his jaw. Removing the battered cowboy hat from his head, he wiped the sweat band with one hand, then spat in the direction of the wire fence, his marble eyes fused to the flinty dirt near where I stood.

"What'ya say, Duke?" Patsy's tone was motherly. "We could move the mares down to the creek pasture for a graze so Jinny—is that what you said your name was?—can see 'em run around. Those other buyers'll be here soon—want a horse for their little granddaughter. Probably they'll ask the same."

Duke pursed his lips into a line so thin it looked as if his mouth were a gash in his face. He nodded. "Yeah." He smiled. "Let's give 'em elbow room."

As he strode off to open the wire gate, I studied the letters of his name tooled into the back of his leather belt. When we'd first arrived, coming to the end of the gravel road and Duke and Patsy's bunkerlike cinder-block house with a bearskin stretched across one side of it, I'd tried not to stare at Duke's huge belt buckle, with its territorial-era silver nugget set in the center. It made me feel as if we'd driven to a different century. After I'd pried my gaze away from the shiny buckle, I'd taken in the panoramic view from the Rocking D's ranch house, perched on a treeless bluff above an unpainted two-story barn, a stallion pen, and one corral. Below stretched the Valley at the Top of the World, its shoestring river fed by spring coulees and creeks rushing down from the white pin-nacles that fenced the valley on the west. Before Washington became a state, this part of the country was known as the Chief Moses Reserve.

As Duke opened the gate, the mares crowded together, eager to get away from the barn and into the open space. When they hurriedly moved away en masse, the stallion bugled after them, then threw him-self against his telephone-pole barricade. The stockade shuddered; the mares broke into a trot. Plunging down the loose dirt of an incline, some began to canter as they fanned out, stopping at the edge of an almost dried-up freshet. They dropped their noses to the ground and began looking for grass. Some of the foals were huge, already the size of yearlings. A few had begun to turn from black to steel gray. The largest one limped. I searched for my mare and found her guarding her timid colt—in equine parlance, a young unneutered male horse is called a colt, a female horse under age five, a filly.

"What's her name?" I asked Patsy. She and Mark and I had followed the herd into the open space, pausing to watch them graze.

"That's True Colors. When we go back to the house, I'll show you her papers."

As I walked toward the mare, she nuzzled her foal, and both quickly moved away. I took baby steps. I stopped, dropped my eyes, looked away. I walked backward toward her. Finally, I got close, but not quite near enough to touch her. I tried to memorize what she looked like: Her only white leg marking was on her left hind, a French anklet with two onyx dots just above the hoof. When I crouched down, she turned her head away, studying me out of her peripheral vision. Her eyes were wide and gingerbread brown. As she regarded me, there was something about the way her eyes softened, the way their warm color feathered into the pink of the sclera where the upper and lower lid met—the color of a desert sunset.

"What a handsome baby you have." I spoke in a low, singsongy voice.

Her foal had a perfect white star in the center of his forehead and reminded me of a breed of horse called an Irish hunter owned by several of my neighbors in New Jersey. True Colors sighed, then dropped her head and searched for grass. The colt eyed me with a combination of curiosity and alarm. I stared again at the mare's white hind ankle, noticing an old scar that made an S from the bulb of her heel up to her fetlock joint. She had no other blemishes.

The blood bay chewed a nub of grass, turned back, and considered me. She glanced at her baby, then again at me. I tried to read her expression. Doleful? "What are you trying to tell me?" I asked, inching my foot closer to her.

Duke shouted something from up near the barn, where he'd remained. Patsy stood about fifty feet away, talking to Mark. She called to me, "Duke says, 'Want 'em to move around a little?'"

"Sure," I said, but regretted it the next instant when I saw Duke lift a rifle and fire it into the air. The echo cracked back at us again and again.

All of the mares and foals bolted as if shocked with electric prods, some getting separated and then calling to each other hysterically. Up at the barn, behind Duke, the stockade shook as the white wave of the stallion's mane rose and fell above the top of the barricade. After a long few minutes, the herd sorted itself out as the dust they'd kicked up settled into the marsh. No horse seemed to have injured itself. What I had seen of True Colors's trot and canter looked acceptable for dressage, the riding discipline I followed. Some of the mares began to mill around each other, anticipating a second blast. Another mare caught my eye: a black bay that resembled "my" mare, but not as refined. The black bay's belly looked as if she had swallowed a Volkswagen. I pointed to her.

"Ain't foaled yet," said Patsy. "True Colors's sister," she added.

The dark bay may have taken an off stride or two when she spooked from the rifle shot. The gray mare with the refined Arab head had a chink in her back; she'd either cantered or walked but couldn't trot. Walking toward the black bay, I noted that she wasn't as tall as True Colors, maybe slightly over fifteen hands—one hand equals four inches. This mare watched me from the corner of her eye as she grazed, and I had no trouble walking up to her. Maybe not even fifteen hands, sixteen hands being the magic height of a dressage horse. But friendly. When I reached out and touched her shoulder, she flinched only slightly, as she would from a fly, then stepped away from me. Gentle, yes, but common-looking. And maybe lame.

After a few minutes, when no shot rang out, the more nervous mares stopped milling, and the herd calmed. The foals took a tug on an udder, then imitated their mothers, searching for new blades of spring grass. Some were so young that their necks weren't long enough to reach the ground, and they pawed the creekbed in frustration. My mare positioned herself and her foal at the edge of the swarm, the same way she'd stood at the edge of the knot of mares when they'd been corralled up near the barn.

"I want that one," I whispered to Mark as we followed Patsy back to the house.

He smiled approvingly. "She's the best-looking. Skittish, though." Our eyes met. I could tell that Mark was as stunned as I was by the otherworldliness of this place.

Inside, Patsy pulled out mismatched chairs from a table—planks laid across two sawhorses and covered with a yellow vinyl cloth—that took up most of the kitchen in their two-room house. Mark, Patsy, and I sat down near the metal utility sink. Duke sat at the other end of the table near the trash burner, where there was only one chair. "Needs his elbow room," Patsy said, dropping her voice. Even though the stove wasn't lit, I could smell woodsmoke eking out of the knotty pine walls.

"Oreo?" she asked, placing a chipped blue willow saucer of three cookies at our end of the table. She put on her reading glasses and fumbled with the accordion folds of a large manila file. "True Colors's papers," she said.

Duke jabbed a filterless cigarette between his lips but didn't light it. I studied the horse's pedigree: Round Table was her dam's grandsire—one of the biggest stakes winners in history. She had very decent bloodlines.

Patsy turned to Mark. "Don't ya got nothin' to say?" she asked. "You ain't said more than two words since you got here. Don't let us hens dominate the conversation." She had a high, nervous laugh. "Coffee?" she asked, jumping up and lighting one of the burners of a black restaurant-size stove. "Don't I got a lotta pep for an old broad?"

Mark's back straightened, and his eyes lit up. "I'd love some," he said.

Patsy unscrewed a jar of instant Nescafé with a strong meaty hand, and pushed the saucer of Oreos in front of Mark. I continued to study True Colors's papers, turning them over to look at the description of the mare's white markings: face, left hind, one cowlick on her neck.

"She's eight years old," I commented. "How long have you owned her?"

"Condensed milk?" Patsy asked Mark. The coffee tasted strong and bitter. Duke lipped his unlit cigarette. A white cafeteria mug of hot water steamed in front of him.

"Bought a load of Thoroughbred mares from an outfit in Yakima. Three-, five-, 'n' seven-year-olds," Duke said distractedly.

Patsy jumped in. "Some was in foal, some we thought we'd race at the Playfair track in Spokane."

"So she's been broken to ride . . . for the racetrack?" I asked.

Patsy didn't answer. "She was in foal," she said after taking several sips of coffee.

"How'd she get that scar on her hind leg?" I asked.

Duke's marble eyes widened, and he was suddenly animated. "Jumped outta the truck when she got here," he said excitedly. He took the unlit cigarette from his mouth and made arcing motions with his arm, tracing the mare's trajectory, his hand almost hitting the black stovepipe of the wood-burning furnace. "We'd just put down the loadin' ramp. I opened the tailgate and the first mare—they was packed tight—"

"Less likely to get hurt that way," put in Patsy.

"Just as the filly closest to the loadin' ramp started to walk down it, some harebrained mare panicked . . . True Colors lit over the side, snagged her leg on something, I guess."

I took a hard swallow of coffee. "Did the vet have to take many stitches?" I asked.

"Couldn't catch her," said Patsy, adjusting the collar of her faded pink flowered cowboy shirt. Pearlized snaps ran down the front of it. She pulled the top snap open. "So we let her range. It's what we did with all the mares when our racin' program fell through. Here's a picture of her first foal." To Mark, she passed a photograph of a sturdy chestnut as bright as copper teakettle. "That there one she's got on her now is her second foal. It was a coupla years after we got the racing mares that we bought our draft-horse stud, Knight of Knights. Your mare had both them foals on the range."

"You seen our stallion down there in the bullpen?" Duke asked Mark.

Mark nodded. No one could forget the one-ton gray pawing the ground and throwing himself against the stockade wall.

"Don't worry." Duke chuckled. "He can't get outta there." His small eyes glistened under the heavy overhang of his brow. "Percherons are natural jumpers," he added wryly.

"You the people lookin' for a jumper?" Patsy asked.

"Dressage," said Mark. "Kind of like ballet on horseback."

"Oh, so you *can* talk." Patsy laughed. "You ride, too?"

"A little," said Mark. "Still learning."

"What about your kids? They ride?" Patsy wanted to know. "I had high hopes of my kids cottoning to ranch work . . ." Her voice trailed off.

"No kids," said Mark.

Patsy looked stricken. "You newlyweds? How long you been married?"

Mark didn't reply.

"Almost nine years," I said after a silence. I braced myself.

Patsy's mouth puckered as if she'd bitten into a sour apple. "Poor Mark." She spat out the words one at a time with a breath in between.

She looked at me judgmentally but added, "Well, I don't blame a body these days for not wanting to adopt."

Mark raised his shaggy Harpo Marx eyebrows. I felt a long way from my world.

"I think I'd like to buy True Colors and her foal," I said. "But I want a vet to check and make sure she's in foal for next year."

Patsy smiled while biting her lip. I wondered why.

A stunning Thoroughbred mare that could foal on her own without complications and raise her baby on the range, showing it where to step, and how not to put its hoof in a hole—what a piece of luck.

"Vets around here are pretty busy vaccinating cows right now," Duke drawled.

"She ran with the stallion until two weeks ago, and I ain't seen no sign of her cycling," Patsy added. "I'm sure he caught her on her foal heat."

"What do you do in an emergency?" I asked.

Patsy looked at Duke and shrugged. "Turn 'em back to God," she said.

Nobody spoke. I took an Oreo from the plate and bit into it.

"We'll keep a close eye on her," Patsy offered. "She shows any signs, we'll put her back with him."

I scraped the white sugary filling off the cookie with my teeth. A Thoroughbred mare that could pasture-breed was hard to come by. Thoroughbreds were bred to do one thing: run fast at an immature age. Most of the sense had been bred out of them. Their hooves were notoriously shelly, their long-term stamina questionable. But this mare seemed to defy those odds. Her feet had good-quality black horn, not a crack or a chip, though the ground was hard and rocky. When I'd seen her move around in the dry creek pasture, she'd trotted sound, no evidence of stone bruises. Given her unprotected, almost feral life, I was surprised that True Colors had only one scar. Still, her distrust of people was a consideration.

"Here's that other mare's papers," said Patsy. "True Colors's sister."

I glanced at the Jockey Club insignia. "This mare's twelve," I said. I didn't want a mare older then ten. All the same, I looked over the documentation carefully.

"More coffee?" Patsy asked Mark. He shook his head. Duke banged his mug on the table. Patsy jumped up and poured him seconds of hot water.

9

"When's she due to foal?" I asked.

"True Colors's sister? Next couple of weeks. She's got a bag on her but no wax; you know, the clear stuff that comes out of her nipples before her milk starts to flow. 'Course, a mare can foal without giving any signs."

The crunching noise of tires rolling over gravel wafted through the kitchen window. I looked outside as a battered white pickup with an oversize camper lumbered up the road toward the house. When the driver braked, the camper lurched dangerously from side to side. A long trail of dust and exhaust slowly drifted toward the stallion pen.

"Them's the buyers from Wenatchee I was telling you about," said Patsy, quickly shelving the Oreos.

The young girl, Ronella, passed her pink plastic horse to her grand-mother and then began to make rapid jerking motions with her arms. "Horsey, horsey," she called in the direction of the Rocking D herd. She pummeled the air. Ronella wore pink cowboy boots, pink shorts, and a pink-striped T-shirt that didn't quite cover her poochy stomach.

Mark and I and the new buyers followed Patsy down to the creek for another look at the mares and foals. Duke lagged behind.

"She's almost seven, but she's still got a touch of the terrible twos," said Ronella's grandmother, a rosy-faced woman with sausage arms. She wore a ruffled Hawaiian-print shirt that billowed over the waist of her size-double-X jeans. Gammy had tiny feet and shuffled along in a pair of white tennis shoes, taking baby steps.

"We had to park her in the camper when we stopped at the casino," Ronella's grandfather told Patsy, his voice put upon. Butch wore regula-tion Wrangler jeans that looked as if they'd been washed and dried to his coat-hanger shape. His tooled-leather belt had a dinner-plate-sized sil-ver belt buckle, and his Western shirt was made out of the same Hawai-ian print as Gammy's blouse.

"She never naps long enough," said Gammy. "Thank Jesus for NyQuil cocktails."

"Jinny here says she's buyin' that mare and foal," Patsy said, pointing to True Colors and her baby. I smiled. Already I was proud of my pretty girl. Butch gazed politely at True Colors. Gammy clicked her tongue.

"Which horsey would you like?" Patsy asked Ronella.

I scanned the herd for the small dark bay, True Colors's sister. She dozed in the sun, her ears lolling. Her head was long but not unattractive. And no chrome—not one white marking on her.

Ronella pointed to True Colors's foal. "Mine," she said.

"No, 'Nella," said Gammy. "That one belongs to this lady here."

Ronella's face broke into a thousand pieces. "Mine!" she wailed, beating her fists against her grandmother. "Mine, mine, mine."

The herd looked uneasy. Most of the mares stopped eating, jerking their heads in our direction. True Colors pushed her baby to the other side of the herd. As my foal lowered his head and crooked his neck to nurse, True Colors gazed anxiously back at us, her head over the foal's back as if to shield him. Her ears were shaped like gilded lilies. Her perfect conformation and her white anklet with the two onyx jewels reminded me of the horse in an eighteenth-century painting at the British National Gallery: *Bay Horse and White Dog* by George Stubbs. Only the background was different. Instead of the English countryside, here there was a desert landscape: one cottonwood beside a bend in the creek.

I called to her, "Don't be afraid, Mom. We won't hurt you."

Ronella dropped to the ground, kicking and beating the scant grass. "Mine!" she screamed inconsolably. Her face reddened; tiny pebbles stuck to her wet mouth and pointy little chin.

"Let's find you another pony, sister." Butch yanked her to her feet by one arm.

"Don't forget about Trigger." Gammy waved the plastic horse.

"That one," said Ronella. Butch held her to his chest as they strode off after the largest foal in the herd, a steely gray colt that limped badly on one hind leg. Mark, Patsy, Duke, Gammy, and I watched as the pair was able to walk up alongside of him.

"How big will he git?" Gammy asked Patsy.

"Well, there's his daddy up there." Patsy pointed up the incline to the stockade next to the barn. "Could get as tall as Knight, but more refined, like these mares here."

"Why's he limping?" I asked.

"Sore foot," answered Patsy without hesitation. "The young ones got soft hooves. Stones, thorns—maybe he caught it in a groundhog hole. He'll come right."

I wondered how she could possibly know.

"And when could she ride him?" asked Gammy.

Mark and I exchanged glances. Did Ronella even know how to ride?

"Probably by the time he's three," said Patsy. "These crosses grow till they're five but have most of their height by the time they're three. If I was to guess, I'd say he'd grow to be sixteen, seventeen hands. Big, yes, but they got good temperaments, most of 'em. And ya know how horses love children."

Mark and I read each other's thoughts. Tiny child with possible developmental problems, paired with a giant unschooled horse. What could her grandparents be thinking?

Butch had gotten close enough to pet the large gray colt.

"Oh, don't that man have a way with broncs," piped Gammy. She shook her head in praise and adoration and wonder.

Patsy agreed. "Jinny here couldn't get closer than a few feet to the ones she's buying," she said, motioning to me.

As Butch tried to lift Ronella onto the two-month-old colt's back, Ronella shrieked joyously. I opened my mouth to object but held my breath and grabbed hold of Mark's arm. The foal's fear overruled his pain, and he leaped sideways, alerting the mares. The entire herd bolted, followed by a tremendous pounding of hooves. Flying dirt and creek stones hailed down around us. The herd moved off, funneling into the creekbed and then running along it like a road. In seconds they'd galloped up the freshet into a canyon and out of sight.

I took a long breath as my heart slammed repeatedly into my chest.

"Horsey, horsey, come back," Ronella cried, and her fists pummeled the air.

"It's okay, 'Nella," called Gammy. "Don't cry, cookie. Grampy'll give you a piggyback. Butch, put 'Nella up on your shoulders. That'll stop her crying."

Patsy, Gammy, Mark, and I walked back to the house. Ronella, her grandfather, and Duke started to hike up the canyon, where the herd had corralled itself in a blind coulee at the foot of a perpendicular granite ridge.

"I hope my new horse and her foal didn't get hurt." Though I tried to conceal my extreme annoyance, I wanted Patsy to know I felt rattled. Appalled, actually. I could tell by the way Mark grabbed my hand that he also felt shaken, as if we'd just witnessed an almost fatal car accident.

"You're a nervous one," Patsy told me, but not unkindly. "Got yourself a city girl, don't ya?" She winked at Mark.

Up at the house, Gammy excused herself and headed for her camper to take a nap. "Been a while since I had kids underfoot." She pressed her index fingers to her temples.

Inside the ranch house, I wrote Patsy a check for a mare in foal and a two-month-old colt. "So," I said, "no way to get True Colors preg-checked?" I was buying a mare in foal and wanted to make sure that was the state she was in. There was no way I could bring her all the way back here to be rebred. Besides, Duke and Patsy were selling out, moving to town—the one with the only traffic light in the county—because, Patsy said, "winter's gettin' to be too hard at the ranch." And because of Duke's heart condition. "Had it since he was a child," she added, "but startin' to affect his circulation."

"I'll watch her for signs of coming in heat," assured Patsy. As if on cue, the stallion bugled, then kicked the barricade. His white mane was so thick that it parted in the middle, falling on both sides of his neck. Even without grooming, his gray dapples gleamed in the relentless sun. He had no shade and, as near as I could tell, no water.

"Price of purchase includes delivery," Patsy went on.

"Middle of August would be best for us," Mark replied. I could see him mentally calculating all the work he had to do. We'd contracted to build the shell of a ten-stall barn and arena. It fell to Mark to finish the interior: build the stalls, hay loft, feed room, tack room, and grooming stall. We had two pastures for our two riding horses, but now we'd need to build paddocks. Suddenly, it felt as if we were in over our heads.

"Sure you don't wanna buy True Colors's sister, too?" Patsy asked. She handed me True Colors's registration papers and a bill of sale. "Then your foal would have a friend to grow up with," she added. "Easier for 'em that way."

It wasn't too late to change my mind. I could buy the other mare instead; she was older than what I wanted and not anywhere near as elegant and maybe lame (what Thoroughbred wouldn't be sore running barefoot on such rocky soil?), but she was more tolerant of humans. We were going to sell the foal next spring and use the money to buy hay. I exchanged looks with Mark. His eyes appeared silver in the indoor light.

I took a deep breath and let out a long, slow exhale. "If the other mare has a healthy filly," I said, "I'll buy the baby."

"Deal," said Patsy, immediately registering my check in her black account book. "Three horses delivered to your farm in August. A mare and two weaned babies."

Done, I thought. I suddenly knew that no matter what happened, there was one thing that I would never regret: saving this exquisite mare from whatever fate fell to her if I walked away without her.

At the time, I had no idea how difficult it could be to wean a foal, so I didn't thank Patsy for all her efforts in what I saw as purely a business venture. I probably should have. Though I'd ridden green horses and rogue horses, I'd never raised a foal. I'd never broken a young horse. I'd never foaled out a mare. I'd never euthanized a horse. I had no idea that breaking an older horse was different from breaking a youngster. I've often wondered: What if, at this moment, I'd been able to look down the long road that awaited True Colors, her foal, and me and taken back my check, forgotten that mare, her foal, and the little unborn one? What if I'd gotten into my car and on the road to home and never looked back? What would my life have been like?

Mark navigated our car south along the miles-long undulating gravel drive. The setting sun stained the sky the rust-red of Japanese maples. The color reminded me of the corner of True Colors's downcast eye as she had turned her head to her foal and then glanced back at me, her expression softening, entreating me not to harm her baby. Without ever touching her, I knew that this was a mare with a good heart.

As we drove, the country felt vast and treeless and empty: a narrow river valley cross-cut by darkening coulees and striated benchland. How had those horses survived on their own in this desolate range? The shadows lengthened. Neither of us spoke. Only a few hours ago, we'd been dabblers, equestrian enthusiasts who owned two pleasure horses. Now we owned five, possibly six—three or four more horses for the price of one, an instant farm family. All we had to do was wait.

Mark flipped on the car's headlights. "What are you thinking about?" I asked.

"About making hay from the grass in the back pasture of our new property," he said. He wondered how much used balers cost, and mowers, and manure spreaders.

As our car begin to climb the steep grade up the eastern side of the Cascades, heading back to the Puget Sound, I closed my eyes and dozed, thinking of my new broodmare. Little did I dream that I would own this horse for a generation, well into the next century, and invest more of myself in her than any other horse: this feral mare, the soon-to-be cornerstone of my farm and life; this albatross, this anchor—this grand passion.

TWO

Four months later, it was August, and an accusatory voice blared inside my head: *What have you done?* Who did I think I was, buying all these horses?

"We could use a wheelbarrow of shavings in both these shelters," I told Mark as we frantically tried to ready our farm for the arrival of two foals and a broodmare with a foal due next spring. Even when I was talking to my husband, *What have you done?* continued to reverberate. I called her Joan Crawford, that critical left-brain voice that rang through my thoughts. For the last month Joan had been screaming more than usual.

The two foals, True Colors's handsome steel-gray colt and the colt's half sister from True Colors's sister—a four-month-old filly that I'd never seen in the flesh—would arrive tomorrow after a long trailer ride over the mountains. True Colors would be delivered in a couple of weeks. Too difficult, Patsy told me, to bring the mare along with her just-weaned baby; Patsy would deliver the mom on her next trip west. Even though I was disappointed not to have my pretty girl, I also felt relieved. Two youngsters would be a handful, and they'd be here in under twenty-four hours. I was frenzied and worried. I'd never bought a horse sight unseen; what if I didn't like the second foal?

A week after she was born in May, Patsy had sent us a snapshot of Filly, a dark bay, like her mother. Filly had a dish face and looked more compact than my memory of True Colors's colt. I pinned the Polaroid on the refrigerator door in the kitchen.

Mark and I had already made two important decisions about the weanlings: what their formal names would be and where to keep them. Names for foals on our farm would start with an A and go down the alphabet. The colt would be named Abercrombie and the filly, beDazzled. We'd keep them where our riding horses lived before the barn was built: In a grassy paddock next to a fallen-down garden shed in back of the kitchen, there was a turnout shelter partitioned into two stalls. They'd be near the house, where we could keep an eye on them. A week ago we'd moved the two 16.2-hand geldings, Willie and Alazan, to their stalls in the giant new structure, and we were now busying ourselves preparing the foal pen.

I inspected the wooden fence of the paddock, making sure that all boards were tight. In the corner of each of the shelter's stalls sat a fifty-pound block of brick-colored mineralized salt. Earlier, Mark had clipped blue plastic five-gallon water buckets to the walls, hung high enough so that a foal couldn't get a hoof in it, and low enough so that the foal could reach it for a drink.

As we bedded the stalls, spreading fir shavings into the corners, I imagined a foal placidly eating hay in each box. Mark leaned on his rake as if it were a staff. We inhaled the comforting smell of wood flesh while studying the view out the shelter's door: The back pasture rolled down to a hedge of cedars that marked our boundary, then slanted toward the river a mile and a half away. Across the Skyqualamie's frothy rapids, the black evergreen spikes atop Haystack Ridge rose into an iceberg-blue sky.

Our farm consists of twenty-plus acres of south-facing slope in the foothills of the Cascades, an hour's drive northeast of Seattle. Long before we bought this property, it was a raspberry farm; before that, cornfields; and before that, giant old-growth cedar trees, none of which remains. The people who sold us the farm had abandoned the raspberry canes and run cattle. Only a month ago our new barn was a shell without power, the former cow pasture infested with blackberry briars, the house a sprawling "ranch" painted yellow and brown, flaking to aqua, the gaudy script letters of the former owner's initials bolted to the chimney. After endless farm hunting—nice house, rocky soil; charming cottage, boggy acreage—we settled here in the unincorporated fringes of a logging village because of the high ground and the fact that the charmless house built on a concrete slab wasn't going to fall down. Now the blackberries had been cleared and the front pasture along the road enclosed by a white fence, but the house was still an eyesore. Every time I thought of my new digs, Joan Crawford ridiculed: *I can't believe you live in that unsightly place.*

But our new land felt magical: well-drained pasture, a pond with a bridge to a tiny island surrounded by cattails, an elderly quince and apple orchard planted by the original homesteaders, and a painterly view. The sun and moon rose between a glaciated V in the mountain pass, always with intense slashes of color—goldenrod, watermelon, smoky lavender. As we signed the land sales agreement, we put aside the rumblings we'd heard about life in the northern foothills—forest fires started by lightning and trees downed by a relentless wind that blew October to March. We'd purchased the farm in the damp of spring; now, in late summer, the long days were sunbaked, the heavens unobstructed. At night, aquamarine cat scratches of the aurora borealis crawled out from the pencil-point tips of a state forest a few miles to our north. Best of all, the farm had a deep well with a powerful thrust of good-tasting water.

"Everything in order?" Mark asked. "What else do we need?"

After thinking about it for a minute, I decided that the foals could use a trough in their paddock. "Something they can't hurt themselves on," I said.

Baby horses are like three-hundred-pound toddlers eager to inspect everything. The bottom board of the fence had to be within six inches from the ground, so that a foal couldn't roll under it and get trapped or escape altogether. Foal pens have to be foal-proofed, just as houses have to be baby- or puppy-proofed. I have often wondered how horses ever existed in the wild. Of course, in the wild, they weren't fenced.

"What if we use a plastic muck bucket for a trough?" Mark suggested. His brow furrowed into his wavy blond hair, which I'd trimmed with my sewing scissors the evening before. Pulling a red bandanna from the back pocket of his jeans, he wiped sweat beads and wood dust from his temples, then continued smoothing the shavings over the dirt floor of the stall, the tines of his rake turned up.

A muck bucket for collecting manure could hold twenty-five gallons of water, and if a foal tried to step in it, he wouldn't get hurt. "Good idea," I agreed. My anxiety subsided an inch.

It was late afternoon. "What to do about dinner?" I asked, thinking out loud. Glancing at the back of the house, I studied the rectangular kitchen window, which a bird had smacked into that morning just as we'd sat down to coffee. I never knew what to do with damaged wild creatures. It seemed heartless to let them die, so I'd run outside into the shrubbery—a maze of azaleas and rhododendrons—to find the bird. Below the window, a young starling lay on its side stunned and panting, its off-black feathers glistening as if they'd been dipped in wax. After locating a dish towel amid our maze of packing boxes, I'd carefully picked up the bird and moved it a few feet into the rhododendron thicket, where it had shade and protection from the cats the former owners had left behind.

Now standing in the foal pen and staring at the smudge the bird had left on the kitchen window, I chided myself for forgetting to check on the starling at lunchtime. My eye followed the line of windows to the west, where a wing of bedrooms made a T with the kitchen. East of the kitchen, above the garage, an upstairs deck jutted out in front of the huge plate-glass windows of what the former owners—the cattle people—had called the Kegger Room, which they had built for their teenage children to drink in and we'd made into our sleeping quarters. While it was clear what we had to do to get ready for our new livestock, we had no idea how to make our house aesthetically pleasing. Incomprehensibly, the house had been built with no view of the mountains. To compensate, we'd had the barn and covered arena built with an unobstructed panorama of the sunrise and southern heavens: breathtaking, when we had the time or energy to stop and enjoy it.

I glanced at my watch: six P.M. The foals would arrive in eighteen hours.

Mark and I have opposite methods of attacking a major project. I take on a large task piecemeal, laboring slowly. Mark works maniacally straight through, pausing only toward the end to survey whatever Colossus of Rhodes he's been making. Looking back at his vast accomplishment, he says, is what gives him the adrenaline rush to finish the job. That's how he hand-dug the trench for the power and water lines from the house, under the gravel driveway, to the barn, a distance of a football field in length. We'd searched the telephone book for someone with a backhoe to dig the ditch. Caterpillars, road graders, and other unnamable earthmoving machinery adorned the neighbors' front yards. Despite many bookings, no backhoe with operator arrived.

The trench was only one of our farm projects. Now that we'd have five horses, our barn cried not just for stalls but for a hay loft, a grain room, somewhere to keep our saddles and tack other than on the floor of our living room. As if the barn weren't large enough, we needed an addition: a covered bin to store wood shavings for bedding. And with more horses, we needed three or four more paddocks. Luckily, we'd been able to purchase an old Mitsubishi tractor with an augur attachment for drilling postholes. Lumber proved to be an inexpensive commodity in logging country; Mark found a gyppo sawmill near the river. Over and over we had loaded the bed of our navy GMC pickup with twelve-foot-long fir boards, finally hauling home enough rough-cut lumber to build eight stalls with a hay loft. Mark tore down the roofless garden shed and used the old-growth cedar siding to wall in the barn's tack and feed rooms.

After commandeering a muck bucket from the riding horses, I secured it in the corner of the foal pen. When Mark connected the hose to the faucet at the back of the house, preparing to fill the new trough, I grabbed the nozzle and took a long drink, then turned the hose on Mark's shirtless sunburned back. He jumped, grimacing as if he'd just bitten into a quince from one of the gnarly trees in our orchard.

"Sorry." I giggled. "Couldn't help it. You looked so hot, and this water tastes so sweet"—no chlorine or metallic tingle, cold, with a deep earthy aroma.

Hand in hand, we trudged to the house to make something for dinner. Complete darkness didn't come until almost ten; we had hours to ready our farm for the foals in case we remembered something else that needed to be done. Pushing open the rickety back door to the mudroom, we pulled off our work boots and went into the kitchen. I won't say that we didn't cringe at the black-and-orange fleur-de-lis wallpaper and matching linoleum, but we were so exhausted that they no longer seemed to matter.

Our first attempt to give our home charm had been to call our property High & Dry Farm, a name with more than the intended meaning. As a teenager, I had lived with my family in a house built over a perpetually flooding river; I'd learned the hard way to pay attention to rising water and the proximity of a house to a floodplain. While Mark and I felt smug at being out of harm's way of the swiftly flowing Skyqualamie, now—finding ourselves the sudden owners of five horses—we feared becoming financially high and dry. What we didn't know then was that the state highway running through the town we lived near—one of only two year-round east-west conduits—was built in an old riverbed and without a dike. When the road to our farm on the high and dry hill later closed due to high water, there wasn't much we could do about it.

Though Joan Crawford yelled that I shouldn't make my husband cook after he'd done a long day's labor, I let Mark make most of the dinner. He was a gourmet; I was still working on the perfect hard-boiled egg. As a scientist, Mark was familiar with measurements and chemical reactions, so his cooking and baking took on an air of professionalism. No recipe stymied him; he could read cookbooks in three languages. For me, even Fanny Farmer was as foreign as Greek. Neither of us had had time to go grocery shopping, so tonight's meal would challenge Mark's culinary talents: dry staples, a few canned goods, and whatever we could forage. An abundance of pig weed—also known as lamb's quarters—grew where the cattle-loading chute had once been; some of the windfall apples from our old trees tasted almost ripe; and what was left of the jungle of blackberries yielded a sea of purple fruit.

After a dinner of lamb's quarters soup, apples sautéed with sausages, and blackberry cobbler, we stared out the window into the advancing dusk. Our house looked better inside if we didn't turn on the lights, so we lit a citronella candle borrowed from our camping gear. The low ceilings had been lowered even further by the cattle people, and the eaves outside the window allowed little light into the kitchen. Even though we'd made over two previous houses, one a redwood Victorian near a navy base in the Bay Area, and the other on the East Coast, a house built of chestnut just before the Civil War, we had no idea what to do with all this particleboard and plywood. Following Mark's gaze out the window into what we called the kitchen garden, I remembered the baby bird. After I cleaned up these dishes, I'd be sure to check on the little mite.

"Those eaves out there," Mark commented, "were designed for a house in Los Angeles. If I cut them back, more light will shine in."

"Great idea!" I cheered. "I'm overjoyed that renovations will begin with the exterior. That way I won't exhibit any 'symptoms.'"

We laughed at what I referred to as my mental disorder, my anxiety about house construction. As a child—before I'd lived in the house on the river that flooded—I had lived in the garage of a house that was never completely built. It had been so miserable and demeaning that, even as an adult, I felt a barely controllable hysteria at Sheetrocking and the nailing of the studs and boards of a new wall. Joan Crawford didn't help matters. As I carried our dinner dishes to the sink, she screamed: *You'll never get this place fixed up if you spend all your time and money on livestock.*

"Enough," I said, feeling a sudden need to visit my horses. Mark got up to join me.

It was a relief to go down to the barn, escaping the new house and the blighted memories it conjured. Hearing our footsteps on the gravel drive, the horses called to us; first deep-throated Willie, then the higher-pitched Alazan. I knew the neigh of each. Tonight theirs were happy voices, both overjoyed that we'd come down to their little village. We were their *people,* and our intentions might include the dispensing of treats. Horses aren't the brightest creatures—nowhere near as intelligent as dogs—but they're highly intuitive. The first thing our boys did was to read our body language, hoping to discover the reason for our visit. Their expressions asked: *Mealtime?*

The two huge sliding barn doors were open for ventilation and the view. Willie and Alazan stood side by side in separate stalls, a ten-foot-high plank wall separating one's copper shoulder from the other's blood-bay shoulder. I threw them each a flake of timothy grass hay—a flake is a section of a bale much like a slice of bread is a part of a loaf—and then checked to see if their water buckets needed filling while Mark picked the droppings out of their bedding with a manure fork.

Willie, my horse, was a stoic bay eight-year-old Thoroughbred crossed with a draft horse, similar to the breeding of the foals we'd just purchased. Alazan was a more animated seven-year-old chestnut Thoroughbred off the racetrack, probably a distant Jockey Club cousin to my new broodmare, True Colors.

"What'll they think of the weanlings?" Mark mused.

I shrugged. "Remember in New Jersey when I took Willie to a dressage show?"

At the competition held at a neighbor's farm, Willie had encountered new horses, none of them causing him to do more than prick his ears as we warmed up in the designated area. As I cued him into a canter, an Appaloosa trotted past us. I don't think Willie had ever seen a spotted horse; he froze in his tracks, the drum of his heart beating into my seat bones and vibrating up my spine. His attention riveted, his eyes widening so that the white sclera blazed out from his head. His posture asked: *Friend or foe?* I'll never forget it. The encounter felt primal: If Willie had decided to flee, I would have been powerless to stop him. I felt on the edge of panic myself, and it took all my strength to rein his head back in front of his chest and resume our warm-up. The first time Alazan saw a pony—a salt-and-pepper-colored Shetland—he tore to the far end of his paddock at a gallop, ripping off a shoe in the process.

The arrival of two foals was sure to undo these normally placid fellows. Horses are creatures of habit; newcomers to the herd spell disruption to the order of the universe.

I opened the five-foot-high stall door and bolted it behind me. Standing next to Willie as he bent his long neck to munch hay from the floor, I felt the heat radiating from his massive shoulder. He had pronounced

Willie eating summer grass in his new paddock. *Mark Bothwell*

withers that were higher than my head and shaped like Haystack Ridge. Slowly, I began rubbing the large bulging muscle at the top of his foreleg, then traced his elbow with my finger, scratching under his belly near his heart and along his ribs. His summer coat had a silken feel. I brushed him daily, and he gave off a clean-animal smell. Willie had steel-shod hooves and weighed about ten times what I did. Something about the rhythmic grinding of his teeth and the gurgling noises that came from his gut felt reassuring. Every now and then he would stop eating, bend his neck into the direction of my scratching, and sigh a peaceful sigh. Outside Willie's stall, Mark began to rake the gravel that paved the barn's center aisle. As Willie leaned into my scratching, I wondered at the partnership between equines and humans—female humans in particular.

When I was an adolescent, having a horse in my life meant I had a friend who was always happy to see me, a warm, large body that I could stand next to and feel protected by, one I could be intimate with, combing his mane like a doll's hair. My horse was a means of transportation as well as an athletic partner in a community of riding friends. Riding levels the playing fields of class and gender—in equestrian events, men and women compete on equal footing. On a horse, I was more than fleet of foot and had superhuman strength. In my more solitary moments, I often pondered what it means to me now, as an adult, to have horses. For one thing, it put me in a partnership with the forces of nature.

I went into Alazan's stall to check his left front hoof, which had just had its shoe replaced. Al's jagged blaze shore like a beacon through the dark. He had thinner skin and a shorter coat than Willie and was finer-boned, with a thick fire-colored tail that hung to the ground. When Mark's horse had started taking an off stride now and then, I had thought it was from a bruised heel. Instead of soaking his hoof in a bucket of Epsom salts, I took the opportunity to get to know my new equine practitioner before an emergency struck, colic being the emergency I feared most.

Dr. Darla, a pretty just-turned-thirty light brownette in date makeup, had appeared wearing every scent on her dressing table. The creases in the legs of her operating-room-green coveralls were ironed straight as rods, her fingernails recently manicured and shellacked. Darla picked up Alazan's afflicted hoof and, over my protests, pulled his shoe. In seconds flat, she took out a paring knife and carved what she said was an abscess

Alazan eats Mark's hat. *Jana Harris*

in the making out of the sole of his foot. Bandaging the hoof in Elastikon, she ordered me to soak it in Epsom salts twice a day for a week. Darla left me with an astronomical bill and a horse I had to keep in a stall. Our "get acquainted" visit had lasted less than half an hour and left me wondering what I would do if I had a real emergency.

Nervously, Alazan nudged me now with his teacup-sized nuzzle. "I'm not going to hurt you," I assured, leaning over and picking up his foot. When I pressed the bulb of his heel as hard as I could with my thumb, he didn't flinch.

"How's he doing?" Mark asked, anxious that his horse not be in pain.

"Seems completely healed," I said. Dr. Darla had made the right call.

Mark offered each horse an end-of-the-day carrot. Before walking up to the house, we stood in the open doorway, admiring the vast snow of stars in the firmament: Mars, Ursa Major, Lyra. We listened to the night noises: the piercing cry of a barn owl, the bullfrogs bellowing in the pond, the horses chewing hay. Though Joan Crawford disapproved of people who took better care of their barns than of their houses, her voice seldom intruded on my thoughts when I was occupied with a horse-related task.

That night I hardly slept. Sprawled on my back in our bed in the Kegger Room, I stared at the glittery white ceiling and the artificially smoke-streaked mirror behind the bar, which, because it was bolted to the floor, hadn't been removed with everything else, including light-bulbs, when the house was vacated. I had commandeered the bar as my desk—one of them; the room was as large as a dance hall and could accommodate big pieces of furniture in place of the pool tables the cattle people had carted away. I'd bought a swivel bar stool for the desk, and when I sat there, I had a view of the barn and paddocks, so I could keep an eye on my horses as I worked. Next to me in bed, Mark stirred, curled up, and slept on. Pulling the covers over my shoulders, I turned on my side, looking out into the night through the huge curtainless picture window next to our bed. Then I remembered the little bird.

Fumbling for a flashlight and finding one so weak it produced only a faded yellow disc, I padded downstairs barefoot. Stumbling around in the kitchen garden, I shone the light through the rhododendron thicket where I'd remembered setting the starling on a bed of dried leaves. My little bird was gone.

We woke at first light, the pumpkin moon still roosting in the crags of an old fir tree to the west of us. Just after I'd turned Willie and Alazan out in their separate paddocks, a battalion of geese stormed in, honk-ing wildly as they flew low overhead. It sounded like stones dropping as each bird, about a dozen of them in all, made a water landing in the pond. Alarmed, both horses jerked up their heads. The geese clucked and hissed as each pair staked out territory: the island, the bridge, the beach. When the geese settled, the horses went back to grazing. A coy-ote with the bushy tail of a fox emerged from a stand of alders and trot-ted down the slope of dried grass to the woods. The moon set. The sun rose, staining the glaciers on the ragged crags of Mount Whitehorse the deep pink of Syrah.

At just past noon, an old brown one-ton pickup pulling a long alumi-num-colored stock trailer rounded the hairpin turn and rolled along our fenceline. My heart thumped as the tow vehicle passed each white post. My foals, the cornerstones of the horse farm that I'd dreamed of since I was a child, were here. I could hardly breathe.

When the truck turned in to our driveway and pulled to a stop, the noise of hooves scrambling on the metal floor of the trailer rang out. I watched as two dark creatures, which appeared to be loose, milled in the back of the trailer behind two larger horses tied in front.

"Welcome," I said as Patsy cranked open the driver's side window. She was dressed in the same pink-flowered cowboy shirt with pearl snap buttons, new blue jeans, and a hand-tooled leather belt with a silver buckle. In the passenger seat was a twentysomething woman with short wavy dark hair and a pleasant freckled face. Patsy introduced her as "my grown-up foster child." The young woman smiled, showing a mouth of small angular teeth.

"Glad to be here in all this good clear air," Patsy drawled, her wind-burned face smiling up at me. I recalled the cloudless skies and dry air of the high desert and wondered what she meant. "Long time no see." She addressed her comment to Mark. "Imagine having smog where we live! Forest fires," she added. "The Okanogan's a tinderbox."

Patsy maneuvered her rig like a teamster and, with a few turns of the steering wheel, got the back of the trailer positioned in front of the entrance to the foal pen. Slowly, she and Mark opened the tailgate. Patsy stood on one side of the trailer, her foster daughter on the other. There was a rapid clattering of horned feet before the first foal jumped out. The second foal scrambled in panic, doing what sounded like a mad tap dance, then threw himself against the side of the trailer and fell to the floor. He rose, trotted in place for a few seconds, then took a giant leap out of the back. Patsy and Mark immediately slammed shut the trailer door behind him.

Two strange animals stood stone-still in the foal paddock, surveying their new surroundings with dazed expressions. Each wore a blue nylon halter; attached to each halter was about twelve feet of yellow nylon rope.

"Not quite halter-broke," Patsy explained. "Ya gotta sneak up on 'em and grab the end of the line to catch 'em."

Mark and I were speechless, amazed that the foals had gotten out of the trailer without catching their lead lines on the tailgate hinges; astonished that they had even survived the journey without hanging themselves.

The filly—beDazzled—was no longer bay but a steely black-gray. She didn't look much like the photo I had pinned to my refrigerator door. All the same, she was adorable. She had a pink heart-shaped upper lip and a tiny white star in the center of her forehead. Her short fluffy mane divided itself down the middle of her neck, and her bottlebrush tail had a tinge of silver in it. I stared at Coltie—Abercrombie—dumbfounded, unable to recognize the foal I'd purchased a few months ago. He was tall and angular, and the blades of his huge shoulders protruded from the base of his scarecrow neck. Something about him recalled a portrait of Abraham Lincoln: gaunt, gangly, unattractive, but with a kind, even mournful eye. The filly was far better-looking, with her round rump, short, arched neck, and narrow throat latch, where the windpipe meets the head on the underside of the jaw. She glanced around, then lowered her muzzle to the grass and immediately started eating. Coltie ran from us. Tripping over his nylon lead line, he stumbled in the direction of the paddock's far corner and cowered against the fence. When neither weanling would have any part of going into their new shelter, it occurred to me that they had never been inside any kind of structure until they had been loaded into Patsy's stock trailer that morning.

"Do they really need those ropes?" Mark asked.

"Ya can't catch 'em otherwise," Patsy said. "Never had halters on till yesterday."

"You wouldn't want to take them off," piped Patsy's young companion. "When I was a kid, I had to put a ten-foot rope on my gelding so's I could catch him. And that was after he was broke. He was a free horse, so's I didn't complain." She added, "Course, I've never been a complainer." The young woman looked to Patsy for confirmation.

Coltie stared at us, the white rims of his dark eyes widening. His flanks moved in and out rapidly, like a panting dog's. I could count every one of his ribs. Filly glanced up at the trailer, then put her head back down to graze. She was round as a melon. Her ears were tiny, and she had two pretty white anklets above the dark horn of her hind hooves, calling up the image of a little girl in a party dress with black patent-leather shoes and white socks. There is nothing in nature that is as white as the markings of a very young animal.

The trailer rattled, rocking from side to side as the two horses within grew restless, stomping their front hooves. One kicked the sheet-metal siding with a hind leg.

"That's Filly's mother in there," Patsy said. "If you wanted her, you're too late. We're delivering her to the Oregon coast today." She threw me a smug expression. The younger woman moved to the front of the rig to quiet the anxious mares.

The Oregon shore was a day's drive away. And if Filly's dam could come with her baby, why hadn't True Colors been delivered as well?

"What about the colt's mother?" I asked Patsy.

"Catched a cold," Patsy said. "I'll be bringing her in a couple a weeks."

I felt a ripple of concern but agreed. True Colors shouldn't travel while sick.

"They all get snotty noses from time to time," the young woman cooed soothingly as she reached her arm between the aluminum slats of the trailer and stroked one horse's neck. Patsy's foster daughter wore a blue pastel cowboy shirt cut just like Patsy's, jeans, and pointy-toed brown cowboy boots with high heels.

"You're still sure that True Colors is in foal?" I asked anxiously. Viral rhinopneumonitis—characterized by a snotty nose—often caused a mare to abort.

"Haven't seen any sign to the contrary," Patsy replied flatly.

Mark and I glanced at each other.

The colt tried to melt into the fence. Lowering his neck to the ground, he put his head in the shade of the corner post, his sides rising and falling rapidly. He didn't seem to notice the lush grass that his half sister was inhaling like a vacuum cleaner.

Patsy started her rig and pulled it forward so that we could close the gate of the foal pen. The filly's mother and the other horse nickered. Filly raised her head and called once, in a high-pitched chime of a voice, then returned to her dandelion greens.

"See ya in a few weeks," Patsy said, grinding the gearshift out of four-wheel drive. "Take care of 'em," she added, checking her face in the rear-view mirror. She put on a pair of wire-rimmed glasses and adjusted an earpiece. "With every mom and foal goes a piece of my heart." She gunned the accelerator pedal and didn't wait for a response.

I pointed to the colt and asked Mark, "Is that the same horse?" Where was my beautiful boy? The sight of the adorable filly chasing a bee from one yellow flower to another cushioned my disappointment, but only for a moment.

Mark shrugged. He seemed unconcerned that our "black stallion" had morphed into, if not an ugly duckling, an odd duckling. "Let's get those ropes off them before they strangle themselves." He headed to his shop in the garage for a knife.

We decided to leave about a twelve-inch length of rope attached to each halter. It was easy to snip the end off of beDazzled's kite string; she had an inquisitive nature and was soon sniffing the cuffs of my Levi's. Her little mouth looked like a rose, petaled in pink flesh. She nuzzled my hand and started to lick my palm. Her ears had tufts of fur growing out of them, and her foal coat felt fuzzy and soft.

"Maybe she wants salt," I said.

Soon I could pet her flat stuffed-toy back and run my fingers through her wild forelock. She had large, widely spaced almond-shaped eyes the color of India ink. When a fly landed on her round knee, beDazzled stomped a perfect bell-shaped hoof. She snaked her neck, which was set high on her chest, and the froth of her mane tossed in the air. Within seconds, her attention returned to the grass.

When we tried to get near enough to Abercrombie to cut his lead rope down to a foot in length, he scrambled, turned all legs, and flew insectlike to the other end of the paddock. I watched as his belly heaved and his black nostrils flared. His inky eyes filled with blind terror and looked like muddy wells that mirrored no light.

Filly sauntered into one of the stalls and started munching hay, then ran out and into the other stall, grabbing more hay. Tossing spears of timothy into the air, she discovered the water bucket, her head sinking into the container attached to the stall's wall. We watched as each swallow moved like a bird's egg down her muscular neck.

"She probably hasn't had anything to drink since yesterday," I said.

We backed off from trying to cut Abercrombie's rope and watched the foals inspect their new home. The two were obviously a comfort to each other, taking refuge in each other's shadows, smelling each other's bums, and chewing on each other's withers. Abercrombie tried to nurse from beDazzled and she tried to nurse off him, which made me wonder if they were really weaned. Each time one tried to nurse, the other went kicking and flailing angrily to the opposite end of the pen as if an assault had been committed. The next minute the offense was forgotten, and they were again trying to nurse.

Every time we got near the colt, he shivered violently from fright. Finally, we gave up on cutting his rope. Backing away from the paddock and shelters, I watched as Filly darted from stall to stall, in one door and out the other. After a while, she discovered that the roof shaded her from the sun and protected her from flies, and she settled in one of the enclosures. Abercrombie hung back but eventually followed. When he grabbed at a mouthful of hay, Filly aimed her butt at him; horse language for *mine*. He cowered in one corner of the stall, discovering the water bucket. He drank. She ate. He drank some more. Though she was smaller and younger by two months, she clearly had the more dominant personality.

"She reminds me of Miss Piggy," I told Mark. With her pudgy ham hocks, Filly even looked porcine, especially when she squealed in excitement. The skin beneath her two white hind anklets was piglet pink.

Miss Piggy sniffed the shavings, then sank to the floor of the stall, rolling with abandon. Wood curls flew against the walls and out the door, handfuls of them clinging to her mane and tail. As I leaned against the high plank fence that walled in the side of the turnout shelter facing the house, I felt her steal my heart. When she got up, Abercrombie sank to his knees in the center of the stall. They seemed to want to occupy the same box. He lay with his legs crumpled beneath him like a fallen bird, still panting. Suddenly, I felt too alarmed to take my eyes from him. From outside, I counted as his sides rose and fell ninety times a minute, almost twice what his respirations should be.

Should I summon the vet, the one I'd called for Alazan? Calling Dr. Darla for my shell-shocked colt didn't feel like the right thing to do. A vet would require this almost feral baby horse to cope with another stranger, one with an overwhelming artificial odor. And what could Darla do for him? In order to administer a tranquilizer and fluids, she'd insist on holding him down, then sticking him with a needle and forcing a plastic tube down his nose and throat.

As I watched the colt's sides heave, I feared he would die. His midnight eyes were so filled with trauma, and his body so rigid, that he reminded me of the starling that had stunned itself hitting my kitchen window. My heart filled with overwhelming sadness. Would this little horse ever fly across my back pasture? Looking at Abercrombie's vacant eyes, I wondered if his soul had fled his body. For once, Joan Crawford and I were on the same dark page: *What have you done?*

All I could think was: *Rest in peace.*

THREE

Patsy wrote that she was making a haul over the mountains, but there wasn't enough room in the trailer on this run for True Colors—too many moms and babies to be delivered to their new homes. Another letter: too many forest fires to chance a trip. The latest: T.C.'s cold had cleared up; now she'd developed a cough, better to wait to deliver her.

Sitting at my kitchen table, I pondered Patsy's communiqués, trying to decipher their true meaning. *T.C. has slipped—aborted—her foal*, I thought sadly. *They're rebreeding her and not telling me.* I stared at my newly decorated kitchen walls.

A few weeks after the foals arrived, our kitchen had undergone a surprise renovation. Mark and I had needed to attend a family wedding, and I'd asked a friend to horse-sit. I'd known Kolika (birth name Doris) since my Berkeley hippie days. Her boyfriend's family was from New Jersey; she'd sometimes visited us on holidays after Mark and I moved to the mid-Atlantic. Now that Kolika and I again resided on the same coast, our friendship had rekindled. A visual artist, Kolika lived in a commune housed in an old hotel on an island off the coast of British Columbia. Despite her unorthodox lifestyle, she was responsible and kind. She was also tall and muscular and could handle a horse. My reasoning went something like this: Kolika had kept horses during her married days in La Jolla, and besides, I didn't know anyone else I could ask to horse-sit for the three days we would be away in the Midwest. Absolutely no one. Kolika jumped at the chance of a paid vacation, if only to get away from what she called the "entrenched powers that be" at her commune, who were converting to a cooperative—whatever that meant.

Unbeknownst to us, Kolika had staged a reunion at our home with several artist friends, all foodies. For three days they'd eaten out of our garden, preparing exotic vegetarian dishes in our kitchen, which they found oppressively ugly. Someone started peeling off the wallpaper, revealing a mold-pink primer, which they had worked over with pastels. After several bottles of zinfandel, they'd decorated the walls with wildly colored fish on legs, leaves with faces, trees with udders, flowers with horns. Here and there an unpeeled swab of gaudy wallpaper was incorporated into the body of some unnamable, otherwise pastel beast.

When Mark and I returned from the wedding, the horses were fine, and the kitchen resembled the kind of vision you might have on LSD. "I told them you'd love it," Kolika informed me, her friends having long since vanished. We stood next to the kitchen island, speechless, our suitcases at our feet. Kolika was so proud of what she called my new "mural" that her smile spread across her tanned face into the viney braids in her cinnamon hair. "Bianca authored the fetal sea horses," she said.

"I thought those were snails," I said.

"Bianca's going through a rough patch," she said carefully. "This mural was amazingly therapeutic. And your riding horses: She really bonded with them."

I felt alarmed that Kolika had allowed a novice horseperson to handle the big and baby equines, but I couldn't think of how to word my complaint even if I'd had the energy to interrupt.

"Bianca's tried every fertility clinic on the West Coast," said Kolika, then changed the subject. "We spent hours currying Willie. Alazan was too jumpy—Bianca was afraid to go in his stall with him. She French-braided Willie's mane. He just stood there. She said she was completely blown away to have such a trusting relationship with anything so much larger than herself. He didn't even try to bite, though she did wonder if he meant to step on her foot—lucky she had shoes on that day. Anyway, she felt truly nourished—her exact words. She's going to make you a mandala from some of the hair that came out of Willie's tail. The only thing that put Bianca off was your collection of whips—"

"My dressage whips?" I asked. A strange woman wandering around in my horses' stalls barefoot? The word *lawsuit* flew through my head.

"She wondered why you beat your horses."

"I don't beat my horses!" I answered, truly annoyed. "I tap them on the butt, or the shoulder, or behind my leg on the flank, when I'm riding."

"I told her you'd never beat a horse," Kolika said, and changed the subject. She explained, step by step, how we should preserve our new mural: spray on Fixodent and paint with Varathane. Kolika pulled a camera out of her army-surplus backpack, pointed it at the wall next to me, and shot most of a roll of film.

"For your scrapbook?" I asked. Kolika's secondary art form was scrapbooking, chronicling her life and the lives of her artsy friends. She had every review of my writing ever published, pictures of Mark's and my impromptu wedding on a dock, photos of our "antique" houses in the Bay Area and New Jersey.

"I can't exhibit your wall, but I can mount these photos and run them by a couple of downtown galleries," Kolika said.

Speechless again, I pressed my palms into my forehead and listened to Joan Crawford, who had a few choice words: *Jana, the only way this house could look worse is if it were vandalized, and that's exactly what happened here.*

"I guess this means we'll start our renovations in the kitchen," Mark said after Kolika had loaded up her geriatric VW Bug and headed back to Canada.

"We can document it with Kolika's camera," I said. "She forgot it." My friend's Leica, with its colorfully embroidered shoulder strap, sat in a chair at the dining room table, where she'd set it down while hugging us good-bye.

In hindsight, Kolika was one of our less disastrous farm-sitters. As long as I've kept horses, the problem of finding competent equine caregivers has been ongoing. Kolika might have trashed a few walls, but she'd taken good care of our animals. She hadn't let her teenage daughters shop in my clothes closet; she hadn't stolen my few items of jewelry (of sentimental value only); she hadn't come to work nearly naked and high on methamphetamines; and she hadn't called us up when we were on the other side of the world to tell us that Alazan had come down with a serious illness and that her boyfriend the vet was putting him on a hundred-dollar-a-day antibiotic. When we returned from that trip, Alazan was in perfect health, but the vet was driving a shiny new truck.

Sitting at the kitchen table a couple of weeks after the foals arrived, I found it difficult to look at the pastel mural. I studied Patsy's letters, trying to read between the lines of her tightly formed script, and traced the wood grain in the table that Mark and I had purchased at the Trenton

Salvation Army and shipped here with the rest of our belongings. Duke and Patsy didn't have a phone, so we communicated by mail. That made it nearly impossible for me to air my concerns about my new broodmare or even about poor Abercrombie.

On the Saturday he had arrived and then collapsed on the floor of the turnout shed, I had ultimately decided to telephone the vet hospital. "His respirations are way too fast," I said, sobbing. A message machine took my frantic call, as if horses have health emergencies only during regular business hours. A woman from the answering service phoned back, giving me the vet's instructions: Take his temperature and get back to her service. How was I supposed to hold a rectal thermometer in an unapproachable three-hundred-pound baby horse for a minute and a half? I comforted myself with a grim fact: If the colt went unconscious, I'd be able to give the vet the information requested.

I had let Abercombie be, checking on him every fifteen minutes, sometimes every ten. In between visits to the shed, I kept an eye on him from the kitchen window, where I could see that his half sister occasionally marched into the shelter and touched her nose to his rump. She would then snatch at a sprig of hay and run outside to rip more grass from its roots. If the colt didn't get up soon, Filly would single-handedly render the foal paddock overgrazed.

Even though he was down, Abercrombie had been doing what is called in equine parlance "sitting up," meaning he was lying down with his neck and head up. But an hour later, he had sprawled flat out on the shavings-covered floor of the shed. I would be heartbroken if he died. My only consolation was that if he passed on, he'd die in peace, not wanting for anything I could give him. He was warm and sheltered from the elements; he'd drunk some water; food was at hand; and he had companionship. Most horses don't pass on under such pleasant circumstances.

After dinner, I walked out to look at the colt, afraid to get any closer to him than the shed fence. He lay unmoving, his eyes glazed and wide open as if he were dead. His barrel had stopped heaving up and down; his respirations were now shallow but still way too quick. Unconscious? His head jerked, then resettled. I never thought I'd be grateful for flies. Meanwhile, Filly—who reminded me more and more of Miss Piggy— jogged into the adjacent box, guzzled water, and began to munch hay. If her pasture mate was dying, she was unfazed by it.

The sun set. In the east, the first stars of evening glimmered above the raggedy snowcapped horizon. I tried to distract myself by watching television. We'd situated the TV in our living room next to our house's only remarkable feature, a stone fireplace crafted by an Old World mason. Mark built a fire. We sat in front of it toasting our legs as we sprawled on a Queen Anne couch we'd bought at Goodwill and re-covered with designer fabric. I dozed off for what seemed like a minute.

Midnight. The fire had dwindled, and the anemic light of television snow spilled over my feet as I fumbled for my shoes. As I stood at the kitchen window, it was too dark to see inside the shed, though the fence posts of the foal pen cast long shadows in the glare of a Day-Glo moon. I walked outside, slowly creeping up on the turnout. The horses down at the barn, Willie and Alazan, must have heard the mudroom door shut, because one of them whinnied. They sensed something out of the ordinary was going on. Had I fed them their evening hay? I couldn't remember. In addition to an acute sense of hearing, horses have a keen sense of smell; Willie and Alazan had no doubt caught the scent of newcomers.

Both riding horses whinnied again. Then something extraordinary happened. Their whinny was answered. Twice! Once by a soprano neigh and then by the voice of a different animal, a foghorn-deep call. Abercrombie was no longer lying on the floor of the turnout stall. Like the injured starling that had hit my kitchen window, the colt was gone. Peering around, I finally saw him standing in the paddock next to Filly, almost a hand (four inches, the width of a groom's hand) taller than she was, the long nylon rope still tied to his halter.

"Did you hear his voice?" I asked Mark, who had followed me outside. "He sounds like a bullfrog." Mark put his arm around me, and we hugged in relief.

Our verbal exchange ignited a volley of whinnies, most of which shot from the barn. Abercrombie stepped nearer to Miss Piggy, and they stood so close that they appeared to occupy the same piece of ground. The pair craned their necks in the direction of the barn, lifting their muzzles into the air.

The next morning at first light, Ms. Piggy (we'd modernized her name) and Kermit, as we now called the colt, were in their paddock nibbling grass. When I brought them hay, Ms. Piggy walked toward me, more curious than frightened; Kermit trotted to the farthest corner, but not quite as if his life depended on escaping me. When Filly let me touch her gun-gray shoulder, I scratched her satiny coat. The sound of her rhythmically chewing pale green stalks of timothy was comforting.

While the filly ate (there seemed to be no end to her appetite), Mark and I cornered Kermit near the old cattle loading ramp, which was covered in blackberry vines. His stork legs folded beneath him like origami as he collapsed on the ground. While I stroked his barrel, my hand moving ever so slowly over his ribs—any rapid movement brought him to the edge of panic—I felt his muscles relax a notch, then tighten. Just as he jumped up and flew away from us, Mark managed to cut his rope.

Before we could halter-break the foals—to take their halters on and off at will—and teach them to lead with a rope clipped to a ring on the halter, they had to be gentled. Gentling a four- or five-month-old horse was a language with which I was unfamiliar. It was important to accomplish this quickly, however, not just because we needed to take the foals down to the barn and acquaint them with their stalls and the

Kermit and Ms. Piggy about a week after they arrived
on our farm. *Mark Bothwell*

other horses, but because we needed to deworm them. Worm infestation can damage an equine's intestinal tract, making a horse susceptible to chronic colic. Deworming medication is traditionally given by mouth, though some anthelmintic products can be added to a horse's grain. These two had never seen grain and had no interest in it, to say nothing of oats adulterated with medication. Even hay seemed new to them. They'd been grass- and milk-fed.

Ms. Piggy was by far the better student. She wouldn't let us restrain her, but she did let us walk up to her and curry her broad back, then knead her rump. As she stood in the early-morning chill, her smooth-muscled shoulder felt like a hot-water bottle beneath my palm. Mark tried to run a brush through the rats in her tail while I occupied her head. Kermit stood a safe distance away, watching intently. I reached down and pulled a metal comb out of my grooming tote, then ran it through her mane. Anything that resembled a scratch was okay with her, especially in the area of her furry magnolia-bud ears and fluffy forelock.

"She's so fuzzy, it's like playing with an FAO Schwarz stuffed toy," Mark said when Ms. Piggy finally let him untangle the mat in her tail.

To train these two little ones, we needed something to use as a reward. But what? Ms. Piggy had nothing to do with a piece of carrot. Taking the orange stick between her baby teeth, she threw it against the wall of the turnout shed. But the second morning after her arrival, a rubber dish of sweet feed piqued Missy P's interest. Instead of snorting at her grain, she investigated the molasses-coated corn, oats, and soy-meal pellets, sorting the shapes with her prehensile upper lip. When I set a dish of sweet feed near Kermit, he backed away, cocked his head, and eyed it suspiciously. So far, all he'd consumed since his arrival was grass (which was getting sparse), a little hay, a few blackberry leaves, and innumerable berries.

Within three days of their arrival, we could walk up to the filly and pet her all over. If we were careful and took slow baby steps, we could approach Kermit without his bolting to the other end of the paddock. He watched as we attached a white cotton lead rope to Ms. Piggy's halter. When Mark pulled on the rope, I pushed from behind, standing to the side of the line of fire of her hind hooves, should she decide to kick. She never did, a good trait in a horse. To reward Filly for taking a step forward, Mark released the tug on the rope, and both of us showered her with praise. When nothing made her move, one of us pulled her off balance, so that she had to step to the side. Again we released the tug on the rope. When all else failed, we placed her rubber food dish a few strides in front of her, lifting the dish to her mouth when she stepped toward it.

In a few weeks' time Mark would go back to work, leaving early to teach an eight-thirty class at the university. I would be on my own, teaching the foals to lead. In October, I would also begin teaching a series of poetry workshops two evenings a week, a schedule that lent itself to animal husbandry. When we first moved to the farm, our commute was fifty-five minutes each way. After living in the Bay Area and near Manhattan, where long commutes were the norm, we considered anything under an hour a "short" drive. Alas, in twenty years' time—post-dotcom era after, 9/11, and following a real estate boom of unbridled development—it had gotten to be a record seven hours to drive to the farm from Seattle on a really bad night. But I'm getting ahead of myself.

In order to handle the foals on my own, I needed more than strength; I needed them trained. Training the foals could not be boiled down to arm wrestling with them—my strength counted for very little against the will of a horse. What I needed was finesse; the use of persuasion, leverage, the adroit maneuvering of two steps forward and one step back. The most important implement in my bag of training tricks was patience. There's an old horseman's saying: *The slow way is the fast way.*

The first step in training the foals was establishing communication. The language between horse and handler relies on more than mere speech, though certainly Ms. Piggy reacted to the tone of my voice, to a harsh *no* and a soothing *good girl* and the happy excitement of a praising *yes!* (Likewise, a horse communicates with his voice—the high-pitched frantic call of the foals when they'd first arrived, the bugle response of the riding horses down at the barn [*This is our territory, who are you?*], a low short neigh from one foal to another when one temporarily fell from the other's sight.) Basically, my communication with the foals was one of body language supplemented by vocal pitch and tone.

As I trained these babies, it was just as important for them to learn to read my signals as it was for me to be able to read their body language. A horse's instinct of self-preservation makes him a quick study of the lexicon of his handler's body. The dictionary of the horse's body language includes the ears: forward for startled, to the side for attention on the handler, pinned back for anger. A horse does even more communication with the other end of his body. Clamping the tail to the butt could mean the horse is cold or that he is guarding his hindquarters from the attack of a hostile or too playful pasture mate. If a horse consistently cocks his tail to one side, it might indicate some pain on the other side of his body. An elevated tail as a horse flies around his paddock is a barometer of high spirits. You always want to avoid getting stung by the swat of a tail. Right now the foals' tails were too short to swat anything, including flies, which continually frustrated them, evidenced by much tail swishing. An exceedingly cross expression crawled across Ms. Piggy's eyes whenever a bee-sized botfly (called a B-52) menaced her. To protect themselves, the foals stood head to hind, one flyswatter tail sweeping the insects from the other's face.

There's a large vocabulary of the tail. Sometimes when we were playing our training game of push-me, pull-you, Ms. Piggy swished her tail violently from side to side, showing anger or distress. I stood clear of her armaments should she retaliate—her hind legs could kick me, her front legs could strike me, her mouth could bite, and the point of her shoulder could knock me down, as could a swing of her butt. Some horses, particularly mares, are slower to put away their weapons than others.

Ms. Piggy never opened her full arsenal. Lucky thing, because we needed to teach the foals the lesson of "I tug on your lead rope and you follow" even sooner than we expected. The grass in their paddock was getting thin; we wanted to move Kermit and Ms. Piggy to more lush pastures so that the paddock could renew itself in time for True Colors's arrival, whenever that would be. I still hadn't received a firm date from Patsy and had started to doubt if I would ever see my beautiful mare again.

A week after the foal's arrival, I pulled Filly off balance, and she willingly took a step. Then she frisked my pocket, looking for pieces of carrot, the first lesson she'd mastered. I'll never forget her expression, the widening of her eyes and the batting of her lashes, when she realized that those orange sticks were . . . yummy! She was mad for anything carrot-colored—orange peels, screwdriver handles, a roll of boundary tape. I'd say it's a myth that horses are color-blind.

On the morning when we decided to introduce the youngsters to the adult horses, the colt still wasn't gentled enough to clip a rope on his halter. We could get close to Kermit and, moving our arms very slowly toward him, we could stroke his corn stalk of a neck—as long as we positioned ourselves on his left side. He didn't want us to stand on his right. If we did, he spun around to stare at us head-on, pulling one of his weapons and kicking out with his right hind leg. It took us a while to read him, but we figured out that the peripheral vision in his right eye hadn't yet developed. He did not want us to stand in his blind spot.

To introduce the foals to our "herd," we began by turning the riding horses out one at a time into the pasture that bordered the foal pen. I started with Willie, the calmer of our two adults. When I brought him through the gate to the back pasture, he stood stone-still, his neck and tail raised at the queer sight. Mark stayed in the barn, babysitting Alazan, who did not like being left alone without his buddy. Willie stared at the foals, then snorted loudly. The foals cowered in their turnout shed, both of them in the same stall, peering out the door, Kermit hiding behind Ms. Piggy. Willie pranced up and down the hundred feet of fence that separated him from the horse leprechauns. He ran and bucked and farted, then calmed to pacing the fenceline. After about fifteen minutes of this, the foals approached him, and he touched noses with them. Then Willie lowered his head and began grazing quietly near their pen. I took him back to the barn and brought Alazan out. Mark came along with us.

Alazan was very immature socially; I had never been able to turn him and Willie out together in the same paddock. Whenever I'd tried, Alazan persisted in taking dangerous liberties, his nose always in Willie's tail, dogging him so relentlessly that Willie eventually kicked his friend out of frustration. Horses don't like other equines walking on their heels. Before we'd owned him, Alazan had been kicked in the jaw, suffering a fracture, yet it hadn't taught him the lesson it should have. Today, however, Alazan was so entranced by the sight of the foals that I held tightly to his lead rope for fear he would run wildly around the ten-acre pasture, possibly (probably) tearing off a shoe and ripping up a hoof.

Ms. Piggy nickered. Alazan tried to bolt away from me, but I held tight. He snaked his neck, trotted in place, and finally settled down enough so that we could walk him toward the newcomers, each standing dead still, not knowing what to make of Alazan's behavior. It took an hour of hand walking Al along the foal pen fence for him to realize that there was nothing frightful (or "fight-full") about his new mates. By this time it was noon, and the only thing on anyone's mind, human or equine, was lunch: hay and an apple each for the horses; waffles and our own apple butter for us.

After they'd been with us for about ten days, the foals were tame enough that we could clip a rope to their halter and restrain them for deworming. We planned to squirt a syringe of creamy medication (though it smells like apples, I have no idea what it tastes like) into their mouths. Dr. Darla arrived in her dual-axle pickup, a sunny smile lighting up her round face. She wore shell-pink nail polish and lipstick.

"Twins," she joked. "They seem to be in good flesh," she added, standing outside their pen. "Look at that bone." She was referring to the wide circumference of the cannon bones in their legs, between the knee and the fetlock. Her midwestern accent caught in my head—she flattened her a's the same way Mark's relatives in Michigan flattened theirs. And she was light-brown-haired, like Mark's sister, who, when she was dressed up as a bride, looked just like Princess Diana. Come to think of it, Dr. Darla looked a lot like Princess Di, whose likeness was then ubiquitous.

The vet handed me several syringes of a mild dewormer. "Starting today, administer one of these every week for a month. After that, deworm each little guy once a month until they're two years old," she instructed. Darla did not volunteer to help us with this task, nor did she venture into the foal paddock for a hands-on examination.

"But the dose is by weight," I said. "How much do you think they weigh?" Since most horse owners don't own truck scales, a horse's weight is gauged by something called a weight tape, a cloth strip stretched around his heart girth. I owned such an item, but I didn't think that Ms. Piggy would stand still long enough for a measurement. Without doubt, Kermit would shy violently away from the strange-looking measuring device, thinking it an instrument of torture.

"Three hundred and fifty pounds," Darla guessed. Her eyes crinkled as she smiled. "Where's your broodmare?"

"Not here yet." I bit off each word. "I wanted to ask you about her. I think she might have slipped her foal. You probably won't be able to do a pelvic exam on her." (I couldn't imagine a vet getting close enough to True Colors to be able to put an arm up her rectum.) "Any other way we can determine if she's in foal?"

Kermit at five months old. *Mark Bothwell*

"Blood test," Darla answered.

"But can we get a needle into her?" Eventually, we'd have to; True Colors needed to be vaccinated for tetanus, which proliferated in settled areas more than on the range. The foals would also need tetanus shots.

"No problem," said Darla, her posture ramrod-straight.

I wished I felt as confident.

The results of the deworming paste shocked us. Within a day, what looked like vermicelli showed up in the foals' manure. In a horse that has been wormed regularly, the dead parasites are usually not visible without a microscope. These ascarids were white and about a quarter inch wide, some of them almost a foot long. The crows—as large as black chickens—picked the "pasta" out of the manure and flew away with it, but, realizing that the ascarids were tainted, they dropped their take, most of the vermicelli landing on the fence. It was a surreal sight, white ribbons flying from paddock rails, blackberry bushes, the old cattle-loading ramp, like remnants of Mardi Gras.

When it was time to move the youngsters down to the barn with the riding horses, we clipped a rope onto Ms. Piggy's halter, left Kermit loose with a halter on but without a lead rope attached, and opened the gate. Our reasoning was that we would restrain and guide Ms. Piggy, and Kermit would follow. We hoped that herd tendencies would work for us, that the foals would gravitate to Willie and Alazan now that they knew each other. Mark stood behind the filly and guided her butt while I operated the head. Kermit stayed close by, glory be. If he'd run off, Filly would have wanted to follow, and since her strength was greater than mine and her training unconfirmed, plan B was to unhook the rope from her halter and allow her to go off with Kermit until we could herd them into the barn.

One step forward, another to the side, we began leading Ms. Piggy through the strange territory of the front pasture, three hundred feet to the barn. Mark had fenced the front field, so if the foals got loose, they couldn't run out onto the road. It felt as if we were traversing the Oregon Trail. Step, rest, step. We passed the strange land formations that would become Mount Manure. Sometimes it took both of us to push Ms. Piggy forward through the prairie of swamp grass and past the old hand-dug well surrounded by a stockade of a fence resembling Fort Laramie. Onward in the direction of the Great Salt Lake—an old porcelain bathtub, sans claw feet, that the cattle people had used as a watering trough.

Slowly, we progressed to South Pass, the barn's sliding door, the foals' two stalls prepared just inside on the right-hand side with Willie and Alazan housed directly across the aisle. A step forward, a step to the side, pause, we let the filly drop her head to munch grass. Kermit veered to the left, trotted to catch up, nervously grabbing bites of clover as he went. When nothing else worked, I picked up Ms. Piggy's bell-shaped hoof and put it down a foot in front of her, then moved to her rear and pushed while Mark took hold of her lead. Until we got horses, Mark had always thought of himself as a dog person, so he tried to get Ms. Piggy to heel like a dog, with just the slightest feel of tension on the rope. For a few strides, it worked. "What a good idea!" I praised. Mark grinned—he was enjoying this more than I was. Later, I would realize what a good brain our little horse had. She didn't rear, or panic, or try to pit her strength against ours. As long as food was at hand, she remained reasonable.

As we moved Ms. Piggy and Kermit along the Oregon Trail, I was struck by their opposite symmetry. The filly was a study in spheres: the beach ball of her barrel, the globe of her rump, the disc of her jaw. The colt, on the other hand, was all lines and angles: the carpenter's square of his shoulder, his long cigar head, barbed ears, and sober triangle eyes; a razor back and hat-rack hips.

When we at last arrived at the barn door, both foals tensed; the change of light to dark spoke of danger. Our riding horses thrust their heads over their stall doors, neighing wildly. Alazan spun, his red mane flying, his fire-colored tail slapping the wall like a broom. I sensed Ms. Piggy's mounting panic as soon as Mark had pulled the sliding door closed behind us. When I unhooked her lead rope, both foals ran for cover, darting into the nearest stall. When Mark bolted the stall's door behind them, Kermit cowered in the corner. Ms. Piggy buried her nose in a pile of hay. When in doubt, eat.

We took a few deep breaths, not wanting to think about tomorrow, when we would have to somehow get both little horses out to their new paddock.

That night Kolika telephoned to arrange to have her camera returned. Bianca had moved into her co-op née commune, and Bianca's brother, a doctor in Seattle, was coming to visit her. If it was okay with us, Bianca's brother would stop by our farm and pick up the camera on his way to British Columbia.

"Maybe Mark knows him," said Kolika. "He works at the U." In the background, somewhere in the recesses of the huge decaying hotel where she lived (not a hotel, actually, but a former home for aged seamen), someone plucked the strings of a guitar.

"What department?" I asked.

Dermatology? Kolika wasn't sure. Mark didn't know Bianca's brother, which wasn't surprising. The university medical center had the second longest hallways in the nation (the longest were at the Pentagon); thousands of researchers worked there.

"Hey, thanks for putting your decorating skills to work in my tack room," I said.

"Your dressage-whip bouquet? Glad you like it," said Kolika. I felt her smile through the telephone. While we'd been at Mark's sister's wedding, Kolika had bunched my collection of whips together like a dried floral arrangement and made that corner of the barn look like a decorator showroom. I only wished my kitchen had turned out as well.

After I hung up, I thought about the foals and how, as soon as I had gentled them, I should accustom them to the dressage whip. Within a year or two, they'd be taller at the withers than my head, and when fully grown, they'd weigh about three quarters of a ton. A dressage whip would help them to respect my comparatively tiny size. Dismounted, if I wanted her to back up, I might press the whip longwise across Ms. Piggy's chest and say, "Back," while tapping her at the base of the neck. Or I might bop Kermit on the nose with the whip handle if I were leading him and he barged ahead of me. If he was a good boy, then I'd say so and stroke his neck with the broad side of the whip.

The phone rang again almost as soon as I'd hung up with Kolika. At first there was no one on the other end of the line, just static. Then a recently familiar voice called through the wires. "Jinny?"

"No *Jinny* here," I said with a laugh. "How about *Jana*?"

It was Patsy calling to say that True Colors would be delivered in a week.

I went into high gear and hardly slept. And I did something I'd seldom done on our farm: I watered the grass in the foal pen in the hope that it would grow. Here in the foothills, it rained almost every day, October to June, but it was late September, and the grass in the little paddock was straw-colored. Mark left early for work, but not so early that he couldn't help turn the foals out in their new paddocks. To get there, they had to turn a corner coming out of their stall and then walk forward in a straight line about thirty feet. I clipped a rope to Ms. Piggy, and together Mark and I guided her from the feed dish in the foals' shared stall to a feed dish in their new grassy paddock. Kermit followed.

Once the foals were out, I was free until I had to bring the horses back into the barn. Ms. Piggy and Kermit chased each other, ran from stinging insects, pawed the ground and rolled, then munched grass and played "touch nose and squeal" through the fence boards with Willie and Alazan. In the early afternoon, I brought all the equines into their stalls before the full heat of the day, when the flies began biting mercilessly. The riding horses came in first. They were always eager to go out in the early morning to graze and even more eager to come back in to the barn for hay and grain. But how to get the foals back in by myself?

I clipped a rope to Ms. Piggy. At first she walked alongside me, heel-ing like a dog, as Mark had encouraged her to do, but after about three steps, she stopped. I picked up a front hoof, putting it down a few inches in front of her. I pulled her off balance. Anything to get her to take a step. Kermit followed. Finally, I clipped a rope to his halter and tried to pull him along with the filly. If one foal took a step, so did the other. When we got close enough to the paddock gate, I unlocked it and swung it open wide. Once I got them to the open barn door, I unhooked both foals. Ms Piggy made a break for her grain. Kermit ran after her into the same stall. The next day I followed the same procedure but closed Ms. Piggy's stall door before Kermit could follow her in, leaving the adjacent door open for him to run into his own stall. Instead, Kermit ran out of the barn yelling high-pitched neighs of distress; Ms. Piggy threw herself against the wall and the door. A cloud of shavings rained down as the riding horses began to roil with excitement in their boxes. I opened the door to Ms. Piggy's stall, and Kermit ran in, almost colliding with his half sister as she tried to run out. In order to separate the two, I'd need to wait until they felt safe and at home here. When that would be, I had no idea.

The Saturday when True Colors was to arrive, we could lead both foals to and from their paddock. Still, it took two people: Mark leading Kermit while I led Ms. Pig. I was really proud of this—we could halter and unhalter the foals in their stalls. We were able to take off the blue nylon halters that they'd worn when they'd been delivered. The headpieces had been on the foals for so long that the band over the nose had made dents in their flesh. It was dangerous leaving a nylon halter on a horse and particularly dangerous leaving one on a foal—baby horses have very fragile necks. If the foal caught it on something, he could strangle himself; if a foal torqued his neck too violently, he could developed something called "wobbles" and be unstable for life. The rule is that if you leave a halter on a horse, it should be an old leather one that will break if pressure is applied. Before the foals arrived, I had ordered two leather weanling-sized halters that we used instead. To this day, I use Kermit's and Ms. Piggy's first leather halters on our baby horses.

Patsy's dusty trailer pulled into our driveway on Saturday, late afternoon. The Indian-summer sun shone citrus yellow, and it made me sad to think that by next month this lemony light would fade to a sidewalk gray. There was only one horse inside. True Colors. She stood frozen, not pawing or tap-dancing on the metal floor of the rig. I had her registration papers in hand. On the front, below the American Jockey Club insignia, her pedigree; on the reverse side, an explanation and drawing of her white leg and face markings as well as the location of her cowlicks, a sort of fingerprint of her identity. Even before I looked into the trailer, I could see that she wore a blue nylon halter with about ten feet of yellow nylon twine attached to it.

"Howdy," drawled Patsy as she rolled down the driver's-side window. "Got your new girl right here." Her short strawberry-gray hair frizzed on the ends. She'd driven over alone this time. When she saw Mark, her smile widened.

Peering into the back of the trailer, I studied the blood bay's leg markings: one white hind anklet with a few black jewels set into it just above her coronary band at the top of the hoof. I moved to the front of the rig. The first thing that jumped out at me wasn't that this horse had the same terrified look in her eyes that Kermit had, but her face. It was covered with sores that appeared to have been doctored with tobacco juice.

"What happened to her?" I asked. I was so startled that I could hardly get the question out. Mark came up behind me. The mare stared at us like a wild animal, looking searchingly through the slats of a cage.

"Just a fungus. Treatin' it with iodine." Patsy averted her gaze. "Brought ya some."

The mare's head was so raw that it was impossible to justify her white face markings with the markings drawn on her registration papers.

"It looks awful," I said. *Awful* was the least of the words that ran through my mind.

"She still coughs some," said Patsy, "but that'll go away. I knew ya wanted your mare, so I brought her, even though she's still got symptoms."

No mucus discharge ran from her nose. A cough was a residual stage of a cold that could hang on for weeks or longer.

"You think she's still in foal?" I asked.

"Don't see any signs to the contrary." Patsy's eyes bugged from behind her glasses. They looked red and watery, as if afflicted by allergies.

"Let's get her unloaded," said Mark, taking charge. "Same drill as last time. Back up to the gate there, and we'll unload her in the foal pen."

"How are them two critters gettin' along?" Patsy asked, putting her truck in gear.

"Fine." I had meant to tell her about Kermit's collapse and the horrendous amount of intestinal parasites we'd found in the foals' manure, but I didn't want to get sidetracked from the latest development. I thought: *Should I keep this mare or send her back? She's sick, and who knows if she'll get well. Or worse, if she'll infect the other horses. And her face . . .*

Patsy maneuvered the rig, and Mark unlocked the trailer's loading door, pulling it open. Inside, the mare stood petrified. When I got closer to her, I could see that she was quivering, her feet planted on the floor.

Joan Crawford spoke up: *Don't unload that horse. She's damaged goods.*

"Jinny, you might have to prod her a little," Patsy told me.

"I'm afraid if she makes a rapid move, she might get caught up in her rope and hurt herself," I said.

"Give her a little credit," Patsy retorted. "This girl's got a lot of horse sense."

I felt like holding my head in my hands. Was this really happening?

True Colors's eyes were so large that the white sclera around them made her look walleyed. She shivered uncontrollably. When I reached in to put a hand on her butt, her rock-hard muscles flinched at my touch.

"Lucky you," said Patsy. "This one's at least halter-broke."

Meaning what? That once, five years ago, she wore a halter, and now a halter had somehow been put back on her?

"We've had a little trouble medicating her face," Patsy added.

When the mare spun around to look out the trailer's exit door, the rope attached to her halter hit the side of the rig, the noise reverberating. True Colors paused for a split second, then, as if fleeing a badger, leaped into the abyss of our foal pen.

"She's kinda head-shy," Patsy said as True Colors ran to the end of the small paddock and stood, her nose skyward.

The mare's mahogany coat sparkled in the afternoon light, which slanted at an oblique angle as the sun sank below the western hills, earlier today than yesterday. I stared at her. True Colors had the fitness of a stallion. She was gorgeous, still reminding me of the Stubbs painting—except for her head, which was tattooed in those odd bloody shapes. She snorted. It would take me days to get near her, and it might be a week before I could start treating her fungus. The way her belly was sucked up into her abdomen told me she was almost certainly not pregnant. So lean, she looked as if she'd never had a foal.

Patsy banged the back door of the trailer closed in preparation for departure. *This is your last chance to send her back,* I told myself.

Say something, screamed Joan Crawford.

Patsy climbed into the cab, started the truck's engine, and pulled forward so that Mark could shut the foal pen's wooden gate, but she didn't stop afterward, just kept driving through the gate of the front pasture and out the driveway. As she turned onto the county road, she gave a short beep of her horn and waved, then cranked up the window, driving on around the hairpin turn and out of sight.

True Colors stared at me, her lovely gingerbread eyes showing their fire-streaked rims. What good feet she had: black horn, well shaped, even though a blacksmith had probably never worked on her. She lifted her tail, which had been chewed short by her foal, and once again I saw her perfect conformation and strong rear end, which in the world of dressage is called an *engine.*

Up until now she hadn't made a sound, but sensing the presence of another equine, Willy and Alazan called from the barn. True Colors gave one short blast of a neigh, followed by another. Even before the first note died in the air, Kermit began braying wildly. He'd recognized his mother! She didn't return his call, just turned her head slightly so that her right eye took in the barn. Frantically, he continued to whinny into the silence, but it was as if she felt that the comfort of her voice would endanger him in some way, and she remained mute.

After an hour of pacing the fenceline, True Colors began exploring her surroundings, walking into one of the turnout stalls, taking a hasty tug of water, and then running out again. Occasionally, she coughed. It wasn't a light hacking cough but a deep, full-bellied expulsion—not like the aftereffects of any respiratory infection that I'd encountered. I sighed. Mark grabbed my arm, and we went inside for a quick bite of dinner: squash soup, sautéed zucchini with tomatoes and mozzarella, apple pie from our just-picked fruit, Mark's specialty. As a wedding present, his mother had taught him to make pie crust. I bounced from the kitchen table to the window to check on our new arrival.

Later, when True Colors stopped pacing, I slipped through the fence boards. The first lesson she taught me was that if I wanted to get anywhere near her, I could not make eye contact. I couldn't look into those lovely dark pools of fallen leaves in rainwater. In fact, to get close to her, I had to turn my head completely away, with my eyes cast to the ground, and walk sideways slowly—very slowly—in her direction.

By the next morning, she'd calmed but was still impossibly skittish. No horse could move faster. She could go from the zero of a standstill to sixty across the foal pen at the drop of a daisy petal, a bird feather, the plunk of raindrops on dusty ground—who knew what made her shy away with so much force. It's called the flight-or-fight instinct. She wasn't a fighter, thank goodness, and never came at me.

Her cough didn't abate, so I sprinkled her hay with water, hoping that wet, dustless timothy would soothe her throat. Though she had no interest in the sweet feed I laid out for her, I watered that as well. When I first offered her a tub of grain, she stretched her long neck—her thin black mane longer than her neck was wide—snorted at it, and bolted away from the foreign smell of molasses. Unlike Ms. Piggy, she would not be coerced by food. How would I train her? Was it even possible?

As I stood near her, a dark green MG pulled into the driveway, top down, and a mid-forties sandy-haired man in walking shorts and a Tyrolean hat alighted without opening the door. The back of his car, I noticed, was filled with coils of rope as well as other hiking and rock-climbing equipment.

Joan Crawford hissed, *Who's the garden gnome? He hasn't washed that chariot in years. Not washing cars seems to be a theme around here.* Mark and I often joked that we had our cars painted more often than we washed them.

"Hallo," he called, lifting a tanned arm to wave. Bianca's brother, here for the camera Kolika had forgotten.

"Giles," he said with a heavy British accent; he and Bianca had grown up in Hong Kong.

"The camera connection," Mark said as we all shook hands.

Giles was jovial and disarming. He and Mark immediately began making small talk about university colleagues they had in common. We invited him in, handed him the camera, and offered him a beer.

"Beck's! Wonderful." Both he and Mark sat down at the kitchen table. Giles was about my height and compact.

"Pretzel?" I offered. I love the crunch of hard salted pretzels. No sugar, no fat grams. Helpful for keeping a dressage body, i.e., a lean butt, not particularly womanly, but it looks good seated on a horse.

Giles studied the kitchen walls. "I see my sister's been here." He laughed, gesturing to a chalk rendition of a fetal sea horse. "So, how do you like living with this?" He didn't wait for my answer. "Staying here changed her life, you know."

"No?" I didn't know. "Actually, we've yet to meet her."

"Then you probably won't." He smiled. "She's leaving for London next month." He shook his head at his sister's impulsiveness. "And she says she owes it all to you—her new calling."

"What calling?" I asked.

"She's on an animal anti-cruelty kick. Horses, to be specific," Giles said. His gray eyes gleamed like dimes. "She's going to work for a fringe group that started out as a fox-hunting protest organization and has gone a little off the deep end. Never mind the murder of foxes. They're now opposing the use of bits on horses. Too cruel."

"Well." I swallowed. "Some bits *are* cruel, but it's all in how they're used."

"Want another beer?" Mark asked our guest.

"Sadly, better not," he said, getting up from his ladder-backed chair. "A long drive, a long ferry ride, and a long queue at the border await me."

We walked Giles out the door and across the front porch, paved in the same stone as our fireplace hearth. True Colors had come into the turnout shed and looked over the stall wall at us as we stood in the driveway. This delighted me, a sign that she seemed to be warming up to the possibility of human companionship.

"One of yours, I presume," Giles said. "Gorgeous. Like something that eighteenth-century Brit, what's-his-name, would paint—Pumpkin, horse of Sir Nelthrope, sixth baronet, with groom." He started walking over to her.

I smiled. "She just arrived yesterday. She's really skittish. Feral, almost."

"What happened to her face?" he said, more to himself than to us.

"Fungus," Mark answered.

I said, "I haven't been able to treat it. The woman who sold her to us told me to put iodine on it." I'd been able to clip a lead to True Colors's halter—we'd cut off her long nylon rope as soon as she arrived—but I hadn't been able to dab those odd shapes of oozing skin. Patsy's assessment that the mare was head-shy was an understatement. True Colors backed away from the shed wall, a set of five evenly spaced planks like a stallion fence. "If I turn away from her—no eye contact—she'll come closer, I think." When I turned my face to the house, I heard her sigh and take a chew. Out of my side vision, I saw her stretch her neck and then take a baby step toward us.

Giles stared at her face, transfixed. "That's no fungus," he said. "That's a burn."

"A burn?" I asked, horrified. "Putting iodine on a burn . . . why do that?"

"Maybe to stop infection, I don't know, but don't do it," he said. "Iodine'll increase the possibility of scarring and . . . nice girl . . . it's painful."

"How do you know it's a burn?" Mark asked. We both stood open-mouthed.

"Burns are my field," he said. "I do burn research." Just then True Colors bent down and coughed, a hack that shook her entire body. "She's probably been in a fire," he added. "Sounds like smoke-induced lung damage. I see a lot of fire victims. Human ones."

My heart sank. Joan Crawford tried to speak, but it was as if she had pebbles in her mouth. The reason True Colors hadn't been delivered earlier became clear to me: When Patsy had delivered the foals, she had complained of forest fires not far from her ranch. But the tall trees were a long way from where she lived, so the fires she spoke of must have been range fires. I knew this to be true because some of my neighbors had gone to work fighting fires in the Okanogan. When Patsy and Duke had tried to load True Colors to deliver her with the foals, the mare must have escaped and run up that blind canyon where she'd galloped the day I'd first seen her. She'd gotten trapped in blazing sage and her head burned, her lungs damaged by smoke. The smoke damage had brought on pneumonia, which was why Patsy hadn't been able to deliver her after they recaptured her. True Colors hadn't coughed once on the day I'd purchased her, but since she'd arrived here, she'd coughed countless times. The telltale cough and the burns were new.

Looking into her face, so filled with harm and misfortune, I momentarily forgot about the pact I had made with her: no eye contact. As she turned slowly away from me, her eyes softened into an expression of resignation. A horseman's saying flew into my mind: *A horse never lies about its pain.* I crawled through the space between the boards of the turnout shed and walked haltingly over to her, putting a gentle hand on her terra-cotta shoulder. Her muscles stiffened, but she didn't move away from me. "No more lies," I whispered, my gaze fixed on her thin black legs and perfect hooves. "We'll take good care of you." As she bent her regal neck and took a chew of timothy, the flesh beneath my palm began to soften, and she leaned into my hand.

FOUR

What could I put on a month-old burn to keep it from scarring? Every time I looked at True Colors, my gaze ran to her disfigured face, and my hands clenched. A friend suggested that aloe might mitigate some of the damage. Though the metal buckles on Patsy's halter irritated some of the burn patches, I was afraid to take it off for fear that I could never get it back on.

It took two of us just to snap the lead rope to her halter. When Mark and I cornered T.C. in the turnout shed, she braced herself and quaked with terror as we approached, every muscle wound tighter than the spring in a jack-in-the-box. Wild-eyed, she stood poised, waiting for the right moment to bound away from us by leaping over our heads.

When I was able to get close enough to clip the lead rope to her halter, the snap's tiny noise sent her swaying forward and back, her beautiful eyes fractured with fear. We had intended to start by leading her around the turnout stall, but she was just too frightened. It hadn't dawned on me that the mere act of clipping the lead rope to her halter was lesson enough for a while. The idea of being leashed to a human was unthinkable to her.

For the moment I put aside making friends with her and tried to make peace. *Brush her while she's free-standing in her paddock,* I thought; what horse doesn't like to be itched and scratched? Don't horses spend hours standing head to tail, nibbling on each other's withers? A scratch is as good a reward as a lump of sugar. (Well, it might have been if she had any use for sugar.) Itching and scratching the foals was how we'd made friends with them, and I hoped that would work with T.C.

Over the next few days, it seemed easier to get close to her in the early morning. Then I realized that it wasn't the time of day, it was what I was wearing; rather than street clothes, she preferred me in my grubby barn jacket, a man's size large royal-blue parka with stains all over the front. Of course, a horse can't know such things, so it mustn't be how I dressed but how I smelled. In order to get near, I couldn't wear any kind of chemical scent—deodorant, soap, hair conditioner, fabric softener. When I put on my well-worn jacket that reeked of horse no matter how often I washed it, True Colors eyed me cautiously though not unkindly, and when she saw me coming toward her pen without any sign of a lead rope, she ambled to the far end of the paddock at a placid walk instead of a frenzied gallop.

Mornings turned foggy on the first of October. After breakfast and barn chores, I slid through the fence rails and slowly placed my grooming tote on the ground before approaching her, holding a natural-bristle brush in my hand. Turning my face away from her, I inched toward her shoulder, never making eye contact with any part of her except her dark hooves. The outside edges of her feet were chipped, but she wasn't long in the toe, which reminded me: I had to make an appointment with the blacksmith to reset the shoes on Willie and Alazan.

Tomorrow two dressage friends who lived up by the Canadian border would be dropping in to see my new breeding stock on their way to Seattle: Liz, a vet, and Kath, a trainer. I'd met them when Mark and I first moved to Washington State—we'd all boarded our horses at the same facility. Liz had offered to help me with T.C., worming her and giving her a tetanus vaccination. Kath was Canadian and not just a dressage trainer but an ace handler. Even so, I felt nervous. I didn't want to traumatize True Colors; nor did I want my friends to get hurt and T.C. branded a rogue. I considered calling a vet but suspected the ones nearby didn't have Kath and Liz's expertise.

Every time I headed for T.C.'s shoulder, the safest distance from a horse's hind hooves, she walked away. We went back and forth like this for about an hour until I began to lose patience, shifting my weight from one foot to the other. My temples throbbed, and I felt near the end of my tether. Meanwhile, the fog had burned off, and the day was brighter than I'd hoped—just high clouds. I had a lot to do before the rains came.

"Stand still, all I wanna do is brush you." My voice was sharp, the voice I used on Willie when I lost patience with him while we worked on walk-canter transitions.

True Colors sprang to the other side of the paddock, where she lifted her long lovely neck and put her muzzle to the sky, snorting into the apple-scented air. I went over to my plastic grooming tote, threw the brush into it, and marched out of her pen.

Okay, if lesson one had been *no eye contact,* then lesson two was *never lose patience* and certainly not my temper. I'd try to brush her again later. As I walked toward the house, the electric charge between us felt so strong that I could feel her mare eyes throwing darts into my back. The sensation made me stop midstride and reconsider: *No, I've got the situation the wrong way around. It's she who feels like my presence is throwing darts at her.* There she was, testing the fence, thinking about how she could get over it and fly away. I heard the squeak of a board as it bent against her weight, pulling at the nails that affixed it to the posts.

Willie, who was turned out in the back pasture, trotted over to see what the commotion was about. True Colors didn't flee him. She stood dead still as he reached his nose over the fence, almost but not quite touching her neck. When she stepped just out of his reach, Willy waited patiently for her to move back. When she didn't, he contented himself with grazing by her paddock fence. She stood stoically, not eating, not doing anything a vexed mare might do, no ears pinned back in Willy's direction or mine, no snaking her neck or striking a foreleg into the air, no wrinkling her upper lip or baring her teeth, nothing that said *stay away*—any and all of which would have been standard mare operating procedure. This was no ordinary horse.

For the rest of the day, I did not look at her or speak to her, other than a few cursory kind words. I threw her a little hay, brought her a tub of grain—which she continued to refuse to eat—and filled her water bucket via the terrifying rubber snake. I didn't dwell on her, coo to her, or tell her everything was going to be okay—not the cold shoulder but the indifferent shoulder. *My pretty girl,* I thought every time I looked at her wounded head, *who will see her worth now?*

Kath and Liz were both thirtysomething, tall drinks of water. Liz was from Texas, with big hair streaked blond and a leathery face. Kath had waist-length brown hair that she seldom tended other than to pull back in a rubber band. They arrived late and were pressed for time, pleading that they could stay only long enough to check out my new horses before traveling on to a big designer show of riding equipment in Seattle. Both women were visibly impressed by the foals and T.C., which raised my spirits immensely.

"They don't look like any range horses I've ever seen," said Liz, whose solo veterinary practice specialized in rural equines—pack horses, work horses, mules.

"Lovely," said Kath as we stood at the fence of T.C.'s turnout shed. Per Liz's suggestion, I'd closed both Dutch doors behind True Colors when she'd gone in for a sip of water. Kath was always looking for brood-mares to put to proven dressage stallions. Her untended hair, unmade-up face, and jumbled teeth gave her a slightly down-in-the-heels look that belied the truth. She'd grown up the only child of a cabinet minister. Liz the vet, Kath's glamorous riding student and business partner, was one of seven children, the daughter of a Texas oil worker. Both had been around horses all their lives.

"If she looks this good now, just think of how her coat will gleam after a few months of Dr. Grass," said Liz, referring to what Irish horsemen called the effects of good pasture.

"But what do I do about those burns?" I asked.

Prone to dark moods, Kath seemed as bright today as a field of mustard. She squinted at T.C.'s face. "You might have trouble justifying her appearance to her registration papers, because the white markings have been altered. I'd call the Jockey Club and ask them what to do."

A deep sadness crept over me. My lovely mare was permanently scarred.

"You're going to have trouble enough getting one tetanus injection into her," I said dejectedly. I kicked the ground with the heel of my paddock boot.

"Her legs are straight, and she's got really good feet. Who are you using for a blacksmith in this neck of the woods?" Kath wanted to know. A blacksmith could make all the difference in the world regarding a horse being lame or sound, especially when it came to trimming a young horse.

"Red Spenser."

"He's super," said Kath.

Kath and Liz worked well together, and our joint plan went off without a hitch. Both women, without hesitation, slipped between the fence boards of the open side of the shed. Before the mare knew what was happening, Liz had snapped a lead rope onto T.C.'s halter and held her with her nose pointed into a corner of the shed. Kath stood at the mare's shoulder and unscrewed the top of the syringe of deworming paste, handing it to Liz. With her free hand, Liz plunged it between the horse's lips and into the back of T.C's mouth. The mare froze, her eyes widening in surprise. Kath pulled the cap off the needle of the tetanus injection, and Liz popped it into the middle of the mare's red neck. T.C. swayed in alarm but remained rooted to the floor. Her eyes flashed. *Traitor.* She wasn't looking at the perpetrators, Kath and Liz, but at me. And then she bent her neck and coughed, her entire body going into paroxysms.

Liz unhooked the lead, and she and Kath slid back between the rails and out of the turnout stall. T.C. bounced from one wall to the other, shavings flying around us.

"She's had pneumonia," said Liz. She combed her frosted hair with her thin fingers.

"Her cough has gotten better since she's been here," I said. Still, it distressed me.

"I don't think she'll get heaves, but keep an eye on that cough; she may need antibiotics." *Heaves* is a term for equine emphysema. A horse with bad lungs is pretty much useless.

"Let her calm a little before you let her out into her paddock," said Kath.

"That might not be until next month," I replied, trying for comic relief.

"Listen to me for a second," said Liz, putting on her professional voice. "You probably won't see the vermicelli worms you saw in the foal's manure, because she's an older horse and has more of an infestation—though she doesn't look like a horse that's never been wormed. Tomorrow the worms are going to start dying and migrating to her midline under her stomach, so there'll undoubtedly be swelling there."

"How do I figure out if she's in foal?" I asked.

"Blood test," both women said as one. Clearly, no one wanted to stand behind T.C. and stick an arm up her rectum to feel for a fetus.

"Give it a little time before you have someone try to put another needle into her," suggested Kath.

Like forever, I thought.

"She'll probably be a little more skittish next time. Just remember, get in, get the job done, get out," Liz reminded.

I so wished that Liz didn't live a hundred miles away. Knowledgeable and capable, a horse genius, she often dealt with difficult horses and usually without a handler. Every equestrian should have such people in her life. I'd been on the farm only a few months, and already I'd called both of them several times, begging advice.

"Do visit Seattle often," I pleaded with Liz. "I'm not sure the vet I use here is going to be able to treat T.C. It has to be a woman, I think; this mare is too terrified of men. She won't let Mark clip a lead rope to her halter. And Darla's the only woman vet listed." I felt like a spurned mistress, begging my beloved to return.

The next morning, with a new day in front of me and the example of Kath's and Liz's expert handling, I tried again to brush True Colors. She looked at me incredulously, the memory of yesterday's assault still in the forefront of her memory. But the sight of her high withers, short back, and the way her hips moved her hind legs underneath her, instead of her legs flying out behind, made me take heart. She was so worth the time I had to spend gentling her. I let another day pass. Already I could see a swelling along the midline beneath her barrel where the dead parasites had migrated. Since she may never have been wormed, there was a possibility of permanent damage to her intestines, but I'd known this was a chance when I purchased her.

Another day went by—more swelling, so much that it slowed True Colors's reaction time (though only by a few seconds) when I tried to clip a rope to her halter. *Good day to groom,* I thought as I gazed at her nibbling on what little grass was left in the center of her paddock. Throwing caution to the wind, instead of walking toward her shoulder, which was as wide and *roja* as the state of New Mexico, I moved toward her massive hindquarters, where her well-shaped black tail occasionally whisked at a fly. The nights were cooling; fewer and fewer insects dotted the air. I needed to get True Colors settled into her stall in the barn before the torrential rains of late autumn set in and well before the first hard frost. And I wanted to fit her with her new halter. I'd come home after a quick trip to the grocery store this morning and found a UPS package on my doorstep—a fancy new triple-stitched halter with most of the buckles covered in black leather, a present from Kath and Liz.

True Colors stood with her hind hoof nearest to me cocked, the way a horse stands at rest, or the way a horse stands if she means to use her hoof as a weapon. I had no way of knowing T.C.'s intentions, especially if she felt cornered. We were in the middle of her turnout paddock, and my hope was that here she didn't feel threatened. I had no lead rope, only an old brush with no smell of newness.

We danced for about half an hour; I'd approach, she'd retreat. Willie walked over to the fence to watch, his gangly body covered by a navy cotton sheet. When I got her into the barn, I knew where I'd put her—in the stall next to Willie. She was eight years old and had never lived in a box; what would she think of living indoors?

With Willie to distract her, I got close enough to slowly reach out with the brush and touch her hip. At first she took a step away, but as I scratched her, she leaned into me. I scratched some more, brushed a very slow short stroke, took a breath, then brushed another slow short stroke. Turning her head, she sighed and regarded me. Brushing her rump was okay, she decided, and for days we continued in this way. When I first approached her, it was with a brush in hand and heading in the direction of her hindquarters. While averting my eyes from her body, I would slowly edge toward her shoulder and her head, where sometimes she would let me clip a lead line (carefully concealed in one of the large pockets of my barn coat) to her halter. This took endless time and tried my patience. My shortage of time and patience was T.C.'s ace in the hole. Unless I was willing to spend both, she wanted nothing to do with me. As I approached her, my body language had to shout, *I have all day, and I'm not leaving this paddock until I get you brushed.*

Friday: The blacksmith was coming in the afternoon to tend to Willie and Alazan. I wanted him to look at the foals' hooves as well. The sun filtered through the low clouds, and I began to swelter inside my jacket. Though it stank of horse, I was afraid to wash it.

I got the two geldings settled into their stalls and was in the foals' box, holding on to Ms. Piggy while Kermit struggled with his grain, when I heard a loud banging noise: Red Spenser's battered red Ford pickup with his motto, *No Hoof, No Horse*, painted in white block letters on the driver's-side door.

Willie had strong, dark-horned hooves, but Alazan's feet were brittle Thoroughbred feet with almost no sole, all of them white-colored horn, which is prone to cracking. Unless Red trimmed, shaped, and shod him once every six weeks, Alazan's feet went flat as dinner plates. Of all the local blacksmiths—sometimes called farriers—only Red knew how to drive a nail into the thin wall of Alazan's hooves without laming him.

After backing his truck into the barn's aisle, Red cut the engine. As usual, he started talking nonstop before he lit the portable propane forge and hoisted the hundred-pound anvil from the back of his pickup. "You on drugs?" he asked.

I laughed nervously. "Hi, Red. What kind of drugs are we talking about? Tylenol, Sudafed?" Blacksmiths are notorious storytellers, and Red was no exception.

Red seemed not to notice. "Lucky I got three levelheaded kids," he said. "'Cause I've got wife problems."

Deciding not to banter further, I led Willie from his stall, cross-tied him in the aisle, and tried to steer clear of any talk other than that of the animal being shod.

Red unclinched and pulled off Willie's old shoes, then pounded out four new steel shoes, all the while talking over the ear-piercing noise. My horses loved Red. He wore no chemical scents and smelled like sweat. He was naturally patient with equines, waiting until they relaxed a leg before he trimmed each hoof with his nippers, then filed it with a rasp.

Blacksmithing isn't merely a trade; it's an ancient art dating back to well before the Greeks, a time when cavalry strength could determine the outcome of war. It takes a keen eye to fit and nail a shoe to a horse's foot without laming him. Think of the hoof as a block of wood: When you drive six nails into it, it usually cracks. At the very least, when a horse is shod, the integrity of the hoof is compromised. As old-timers say, shoeing a horse is a necessary evil. A smith who can shoe a horse so that he is lighter on his feet than he was when he was barefoot is considered a kind of genius. Sadly, the horseshoeing lore of the ancients is lost; it wasn't written down, regrettably. Blacksmithing can be learned but isn't easily taught. Red had a gift.

After maneuvering Willie's left hind hoof—my horse was always touchy about lifting this particular leg off the ground—Red tossed his ginger-colored hair off his forehead and wiped his brow with a red and white bandanna. He had red hair all over what I could see of his slight body. Everything about him was red—nose, eyes, shirt, suspenders, even his appointment book when he could find it. He often arrived hours, sometimes even days, late.

When we finished shoeing Willie and Alazan, we stood in front of Kermit and Ms. Piggy's stall, looking in at them. "I want you to look at the foals before you go," I told Red. "I think they're still too wild to let you trim them, but maybe next time."

"Two-forty-five," Red said. "You're a schoolteacher, do you know if that would be high if that was your cholesterol count?"

"I really don't know what's high." I watched the foals munch their hay.

"The wife told me to pick up something at Safeway—razor blades? Matches? Baking soda? I have trouble with my memory, so I got my cholesterol tested at the pharmacy while I waited for the answer to come to me."

"Write it down," I suggested, trying to keep my answers brief. Now that we were finished with shoeing, I wanted Red's input on the foals.

"Write it down?" He grinned. "That'd be cheatin'. Hey, what color're them two?" he asked, his attention turning to Kermit and Ms. Piggy. "Do you think if I ordered three fishwiches instead of three Big Macs, my cholesterol would go down?" Red didn't have a pound of fat on his lithe body.

"You want me to halter them?" I asked as Red opened the stall door and went in.

"Nah. This time we'll just let these 'bout-to-be-gray babies get used to me." Red scratched Ms. Piggy with a sunburned hand. His fingernails were black with oakum.

"She's the friendlier one," I said. "I guess she's my favorite." I stared at Ms. Piggy adoringly, wondering if Kermit would ever get over his fright of humans. "He's sooo timid. And he doesn't want you on his right side."

"Not unusual," said Red. "Had a few like that myself. Horses by nature is cowardly, 'cause in the wild, they's preyed upon. And who knows?" He turned around and grinned at me with a mouth of widely spaced spiky teeth. "You might be a lion, or would that be lioness?" He turned to Ms. Piggy. "Looks like a carousel horse."

Red patted her shoulder and ran his hand down her foreleg, pinching her ankle. What luck to have her come into my life, and to think I bought her sight unseen. When Ms. Piggy lifted her hoof, Red held on to it for a few seconds until she pulled it away and stomped the ground. Red walked around in front of her and did the same thing to her right leg. When Red turned his attention to Kermit, the colt swung his butt threateningly in the blacksmith's direction and put his head in the corner. Red didn't flinch; instead, he scratched the top of Kermit's rump, his index finger moving across the croup until the colt's pelvis dropped beneath Red's touch.

"He's so birdlike," I said in dismay.

"Pretty big wingspan. American eagle, I'd say."

Red had horse sense. It took physical strength to be a blacksmith, and it took a special kind of temperament, firm but kind and with endless patience.

"Piece of cake," he said, giving Kermit a good-bye pat. "We'll try to trim 'em next appointment. He's a little long in the toe. Should be in separate stalls when I work on them, though."

"I hear you." Weaning the foals from each other lay heavily on my shoulders.

"Who's the horse up by your house?" he asked.

"My new broodmare," I said, trying not to appear too proud. "The colt's dam."

Red drove up the gravel drive. I walked behind his truck to open the gate for him. He let the engine idle as we walked over to True Colors's paddock and stared at the bay mare. We had a good side view of her—a conformational shot, it would be called if we were taking a photograph. She regarded us with a stoic expression, then pricked her ears.

"Good-lookin'," Red said, as if talking about a woman. He unclipped the double-end snap that chained the gate to the post and walked into the paddock. He looked to the ground, hunched his shoulders like an old man, and when he took a step toward the mare, he limped. True Colors stared at him but didn't move as he approached, stopping about two yards from where she stood. After a few minutes, he turned around and slowly walked out of the pen.

"She's supposed to be in foal. What do you think?" I asked hopefully. Red and his wife raised Paso Finos, so I looked to him for expert advice.

Red shrugged. "Too soon to tell. Who's your vet?"

"I've been using Darla." Though the sky was flannel gray, the air felt unusually warm for a Northwest autumn.

"Purdy lady," he said. "And smart, that Darla."

"Glad to hear it." I needed a veterinarian who nipped problems before they took root. I just wished she were as good a horse handler as Liz.

"Married her boss," said Red. "About twice her age. Smart girl. What're her gaits like?" He mopped his brow with his bandanna, then flicked it in front of him. As the handkerchief cracked the air, True Colors turned toward us, then trotted diagonally over to the back pasture fence and started galloping frantically back and forth.

"Skeptical, ain't she? Lots of spring in her stride. Really bends those hock joints, like she's got elbows in her hind legs. Shoulder looks like it's electric." Despite her burns, T.C. was gorgeous. "But wild as a Viet Cong," he went on. "Got excellent feet on her; best Thoroughbred feet I've ever seen. Hell, she even looks like a Cong; just as skittish. Did I ever tell you that I used to hang out of a helicopter and photograph 'em while my buddies was shootin'? Little men in black pajamas, red-complexioned, black-headed, zipping back and forth—just like she's doin' now." He gestured. "I put a camera up to my face and held the lens there the whole damn time I was in the war. That's how I got through it."

Most of Red's talk that wasn't about horses was about his family and Vietnam. He lit a cigarette. "Shoulda never gone. Shoulda stayed and fought the drug war here at home." After a pause, he continued, "Some people call her a home wrecker."

I'd lost the thread of our conversation. "Huh?"

"Darla. None of my business. Besides, my home's already wrecked. My three daughters are real levelheaded, and if they weren't, I knowed how to fix 'em." Red took a breath. "Cut their hair with hedge clippers and blacken their front teeth. Then no one'd look at 'em. But the wife? Don't know what to do about that woman; never ever gave me a day of trouble before." His sunburned brow furrowed. "Always such a careful person, cut down to a pack a day when she got pregnant. For years I was scared my girls would get hooked on drugs, and then about a month ago I found a Baggie of white powder hidden in the door of the wife's car."

I could never tell when Red was pulling my leg.

"You sure you're not on drugs?" he asked, slamming the door of his truck and stepping on the accelerator.

After Red's noisy pickup pulled out of the driveway, I leaned over the fence and stared at True Colors with new eyes.

That was probably exactly how she felt: *hunted*.

The next afternoon was clear and cool, the sun angling in like a strobe as a gray feathery wind blew. I had a new plan for True Colors. She'd never had an owner. She'd never had a keeper, either, or what is called in equine circles "a person." Until very recently, she didn't know what it was to be kept. Today I saw her in a different light. Could animals suffer post-traumatic stress syndrome? I believed that surely she had. *Why should I bond with you?* I could hear her thinking as I camped out in her pen. I put aside training and even gentling. I wasn't trying to groom or photograph her or anything that could be construed as hunting.

My new plan was to become a part of her landscape.

FIVE

Sometimes in the wee hours, when the otherworldly noise of coyote howls jarred me from sleep, I lay in bed, having completely forgotten that I owned a horse farm. In the fog of half sleep, I would be back in New Jersey, where we'd lived for nearly a decade.

"You're from Frisco?" people asked Mark and me when we first moved to Princeton. *Where's that?* I wondered. No one in my native state called San Francisco *Frisco* or California *the coast*.

Six months before landing in New Jersey, I'd been a horseless Berkeley poet living with a Stanford biochemist. Mark and I had met at a Ph.D. party in the Berkeley Hills, a celebration that featured a claw-foot tub of 190-proof laboratory alcohol in a 1920s cedar shake house. I was reclining on a window seat in one of the classic East Bay structure's bay windows that overlooked a cluster of Monterey pines. A tall blond man walked through the front door. He wore a short curly ponytail, one gold earring, and a black motorcycle jacket. It was love at first sight.

After a year, Mark landed a position at Princeton, losing his ponytail and earring. I found a job in the arts in Manhattan. We married and moved across the country in our little red Datsun pickup.

Being in weather that was cold enough to snow was beyond anything I'd experienced, except for two flukey days at the University of Oregon, where I'd gone to college. I kept asking, "When can we go home? Can't you get a job in California?"

We moved to the countryside, where the rolling hillocks of the Sourland Mountains sloped toward the Delaware River, into a federalist manor in need of repair and paint.

Cleanup took months. June's heat and humidity hit like a debilitating influenza. Nights were so hot I couldn't breathe, so I'd sleep on the coolest place I could find—a closet floor. What saved me was the comfort of fireflies and their amazing light show.

One or two neighbors dropped in, remarking on the property's face-lift. The women in Princeton's exurbs, as the writer William Least Heat-Moon noted in his memoir, *Blue Highways,* dressed like well-clipped mortuary lawns: green skirt, pink top, alligator logo. I wore brightly embroidered Guatemalan *huipiles.* Worse, my husband and I had different last names. "Why would you keep your maiden name?" more than one neighbor asked. But in Berkeley in the 1970s, a woman who wed and took her husband's name was not to be trusted.

"When can we go home?" I begged Mark.

I missed California's Mediterranean climate, my women's writer's group, Cody's Books, and Peet's coffee bar on Rose and Vine streets, where, before I married, I'd lived in the garden shed of a house owned by an author of young-adult books, a stone's throw from a tiny new café, Chez Panisse. Someone had told me before I moved to Princeton that one thing I would learn from living amid the deciduous ivy walls was that you could never be tall and blond and thin and rich enough. I'd used Born Blonde on my hair since I was fifteen, watched my weight, and still I felt like a wart.

In October, the maples and pin oaks of the Sourlands turned the colors of a forest fire. A hunt club trotted past our house, then up the driveway of the commercial-airline pilot who lived next door, along his grassy well-mowed airplane landing strip, disappearing into the stubble of soy and cornfields beyond. One weekend a public-address system announced the particulars of a horse show held on the grounds of another neighbor's farm. I listened, transfixed, from our screened-in back porch, as horses jumped a cross-country course of fallen trees and rail fences. Riders flew along the ridge at the top of the airfield, wearing colorful racing silks.

"Why don't you take riding lessons?" Mark suggested.

"Horses take too much time and cost too much," I replied. "Are you looking for a job on the West Coast?"

"But you love horses," Mark insisted.

For my birthday, Mark gave me riding lessons at a private stable half a mile away. Once a week during the winter, I reported to the picturesque red barn with the copper running horse weathervane atop its cupola, arriving early so I could visit with the school horses, Flybynight and Dixie Lee. Equine geography, so familiar to me as a child, flew back from memory: their big fragrant bodies and the amazing warmth that radiates from them—how temperate a barn feels compared to the chilly outdoors. I'd forgotten their subtle affection, not as readily gained as that of a dog. A horse is much less eager and less trusting, and his affection can easily be missed, but when it isn't, oh, the camaraderie. Soon the two school horses recognized me and whinnied when I arrived. It felt as if we shared a secret. As they stretched their necks over the stall doors, waiting for a pet, I noticed the varying differences in their anatomy: Flybynight, with high dinosaur-plate withers and the narrow haunches of a greyhound; Dixie's bulldozer rear end, with a tail as thick as a tree trunk.

I struggled. After each lesson, the muscle soreness in my thighs didn't wear off. It took months for my legs to adjust and my mind to register the new demographics. Most of the other students weren't teenagers but middle-aged women; the price of equine sports is high. Many of the horses in Red Barn Stable had been imported from Europe. People rode not in blue jeans but in German-made breeches with upholstered leather seats. Helmets were required. Women wore black leather gloves and jewelry: diamond-studded white-gold earrings that matched the silver in their spurs. Surprisingly, I felt less wartish in this milieu. After a few months, it all came back to me: the basic riding skills I'd learned as a child.

As summer approached, the two-hour commute to my job as director of a poetry reading series at an Off-Broadway theater in Manhattan began to feel arduous compared to a restful life of watching fireflies from the window of my upstairs writing studio. One warm afternoon, as I walked down the driveway along our always-in-need-of-trimming hedge to the mailbox, I braced myself for the usual rejection letters but found a single hand-addressed envelope. Ripping open the letter, I couldn't believe it: a surprise literary grant! Not a lot of funding but enough to buy shutters for our house or . . . I couldn't decide, and the grant came with no strings attached.

"Buy a horse," my husband said.

"I don't want a horse," I told him.

Mark immediately purchased several bundles (called squares) of locust posts and rails to fence in part of our lawn, which he was tired of mowing. We had an old slate-roofed shed that served as our garage, but the airline pilot had bought from the former owners the big barn that once belonged to our house. The moment our flyboy neighbor saw that Mark was building a corral, he banged on our back door and offered us a stall in what was once our house's stable. As he stood in our kitchen in his dress uniform, our jaws hung open. We hadn't talked to him since the day we moved in. Cappy, as he was called, assured me that I could ride up his airfield as long as I kept my horse on the edge of it. That was the rule: If I stayed on the edge of the field and did not damage the crop, I could ride for miles.

The woman I took lessons from sniggered when I told her how much I wanted to spend; she knew of no horse in my price range. Studying the classifieds of the local paper, I relied on my instincts and bought Junipero—his Hispanic name pleased me—a 15.2-hand, fifteen-year-old sorrel quarter horse with a long wise face. Quarter horses had a reputation for bombproof temperaments and gaits that were easy to sit. Juni, pronounced with an H sound instead of a J, was owned by a teenage girl who wanted a flashy Appaloosa so she could pursue her goal of becoming a rodeo princess.

The afternoon Junipero arrived, my life changed. I suddenly but joyously felt the weight of owning a zoo-sized animal that was totally dependent on me—one I had to feed and water three times a day, keep clean, pick up after, watch for signs of distress, blanket, unblanket, check for loose shoes, check for broken fence boards, restrain for the vet and blacksmith. Neighbors we'd never met started dropping in. "What kind of a horse?" they asked. What kind of riding did I do? Many apologized for not introducing themselves sooner. Was I interested in taking dressage instruction in an arena located up the airstrip and across the soybean field at the farm where the horse show—which I learned was called an "event"—was held?

Within a week of owning Juni, I was asked to join a ladies' group lesson taught once a week by a woman who had trained with the U.S. Olympic team. Messages on my answering machine invited me to trailride on Thursday afternoons. My little brick-colored horse showed himself to be a solid citizen in the company of other horses, which led to suggestions that I come out on Friday mornings to exercise the hounds. When we received an invitation addressed to Mr. and Mrs., asking us to join the local hunt club, I felt as if I'd fallen into a parallel universe.

Put a horse on your front lawn and change your life. The interior of our house began to take on an equestrian theme after Kolika came for a weekend.

"I love this place, there's so much space," she said, windmilling her arms.

"The people we bought it from told us that someone stole the shutters off the front windows because the place looked abandoned."

"No, no, no." Kolika shook her long mane. "Think French country estate," she insisted. "Think tiny Prussian-blue running horses on an off-white background for the dining room." She trotted down the wide slate hallway, her long tie-dyed skirt billowing behind her. "On the stairs . . . What kind of budget are we working with here?"

"Budget?" I asked. "Are you kidding? All our extra money goes to buy hay."

I fell into a tight friendship with Dot, my new riding teacher, about forty and divorced. Dot's mother headed a national dressage organization. The United States Dressage Team was headquartered thirty miles away at what was once Diamond Jim Brady's lavish country estate. One bright spring afternoon, Dot almost physically dragged me to a private schooling session in the estate's sand garden. The Victorian barn had been completely restored. Inside, arched stall doors outfitted with brass fittings and black wrought-iron hinges seemed a living museum; I felt transported back to the late nineteenth century. One by one I watched a visiting German clinician ride each of the American team's horses and transform it into a Pegasus. His name meant nothing to me, but later, I learned that Dr. Reiner Klimke was one of the world's most celebrated riders. Watching him was witnessing history.

Due to Junipero's conformation, he wasn't suitable for dressage: His rear end was too high, and his neck set too low on his chest. But he was such a kind horse as Mark attempted to post his trot. When Mark leaned too far back, losing his balance, Junipero halted and stood placidly chewing his bit, waiting for his master to right himself. As I watched Juni from my study window, he seemed lonely, standing all by himself in his paddock. In the wild, a horse was part of a herd. He needed a friend. If we owned two horses, Mark and I could ride together.

Dot knew the perfect dressage prospect. I should have guessed by her

name, Devil Mist, that the quarter horse–Thoroughbred had a temperament as hot as the oven Mark used to bake gourmet pizza. She was the
horse I should have had when I was fifteen, I thought the first time I
dared ride her outside of a fenced area. She jigged and never walked. She
cantered at the drop of a leaf, her shoulders immediately drenched in
a frothy nervous sweat. Our neighbor gave us another stall in his barn,
and we built a second paddock. Devil disliked Juni; her ears were constantly pinned in a fit of pique. He, on the other hand, adored her. Oh,
but the loveliness of the arch of her neck and the rainbows that the winter sun found in her long black tail.

One finger-numbing January night as I bought grain to her in a five-
quart bucket, she lunged at me like a Rottweiler, biting me on the ribs
with such force that I doubled over in pain, spilling her grain into the
bedding. Most days nothing I did gained her affection. But her talent
at dressage—when she was in a cooperative mood—kept me attached
to her. When she moved sideways, her front and back legs crossed like
scissors; at the trot, she exhibited tremendous lift. Her muscles had the
elasticity of rubber bands. If only I could quell her temper and keep her
mind on her work so we could dance as one. Her powerful grace fueled
my desire to partner with this incredible beast; I'd never felt such a riv-
eting force.

Mark started riding Juni regularly, even though the little sorrel quarter horse was a mite too small for him. Mark had never ridden before
we moved to New Jersey, but he was fearless. I struggled with Devil, but
the mare never quieted. She had to go.

I searched for my next horse on my own without a trainer's advice.
There's a horseman's saying: *New owner, new life.* Willie was a large bay,
age five, some sort of Thoroughbred-draft cross, my first experience with
what were called warmbloods—part hot-blooded Arabian or Thoroughbred and part cold-blooded work horse. According to the hunt staff, he
was dangerous, though everyone was tight-lipped as to just how. I never
found out. He was kind, like Junipero, but with ground-eating strides.

Willie was delivered on the charcoal-gray afternoon when the mayor
of Philadelphia ordered the police to firebomb the Move commune on
Osage Avenue. Two hundred and fifty people were left homeless when
three city blocks caught fire; twelve people died. Smoke from the disaster traveled all the way to the Sourlands.

A few weeks later, I rode Willie across the soybean fields to a dressage lesson with Dot at Meadowberry Farm. The farm's owner, whose daughter was a steeplechase jockey, took a lesson that day. The trim, wavy-haired woman told me about a Thoroughbred in Maryland that wasn't suitable for racing but had dressage potential; he was looking for a good home where his new owner promised to put some training into him. "He's a tall, handsome chestnut, just the right size for your husband," she said. That's how we acquired Alazan, the grandson of Nijinsky.

As I fixed dinner one night about a month later, Mark came home from work and asked me the oddest question: "What do you think we need to do to this house to sell it?"

"What are you talking about?" I asked.

"I thought you wanted to move back to the West," he told me.

"I did?"

"Of course you did," he said, eyeing me skeptically. "You ask me every five minutes when we're going back."

"Oh, oh, oh," I said, "but that was before I started riding."

"I got a new job," he told me, "in Seattle."

"What?" I was stunned. "But I like it here; I don't want to go back."

"Sure you do," he said. "We'll buy a farm and raise horses."

SIX

Nervously, I waited for Dr. Darla to come and give T.C. a pregnancy test. What would I do with this mare if she weren't in foal? The vet appointment was midweek, which gave me plenty of time to catastrophize. I'd suggested to Darla that she bring an assistant, but all the same, I dreaded her arrival. I had a gut feeling that Darla and T.C. weren't going to get along.

Otherwise, I felt buoyed by the progress I'd made with the foals and even with True Colors. For a week, I'd camped out in her corral a few hours each day between rain showers. True Colors always greeted me with a slightly alarmed expression on her otherwise stoic face. Then she moved to the other side of her enclosure, sometimes grabbing at the hay I had put out for her. Slowly, she became less gun-shy, but she never let down her guard.

A few days before we moved T.C. into the barn, we tricked the foals into separate stalls. When Mark had finished the inside of our stable, he'd built a foaling box double the size of a normal stall, one that could be partitioned into two regular-sized stalls. The partition was ten feet high, a wall no horse could jump from a standstill. We lowered this wall to about five feet. The foals could see each other over the divider, and touch noses, but were too small to climb over it. As long as they could see each other and touch, they didn't panic in solitary quarters. Our plan was to add boards for height as the little ones grew, which they were doing like Jack's beanstalk.

Foals start to look cartoonish at six months of age. First their hindquarters grow—they resemble hot rods with jacked-up rear axles—then the front end catches up. Kermit's hindquarters towered so far above his withers that he looked as if he were walking downhill. Ms. Piggy, on the other hand, continued to look like a study of spheres. Her wide, intelligent eyes and small pink nose filled me with joy. I loved to hold her muzzle, stroking the sea grass whiskers on her lower lip. An attention junkie, she even let me kiss her pointy snout, which curved in the shape of a heart. I could now comb Kermit's mane—as long as I stayed on his left side.

A day before Darla was to arrive, Mark and I led True Colors to the barn. At the entrance, she balked. If the black cave had not smelled of horse, she never would have gone in. It took two people to lead her, one to hold the rope and the other to herd her from behind, assuming she didn't bolt at the noise of the lead line being clipped to her halter. Her reaction was often worse when I unclipped the rope; something about the noise and the sudden lack of pressure on her poll—the top of her head—caused by the removal of the lead made her flee with all the force of her feral 1,250 pounds. Sometimes she got away from me with the rope attached, and many a time, even though I wore gloves, a scarlet friction burn raised itself on my palm, along with the sensation of my right shoulder being dislocated. It could take as long as an hour to catch her, but—and this was improvement—when I did pick up her lead rope after she'd gotten away, she didn't bolt. I wouldn't say that her eye softened, it just turned the hue of resignation. Not that I was making eye contact. Eye contact was still verboten.

After we got her situated in a stall next to Willie, it was time to take off T.C.'s old nylon halter and fit her with her safer leather halter; its leather-covered buckles would be kinder to her burns. Her wounds had mostly healed, her cough had abated, and her face was speckled with fresh pink skin. When I could get close to her, I scrutinized her burn marks for new hair.

Carefully, I laid my plan. I would make my attempt after she'd been turned out and brought back into the barn to eat. If it was raining, I'd wait for it to stop, because the noise of rain on the barn's metal roof, even though it was insulated, distressed her. As True Colors munched timothy, I entered her stall but didn't approach her. Instead, I picked out the manure she'd just dropped. Though the manure fork and muck bucket still made her anxious, she'd become a little more accepting of them. Then I began to brush her rear end, working toward her head. Turning my face away from her, I carefully undid the nylon halter's buckle near her left ear. When the halter fell to the floor, T.C. jumped backward, snorting as if it were a predator. Eyeing the pile of blue nylon suspiciously, she sniffed it, then took a nibble of hay. Slowly, I reached down, picked up the halter, left the stall, and returned with the lovely new one. I rubbed the halter across her flank, like a grooming cloth, before backing up in the direction of her muzzle. When I let her smell the gift halter, she flew to the other side of the stall. Feet planted, she trembled all over. I spread the nose band as wide as I could, holding it in both hands, but couldn't get it near her face. I took the halter apart so that, instead of putting her muzzle through it, I could put the halter around her face. Just as I got the strapping over the bridge of her nose, she snaked her neck, flinging the halter against the wall. The noise startled her. After an hour, I gave up. Now I wasn't sure I'd be able to put the old halter back on her. Good reason to cancel the appointment with Darla tomorrow, I thought, then remembered that the foals were due for tetanus shots.

It took countless tries. I had to turn my face away from True Colors while doubling the crown piece of the old halter back on itself. The very touch of a strap anywhere near her ears sent her reeling with fright. When I finally got the old halter back on, I buckled it way back on her neck, then, in slow increments, pushed it forward until it sat just behind her ears before I tightened it. Slowly. Since I couldn't look in her direction, I had to do it all by feel. That was when it came to me: The only reason she had allowed me to put the old halter back on was because of the smell. The new halter smelled of recently tanned leather, which to her must have been the odor of slaughter and quicklime. There are no how-to books on returning an injured feral half-ton beast to health and domesticity. I was on terra incognita.

That night I went to bed emotionally exhausted but not beaten. I rose early to get the barn in order for the vet's arrival. When a fancy dark green veterinary truck pulled in, all horses were in the barn, the foals wearing new weanling halters.

"Hi, there." Darla smiled. She wore midnight-blue mascara and had brought an assistant, a mousy-haired woman with a less starched appearance. "Today we have two tets and one preggers check," she went on, smiling her pretty white-picket-fence smile as she read from a clipboard. She didn't introduce her assistant.

Her cutesified professional jargon was meant to disarm me but had the opposite effect. "Let's start with the foals," I said.

"Ooh, they've grown," Darla crooned. "What color *are* they?"

When I gave a one-word answer, "Gray," Darla disagreed: "That can't be." She put her well-manicured hand to her seashell-pink mouth. I wondered if she'd ever seen a young horse graying after being born black or bay.

The assistant spoke up for the first time. "You've seen gray babies." She gave Darla an incredulous look.

The assistant held on to Miss Piggy as Darla stabbed her in the neck with one delicate stroke. Filly jerked backward only slightly, eyes widening, as Darla pulled out the hypodermic needle. "Just a teeny bee sting," Darla told her, patting the dish in Ms. Piggy's cute head. Kermit wasn't so easy. He obviously had a more sensitive nervous system and practically hoisted the assistant off the ground when Darla injected him. The vet's hand moved as if throwing a dart at a board. *Thwank.* Darla stayed in the stall with Kermit afterward, trying to befriend him; his inky eyes were wide with betrayal.

True Colors was next, and already I felt defeated. The assistant held the rope, but when Darla entered the stall with a needle and syringe with which to draw blood, T.C. puffed up, sidling first one way and then another before starting to crow-hop on her hind legs, pivoting away from the vet.

I had an idea. "If you put on my barn jacket, you'll smell familiar," I told Darla. How to be diplomatic about this? I couldn't tell Darla that her perfume offended my horses. I held up my grubby blue jacket. Darla looked almost frightened. But the assistant thought it a good strategy.

"Well . . ." Darla stammered.

"You have an old jacket you use for chores?" the assistant asked Darla.

"No," she said, looking honestly pained. Reluctantly, she put on my coat, a men's size large that hung below her knees. She pulled on a pair of surgical gloves.

"The smell of latex will really put her off," I warned.

Darla closed her eyes and swallowed. She'd probably never encountered a situation like this in vet school. Clearly, she hadn't had the real-life situations like the ones Liz handled every day.

It took a good deal of time to get the blood out of T.C., but it was a fait accompli largely because the assistant suggested that Darla draw the blood from True Colors's hip, where she was less sensitive, rather than from her neck.

"I hope I don't have to do that again," said Darla with a forced smile.

She took off my jacket, held it between two pincerlike fingers, and handed it back to me.

The assistant labeled the vial of blood. "If it works, go with it," she said matter-of-factly. I wondered why Darla didn't always travel with this no-nonsense woman.

"We'll have the results in a couple of days," Darla said, resuming her air of authority.

The idea of being turned out to pasture in the morning and then brought back in at the end of the day with the rest of the horses was completely foreign to True Colors. Gates flummoxed and often terrified her. Even passing through the stall door made her anxious, so just leading her to pasture was a problem. Somehow it worked better if Mark and I herded her, because once we got through the open pasture gate, unhooking the lead rope was traumatic for everyone involved. At the end of the day, it was easier to herd T.C. back to the barn and into her stall after bringing the other horses in. She could hardly avoid the barn: The riding horses and the foals called frantically to her until they saw her enter the aisle and then struck up a happy chorus of relief-filled nickering.

It began to occur to me that the other horses recognized her as the de factor head of our little herd. Not that she was an alpha mare; as near as I could determine, she had no bossy characteristics whatsoever. It was with this in mind that I decided, on the day after Darla's visit, to try to turn T.C. out with another horse: Willie. He had a forgiving temperament and possessed the horse equivalent of street smarts.

First Mark and I herded True Colors into the back pasture. We watched as she galloped away from us in the direction of the woods and then stopped to cough. After she wandered around, searching for a patch of stunted clover, and stood about three hundred feet away from the gate, I got Willie from his paddock. Leading him into the back pasture, I turned him loose, leaving his halter on so that if things went wrong, I could easily move him to safety. He froze, staring at T.C. She lifted her head and stared back for a moment, then returned to grazing. The frosty nights had caused the sugar content of the purple clover to rise to the level of maple syrup. A less mannerly gelding would have trotted over and inspected her privates, which might have garnered him a good swift kick in the groin.

My husband and I stood at the fence for about fifteen minutes, watching the two horses keep their distance. Both of us felt nervous. Had T.C. ever been turned out with an adult male horse other than the herd stallion? Had I put my big kindly Willie Africa in danger?

"Now that we've finally got her settled, it would be a shame for her to get hurt," Mark said. He drew a breath as the gelding walked within a hundred feet of True Colors, then put his head down to graze, his face pointed in her direction. She continued to munch grass, keeping a watchful eye on him. When he approached, I heard no squealing. There wasn't any kind of standoff. No fireworks. Relieved, Mark and I walked back to the barn. When I glanced over my shoulder to check on them, they grazed side by side as if they had been pasture mates all their lives.

That afternoon when I brought the horses in, I noticed that Alazan had thrown a shoe. "Drat you," I said, playfully socking his copper shoulder with my fist. Al was mentally six months old and had all the sense of a toddler. I trudged up to the house and called the blacksmith, then went back to the barn to wrap Alazan's foot with duct tape so that he wouldn't bruise the sole of his foot and cause another abscess.

"Good thing you're so good about having a hoof soaked in a bucket of Epsom salts." I kissed him on the soft flesh of his nose, just above one of his comma-shaped nostrils. I often had to soak his feet. Whenever I had to soak two bruised feet at the same time, I began to feel that Alazan was a losing battle. But on the one occasion when I had had to soak three hooves at the same time, Al took his medication like a champ, standing perfectly still. I lacked enough five-quart rubber buckets and used my favorite yellow plastic salad bowl, which—not surprisingly—cracked under his weight. The bowl was now usable only for holding popcorn; I kept it as a memento.

When I'd telephoned Red to shoe Alazan, his wife answered. She was brusque, telling me that her husband couldn't come by until the beginning of next week. I'd never met her, but someone had told me that she worked at the county jail's infirmary; maybe that was why her husky smoker's voice brought up the image of Big Nurse in *One Flew over the Cuckoo's Nest*. Imagine my surprise when, at five o'clock, just after the sun had started to set amid a lavender-watermelon haze, I looked out of my living room window and saw Red's battered Ford truck idling in my driveway.

We positioned Alazan in the aisle under one of the overhead fluorescent lights, and the blacksmith quickly reshaped Al's bent shoe on his anvil. "The wife's got a bit of a weight problem," Red told me as he picked up Alazan's hoof.

It never ceased to amaze me how Red could rail angrily about his personal life and not upset the horse he was working under. Miraculously, he seemed to have a calming effect on Al, who stood placidly on three legs as Red tore off my duct-tape bandage, then rasped the ragged hoof.

"What can I do to keep him from pulling a shoe?" I asked in a pleading tone as I held on to Alazan's lead rope. I couldn't count the hours I'd spent nursing the big chestnut's feet.

"Turn him out in bell boots. Same as you ride him in," Red directed, then rattled on, "So when I came across some white capsules in an envelope with the return address of the hoosegow's sick bay, I just thought they was diet pills. But when I found some vegetable matter stuffed into a money roll that was supposed to pay my bridge toll, I knew I had a problem. When I confronted her, she denied everythin'." Alazan pulled his hoof away. "I was all done anyway," Red told the horse.

"Then she accuses me of havin' an affair." He threw his rasp to the ground, but somehow Alazan intuited that Red's anger wasn't directed at him. "I got some spare time today; let's have a look at them foals now that ya got 'em each in their own box."

I returned Al to his stall. Red pulled back the latch to Ms. Piggy's box, and the filly searched his pockets for sugar cubes.

"Do you want them haltered?" I asked. It's not natural for a horse to stand on three legs, and it takes time for a foal to learn how to balance itself for a blacksmith.

"Just leave her loose," said Red. "I'm only goin' to work with her fronts this time." I handed him his nippers and rasp, which reminded me of a huge fingernail file with a wooden handle. After he got Ms. Piggy to pick up a hoof, Red turned slowly with his back facing her, then practiced wedging her foot between his knees. The filly chewed on the back of his hand-tooled belt, showing little resistance as Red nipped the toe off her hoof.

"So I told the wife that if she was on drugs, I was going to the cops. 'Course, she laughed. I got too many DUIs to ever wanna see a cop again." I wondered what Mrs. Red was really like and what the real truth was. Piggy pulled her leg away from him and slammed it to the floor. Red moved to the other side of the baby horse and picked up her right hoof.

"She was a pretty good girl." I smiled, stroking the white star on Filly's head.

Red headed for Kermit's stall. When he tried to pick up the colt's front foot, Kermit reared back on his hind legs, falling sideways into the wall. I gasped as the spider-legged foal scrabbled to right himself. Red pointed the foal's head into a corner and tried to pick up his long black foreleg. This went on for some minutes as Red railed about the wife. "So I asked her father if he would come with me to the drug-intervention program at Death Valley General." The local hospital was often referred to as Death Valley because of the many fatal collisions on the state highway.

Kermit's eyes glazed over. He let Red hold his hoof for a minute without struggling. Red wasn't able to manipulate the nippers, so he quickly rasped the toe before giving Kermit back his hoof. "The wife's dad wants to find out who her dealer is." Red reached for Kermit's right hoof.

"Careful," I called from outside the stall. "That's his bad side."

Red went on with the business of trimming as if it didn't matter that Kermit's peripheral vision hadn't developed. "They ain't got patience enough to let me do their hinds," he told me. "Next time. Even the little critters I got at home only got patience enough for two hooves at a sitting. They done good, these babies."

I smiled with relief and pride.

"Let's take a look at the new girl on the block." Red marched into True Colors's stall. "Better with no rope or handler," he said. "We don't want her to feel ganged up on. Just gonna look at this lovely lady's feet. Just looking." True Colors tensed as he patted her neck, running his hand along her sloping shoulder. When she wheeled around to evade his touch, Red left his hand on the top of her back. "Not gonna hurt you, Miss Lady."

He turned to me. "I never killed nobody, not even in 'Nam, not for sure. Hell, I might go out and rough someone up, spray-paint 'drug dealer' across their driveway, but I wouldn't really hurt nobody."

True Colors's deep fear of humans flashed from the white sclera of her eyes. She darted from one corner of her stall to another like a bird that had flown through an open door and found itself trapped in a house. Willie trumpeted a series of sharp neighs. Unfazed, Red stood still as a tombstone in a blizzard of wood shavings. "Sister," he said softly, "this is foolishness. I ain't gonna hurt you." A horse listener, Red knew how to read a horse's body language. "She reminds me of a bronc I drew in Denver when I was on the rodeo circuit."

"You rodeoed?" I asked.

"Thought it would be a good way to meet girls." Red sniggered. "Didn't take me long before I figured I'd meet more girls in the service and have fewer broken ribs."

When she saw that Red wasn't frightened by her panicking, that he might just stand there in her stall all day if it suited him, True Colors burrowed into the darkest corner and dropped her head to the floor. Red scratched her hindquarters, then backed slowly toward her shoulder. Putting a hand on her elbow, he ran his fingers down her foreleg. When he pinched between the splint bone and tendon, just above her fetlock, she didn't pick up her foot. He released the pressure and tried again. On about the fifth attempt, she rapidly lifted her foot, then slammed it back on the floor.

"She ain't such a piece of cake as the others," Red told me. "But that's okay. We'll try her next time with a mini-rasp so as not to scare her. Face looks better," he added. "Probably'll scar. You know"—he looked directly at me—"she's scared, trembling, even, but she don't wanna kill me. She don't even want to stomp on me."

He gave True Colors a soft pat on the flank, and I could see by the way her flesh met his hand that she had relaxed an inch. As he walked out of her stall, True Colors wheeled around and stared after him, not in fury but with a curious expression. *There's hope for this horse,* I thought.

"See ya in a coupla weeks for your regular appointment," he said.

After paying Red in cash—I got a 10 percent discount, and cash always made him happy—I went up to the house. The light on my answering machine blinked. An unfamiliar woman greeted me by name in a businesslike voice and went on to say something I didn't quite catch. I hit replay. It was the office manager at Valley Equine Clinic: The blood test was back. True Colors was not in foal.

SEVEN

I'd been pacing from the kitchen up the stairs to my desk in the Kegger Room and back for so long that I'd worn a trail while waiting for Kolika to stop by and give me some decorating tips. The biggest question of all was what to do with True Colors.

Inspired by a long-ago visit to the Newport summer house of those intrepid horse lovers the Vanderbilts, I'd filled the upstairs Kegger Room with floor-to-ceiling potted palms in huge terra-cotta pots. Mark had installed a ceramic woodstove with a glass window, and the heat from it, combined with the light and the greenhouse effect of the many über-sized windows, gave the Kegger Room such a tropical feeling that we now called it the Winter Palace.

I couldn't sell T.C. to another breeder; the scars on her head made her registration papers questionable, and she was impossible to handle. Euthanizing her was not an option. I could give her away but feared that she might come to harm. She did have value, and I felt responsible for her.

The dripping eaves of early winter's endless gloom didn't help my mood. First the snowy peaks vanished into an oppressive cement ceiling of sky; then the mountain wind kicked in, and horizontal rain shot at the kitchen window. The hours of light shrank as if they'd been rationed. I turned to problems I could solve: T.C.'s new halter, for one. If I used it on another horse until the newness wore off and the odor of horse seeped in, T.C. might not reject it.

Staring out the window, I watched for Kolika's battered VW, then glanced at the new scuff marks in front of the stove. Yesterday I'd invited two junior high school girls, neighbors with horses who'd ridden up for a visit, to bring their ponies inside the kitchen. There was nowhere to tie the ponies out of the wind and no extra stall in the barn. I seldom got visitors and hardly knew my neighbors, so I thought: *I hate this floor, why not?* Strangely, the unshod hooves of the woolly ponies hadn't done an inch of permanent harm. It hadn't troubled the little beasts to be led through the mudroom door and into the kitchen. Vicki held one bay pony by the rawhide reins of his bridle, positioning him next to the hum of the refrigerator. Angel held the little bay gelding next to the cooking island. For about an hour we'd talked and sipped instant cocoa.

The girls bubbled with questions, few about horses. I was a teacher, but not their teacher, and had color-crayoned walls, so no subject seemed banned—periods, stepmothers, and other problems of fractured families.

Now, bending over to buff the linoleum with a rag, I thought I heard a car's engine, but it was a fierce gust of wind. There seemed no way to predict when it would cease. If it were accompanied by rain, I was afraid to leave the horses turned out for more than a few hours else they chill to the bone, especially the little ones. Even True Colors eagerly headed in from the back pasture to her stall, preferring to be herded and not led. Had I accidentally found an inroad to training her? The cold wet of western Washington winters stood in sharp contrast to the dry snow of her high-desert home. Though I turned the riding horses out in waterproof blankets, the idea of putting a turnout rug on T.C. was unthinkable. The mare went wild with fright, throwing herself against her door, when she heard me in the next stall as I heaved Willie's size-82 Gore-Tex blanket across his back.

When Kolika arrived, she carried a rattan basket of clothes into the house. "My laundry," she said. "I thought I could use your washer while we talked."

Kolika had left the commune and relocated near Seattle. Now she was a single mother of teenagers with a longtime live-in boyfriend and a start-up home-renovation business that employed her whole household.

"It may look awful, but I know why the last owners painted the outside of this house mustard yellow," she told me. "It's so dark around here."

I agreed; Mark had painted our last two homes yellow, which suited their Victorian style, but yellow with brown trim flaking to the aqua undercoat didn't suit this house—a "rambler," in real estate jargon.

"Stonehenge gray with white trim," Kolika declared, talking with her hands. Even though she did manual labor, she had long, well-crafted nails. My hands were my worst feature: fat knuckles and no fingernails. "For a little color, go with old barn red for the exterior doors," she added. "How're the horses?"

After Kolika got situated, we walked down to the barn between rain squalls.

"Hi, Alazan." Kolika ran her finger up the thin snip of white like a lightning bolt to the star between his eyes. "You drama queen," she told him. Very people-oriented, as ex-racehorses often are, he was always the first to jut his head over the stall door. The foals could barely reach their snouts to the top of their doors. Ms. Piggy pressed the side of her face and one large eye into the bars that fronted the stall walls facing the aisle, as if staring out from inside a birdcage.

"They've grown!" Kolika smiled at Kermit, whose ears pricked in alarm. "Still the shyest boy in the class." One of the things I loved about Kolika was the way she attributed human qualities to horses. She turned to Pigster. "The girl with all the charm. And this lady's gained weight!" She gazed in at True Colors. "Will her head always look like that?"

My throat tightened. "I guess so."

Per usual, True Colors stood at the back of her stall, not taking any notice of us—unlike the others, who always greeted visitors by nickering. When no treats appeared, Willie and Al tossed their heads, their liquid brown eyes filling with want. True Colors never begged and seldom jutted her head over the door even at feeding time. She still hadn't cottoned to grain. She ate some of what I fed her, but it took her the entire night, and that was after she dumped her grain dish onto the floor. This mare had yet to eat a carrot or even a piece of apple. Every night at five o'clock, when I threw her dinner hay into her stall, she would stare at it for a few minutes, then walk over to smell it, sorting through it with her prehensile nose, but she preferred to eat when there were no witnesses. On the rare occasion when I forgot to throw her hay, she never roiled at the injustice, as the others did if forgotten. Instead, she stood still, turning her head as if glancing at her hindquarters. In a normal horse, this would indicate that her gut hurt and colic should be suspected—not true in her case. I often wondered: Why did she nervously sweep her gaze around her body's perimeter from time to time?

"She's a riddle wrapped in a mystery inside an enigma. *But there is a key* . . . " I paraphrased Churchill talking about complicated matters of state. True Colors wasn't evil, though just as unpredictable. Would coping with her always feel like strategizing an international crisis?

"Such a pretty girl. That's really too bad about those burns," said Kolika.

Dark-pigmented scars speckled True Colors's head and ears; several of the bald patches were now encircled by white hair. It looked as if someone had thrown bleach in her face. "I don't know what to do with her," I told Kolika. "Next time the blacksmith comes, I'll ask him how to sell a horse as rodeo livestock." True Colors was so wild that being a bucking horse was the only possible life I could imagine for her.

Back at the house, Kolika showed me a scrapbook she'd filled with ideas for the kitchen. "Here's the look you want," she said, pointing to an *Architectural Digest* clipping. "Once you raise the ceiling, you could install a plate rack."

Suddenly, my old phobia rose up—that feeling of living in a house perpetually under construction. I took a deep breath. "No doubt about it," I agreed with some effort. "Raising the ceiling is the key to making this place livable."

But what was the key to civilizing True Colors?

I always called Red the night before to confirm our appointment for the following day. This time his wife answered. She told me that if I had made an appointment, of course Red would be there. I wasn't convinced. Sometimes Red ran out of daylight and went home. Try another blacksmith? I had, and he'd lamed Alazan.

Just before ten the next morning, Red's truck idled in the driveway. "You're early," I greeted him. Red wore a baseball hat and was eating what looked like a fast-food fish sandwich. Luckily, not only were the horses in the barn, but the rain and wind had ceased and—the fates were with us—the sun was out. Natural light was the best illumination for shoeing a horse. It also helped that the horses were warm and dry, their joints bent more easily, and a dry foot was easier to trim and shoe than a wet one.

We started with Willie. He had no qualms about being shod, was well mannered and docile. He did tense up when Red took a red-hot horseshoe out of the forge and held it to Willie's hoof to size it. The sizzling noise, the smoke, and the smell of burning hair made his eyes widen, but being a trusting beast, he stood perfectly still. Alazan was not so trust-ing. It could take two hours to shoe each animal, so I was glad Red had arrived early—by three, the light would start to fade.

The foals were next. Red wanted to trim the youngsters outside their stalls in the aisle, a big step in becoming a grown-up equine. "Hey, it's scary," he said. I held Ms. Piggy as she stood atop a black rubber mat purchased for this purpose. "That's what the doctor at intervention ther-apy told me. On drugs, she's a different person. 'She could walk right out of your life, so be prepared,' he told me." Red picked up one of Ms. Pig-gy's front hooves. "Me 'n' the kids go to intervention therapy together, and in order to do that, we gotta go behind the wife's back."

Ms. Piggy tried to pull her leg away from the blacksmith. When that didn't work, she sat down on her haunches like Gumby. "Let's give sister a break until we're done with the colt." Red's strategy was to make the right thing easy.

Kermit pulled a perplexed expression. He tensed as Red whittled away at his hoof. His peripheral vision had developed, but not com-pletely. Three hooves out of four: not bad.

"Why don't we get the new girl out here in the aisle to trim her feet," Red suggested. Sore from bending over, he leaned back, stretching his spine.

Luckily, T.C. had her halter on. I was now able to remove it at night, but in the morning it took me as long as fifteen minutes to get it on before turning her out. Slowly, ever so slowly, I would lift the crown piece over the top of her neck, trying not to frighten her—when she shied and swung her head, she sometimes whacked me on the ear. I led the mare from her stall, her steps quick and animated. Red patted her shoulder; her flesh tensed, feeling wooden.

"Got a nice coat on you, Princess, and shiny, too," he said. "Shine is unusual this time of year." Red stroked True Colors's neck. Her winter coat had grown in short but thick. She stood rooted to the rubber mat, every part of her rigid; only her gingerbread eyes moved. When she jerked backward, Red gently touched her from behind, and she jumped forward, then stopped dead. He didn't use a nippers or a regular rasp but filed each front hoof with a short piece of iron that looked like a carrot grater.

"Do you think I could sell her to someone who manages rodeo bucking horses?" I asked. "She's not in foal, and I don't know what to do with her."

"Breed her again next spring," Red offered. It seemed the obvious solution.

"But she's so wild; I don't think anyone could manage her." I didn't say that I feared she would come to harm in the hands of others, even professionals.

"Don't know," he said thoughtfully. "Rodeo livestock is sold on contract. They have outfits that raise horses bred especially for their action—follow special bloodlines. Most of 'em animals is pretty tame. Have to be to get transported around like they do."

"Oh," I said dejectedly.

"Hell, it's scary," said Red. "In order to go to therapy, me 'n' the kids have to get our stories straight and hope the wife don't get suspicious when we're all gone at the same time. Don't like lying, but the alternative is havin' a doper for a wife and mother."

When Red moved toward True Colors's rear end, then leaned on her left haunch, the mare began to tremble. He ran his hand down her hamstring, over her hock, down her long cannon bone to her pastern joint. The last thing I remember was watching the muscles in his arm flex as he pinched, trying to get her to raise her hind foot.

Suddenly, a cyclone of rock shards flew in every direction. I was thrown to the ground, my cheek pressing into the gravel floor of the aisle, my hip and the lower part of my body sliding over the rubber mat as I tried to hold on to True Colors's rope. With a thud, Red fell against the door of Kermit's stall; he groaned, the lock rattled, and the door frame shuddered. As Red sat up with his back against the wall, we heard the rapid-fire rhythm of a horse galloping away from us. The other horses bugled in alarm.

I hobbled to the barn's back door. My palms stung. Looking along the track that ran in front of the paddocks to the back pasture, I saw a bay horse flee as if from battle, a blue lead line flying behind her like the tail of a kite. "Shit. I'll never be able to catch her," I said.

Red pulled himself to his feet. "Guess she don't wanna give up her weapons," he said. "Some of 'em just don't. I shoulda knowed better."

I thought Willie would leap over his door. Ms. Piggy's shrill voice cut into the cold afternoon. Kermit, who looked terrified, bellowed ceaselessly. Alazan neighed and trotted in place. I put my hands over my ears. "Calm down," I told them. It did no good.

"I'd better go try and catch her," I said after I'd written Red a check. I couldn't remember where I'd hidden the cash I'd taken out of the bank to pay him.

"Need help?" Red asked, heading for his truck.

I tramped around the back pasture for the rest of the afternoon, following True Colors. Every time I got within fifty feet of her, she flew off into the woods or up to the leafless pie cherry tree by the old bathtub watering trough. The only thing that slowed her was the lead rope getting tangled around an ankle. My heart sped; would she fall, breaking a leg? Then I saw how quickly she learned to avoid it, to hold her head at an angle as she ran so that the rope flew away from her churning hooves. Up at the barn, horses called. She never answered but stopped now and then to graze on a tuft of dry grass. Whenever I approached, she shot off in another direction.

A purple dusk settled around us. I gave up following T.C. and walked up the incline back to the barn to feed the others, my rubber boots catching in grass flattened by the wind. I was exhausted, my body already sore from striking the ground. Once inside, I saw that the horses had kicked all the bedding out of their stalls. When I tossed them each a flake of hay, they only grabbed at it. Willie looked hangdog and refused to eat. Kermit coughed, oats dribbling from his mouth. Alazan paced the front of his stall like a caged ocelot. *They'll colic if I can't get her back inside,* I thought.

True Colors stood on the brow of the hill in the fading maize light of early December. Sometimes at dusk the sun brightened, and light that looked artificial shot horizontally in from the west in a last illumination of day. Kolika was right, T.C. had gained weight. Then it struck me that something was odd about her belly, the way it bloomed from her rib cage, hanging like a basket of fruit. Could True Colors be in foal after all?

I went back outside to try to bring her in. At about seven P.M. the wind began thrashing the trees. I felt cold to the skin and gave up. The heavens went dark with only a scrap of moon. Rain pelted the ground. Soon there was standing water everywhere; candles of lunar light flickered on the surface. When I walked into the barn, the other horses were still undone, and Willie hadn't eaten. Not even a carrot quelled Alazan. I trudged up to the house to call Liz; my rain-soaked jacket felt pounds heavier. In spite of my discomfort and worry, I was smiling at the thought of T.C.'s baby.

While I shuffled through the papers by the telephone, looking for Liz's most recent private number, Mark walked in the door, home from work.

"T.C. got away from the blacksmith hours ago. I still can't catch her," I told him.

"So why are you smiling?" he asked, scanning the kitchen for dinner.

"I think she might be in foal after all."

Mark raised an eyebrow and embraced a tall, slender Ballard's beer.

Liz's husband told me that she was at a convention in Denver. I tried Kath. Her answering machine gave a number in Montreal. It was late on the East Coast, after ten.

"When's dinner?" Mark asked.

"Maybe we should boil some water for spaghetti," I said, unable to remember my cooking plan. All I could think of was T.C. and a baby. But Mark loved pasta. "There's anchovies in the pantry." I waved in the direction of the new alcove. During the torrential rain of autumn, Mark had gone stir-crazy and begun knocking out the Sheetrock, putting in shelves. Even Kolika approved.

"I'm hungry." His mouth formed an upside-down horseshoe.

"Here's a tomato to dice." I reached into a colander on the kitchen island where I kept fruits and vegetables. "There's herbs drying in the mudroom."

"What about you? What are *you* going to do?" His tone accusatory but humorous.

"Why am I not making dinner?" I laughed. "I have to call the vet." I searched for Darla's number in the pile of business cards we kept beneath the built-in china case that separated the kitchen from the dining room. The night clerk who answered assured me that Darla would return my call.

When Mark opened the storage cabinets beneath the cooking island, lids and saucepans poured out, crashing to the floor.

"What happened to this linoleum?" he asked. "Has a horse has been here?"

I flipped a stove burner to high. "Here, let's fill that five-quart pot with water," I said, avoiding the question. "If you dice the tomatoes, I'll finish the sauce."

Darla called back almost immediately. Explaining the situation, I asked, "Are those blood tests ever wrong? To check if a mare is in foal?"

"Oh, no," she said confidently.

"But True Colors has this belly on her," I said.

"It's just foal belly, edema plus fat. Mares get it after having several foals. I guarantee you," she said, "that mare is not in foal. And if she were, it's way too early for a mare to start showing."

Was it too soon? Mares generally start showing at six months, though it varies with the mare and how she is built. True Colors had looked so svelte when she arrived. In just a few months' time—mostly spent being so frightened that she didn't eat—how could she have put on what looked like a beer gut?

As I thanked Darla and apologized for interrupting her evening, I was already mentally dialing Kath's international phone number. After a long pause, a voice said (in French) something like "Little Sisters of the Holy Sepulcher Retreat."

My God, what had I barged in on? Had Kath checked in for treatment? I shouldn't have called. All the same, I handed the phone to Mark, who knew enough French to navigate science texts and cookbooks.

"Ask if we can speak with Kath," I pleaded. "I think she can help our horse." Mark looked at me as if I'd just landed from the planet Krypton. "Please."

Finally, Kath was on the phone. "S-sorry to call so late," I stammered. "I have a question I think you can help me with."

"*Oui,*" she said. Nothing about her voice sounded depressed or put out.

"True Colors is starting to get a belly on her, and I was just wondering . . . those blood tests that they give mares to see if they're in foal, are they ever wrong?"

Kath chortled as if standing next to me and not thousands of miles away. "Depends when they're given." The information rolled off her tongue. When it came to equine care, she was a marvel. "If blood is drawn after the mare is more than three months in foal, they're inconclusive."

"Meaning?"

"Meaning they don't show anything. Waste of money."

"So if True Colors was more than three months in foal when she was tested, and the test came back negative, she could be in foal?"

"Absolutely."

"Wow! By the way, thanks for the halter."

"I hope it fits," said Kath through a break in the connection.

"Oh, yes," I lied. After using the halter on Alazan, I had started to inch the crown piece toward T.C.'s ears, but she still sprang away like a jungle cat.

A gust of wind slammed the side of the house. First the kitchen lights flickered, then the telephone connection broke.

"I've got to get that mare into her stall and the barn closed up," I said, trying to think how to manage it.

"What about dinner?" Mark asked. Our agreement was that he cooked on weekends and I cooked during the week. As I pulled on my wet parka, he reached for a cleaver, hacking at the Roma tomato until it bled across the cutting board.

I flew back to the barn. Wind rattled in the skeleton trees. It was so wet that I felt as if I were walking through a storm on the high seas. From the top of the driveway, I heard one of the giant sliding doors banging against the barn wall and hurried to secure it. If True Colors wanted to spend the night outside in this, then more power to her. But I cursed my present circumstances. How was it that Kath, who didn't have a college degree, knew more about equine reproduction than a vet?

When I flipped on the overhead lights, a wind hurled shavings grit at me, and little pieces of wood shrapnel stung my face. The horses, however, were calm. All trumpeting had ceased. What had quieted them? I wondered. Struggling to advance the heavy door along its trolley, I pulled against a wind so strong that the door billowed in the middle like a sail. After battening down the hatches, I went along the aisle, picking up horse blankets that had blown off their hooks.

Willie raised his head and nickered softly, his ear cocked as if waiting for a reply. When I saw his ear rotate, a thought struck me.

I marched outside; the arena gate had blown open. In the weak light that filtered over the top of the barn wall, I saw a horse standing in the covered arena. The rope was attached to True Colors's halter, but she stood peacefully, one hind hoof cocked. Turning her head slightly to acknowledge me, she didn't run away. I crept forward and, just in case she could see in the dim light, averted my eyes.

I took hold of the rope, which was wet and encrusted with sand. She didn't flinch but seemed to follow me, rather than me leading her, as we headed back into the barn. When the other horses saw her, they nickered, though not in distress. After I opened her stall door, she followed me inside, where I gradually approached her head and, in stop-time movements, removed her halter. She stood next to the wall that separated her stall from Willie's. Her muscles weren't relaxed, but she wasn't rigid with fear, either; she assumed something close to a resolved posture.

"You're as soaked as wet laundry," I told her. Water dripped from her mane and tail. She turned and looked at me, and for an instant, our eyes met. In that moment, I felt that she accepted me as her keeper.

I patted her wet shoulder, giving her a little scratch. "We won't trim your hind hooves next time," I told her. The irony was that they hadn't really needed trimming. Her front hooves had needed the toes shortened; she no longer ran on the range, where the hard ground sheared off new growth. But her hind hooves, though ragged, were perfectly rounded and without cracks. True Colors sighed deeply and waited for me to leave her stall. The minute I latched the door behind me, she lowered her head into her hay. I turned and looked in at her.

"Never again will I ask for your weapons," I promised.

EIGHT

By mid-February, there was no denying it. True Colors was in foal.
After months of low-hanging skies and early darkness, the hours of light began to lengthen at a noticeable clip. Evergreens had bright new growth on their spiky tips, and the pussy willows started to fur. When Darla got out of her truck on the day she arrived to give spring vaccinations, her jaw fell to the base of her slim neck.

"Oh my God! Hide her in the attic! No, it's too late! Look at the belly on Colors!"

"I've been watching that bulge, believe me." I grinned. "Like a pot to boil."

I wanted this foal so much it was an overpowering feeling. The answer had nothing to do with my having gotten a raw deal on a horse. Months ago I'd decided that if I could find no use for True Colors, she could live here as long as I did—a sad waste of a horse, but so be it. Other than the fact that she couldn't be caught, she wasn't much trouble. She was kind, never bit or kicked anyone, equine or human. And she had a stabilizing effect on her stablemates; whenever I took her into the arena to see if I could work with her—to back up when I pressed my palm against her chest, to move away from the pressure of my palm on her side—the other horses cried until I returned her to her stall.

True Colors, on the other hand, never cried for the others when left alone in the barn or field. She might stand in the back of her stall looking anxious, eyes flashing, but she uttered not a peep. And unlike most nervous horses and most Thoroughbreds, she was an easy keeper. She hadn't learned to like grain; she never begged for food and never anticipated feeding time. She wasn't like any boss mare that I'd ever encountered. She was more like an anchor.

I almost couldn't believe the happy turn of events. Another foal like Kermit, I hoped. He'd grown stately; though still shy, he gave the impression of a prince instead of a frog. T.C.'s unborn baby meant more to me than a new addition to the stable, and I often lay awake nights, trying to decipher what this foal symbolized for me. It would be the first foal born on our farm, establishing us as a family. It would also fill a void in my past.

"Why horses?" my mother used to ask me. "Begging for a horse for your birthday is wishing for the moon."

So went the conversation between us. It started in our first home, where I'd slept on the living room couch; continued through the second, which my father built in the vacant lot next door; and went on when we moved to the country, where, for a while, there was no house, so we camped out. At age six I wondered, *What's wrong with asking for the moon?* We lived amid California's oak-studded brown hills in an era when atoms were smashed in a linear accelerator just down the road. The moon, or traveling to it, was in the near future—even for girls.

"Why horses?" Mother wanted to know.

Because horses were powerful and I was not.

"Go read a book," she told me, turning the page of *Sunset* magazine. "Horses cost too much, and they take up too much time."

My parents were building their dream house in one of California's wealthiest suburbs. Vaulted ceilings, marble floors, a walk-in stone fireplace off the chandeliered lanai, and a sunken foyer, rooms with names I had trouble getting my tongue around. My parents were building Casa Grande literally by themselves while we lived in the dream house's three-car garage and the two tiny rooms attached to it until the house was built. A vintage black Lincoln Continental took up center berth of the garage, covered in bedsheets to protect it from dust. Mother, Father, and the baby slept on the cement floor on one side of our car in front of the television, my brother the Little Guy and I on the other. If I was good, I could sleep in the car. I wasn't good very often.

My father wasn't a builder. He rarely spoke, but when he did, his attention belonged to my mother. He had an Ivy League education but worked at a meatpacking plant next to the stockyards. My parents' scheme was to live in the garage for the year it took to build the house. Meanwhile, Mother gave dream-house tours to my classmates' parents who dropped by to see the new baby.

"Let me show you *the house*," Mother said. Waving her tanned arms, she pointed enthusiastically to concrete pilings in the foundation that my father had dug with a pick and shovel. "Playroom," she explained, pointing. "Master bath." Everybody knew about the dream house, which had gotten a lot of publicity when my father unearthed several skulls. Digger Indians, said a man from the university who came to investigate.

The property sat on the eastern side of the coastal foothills in the shadow of a redwood enclave where, I later learned, Ken Kesey had experimented with hallucinogens and Tom Wolfe took notes for *The Electric Kool-Aid Acid Test.* While some happenings in La Honda went on in secret, the goings-on at the garage house felt like a zoo exhibit.

Back when my father was building the garage, we lived in the swimming-pool dressing rooms, doorless, roofless enclosures constructed out of grape-stake fencing. Mother cooked on a stone firepit in a gravel picnic area. There was no bathroom. We used a gallon can, which was a secret. Authorities would take us children away if they found out. Though I had night sweats about sleeping out in the open where wild dogs might eat me, the idea of being taken away paralyzed me with fear.

The first summer, when we lived in the dressing rooms, we bathed in the dream-house pool. The pool had belonged to the house in back of us in a subdivided walnut orchard; its owner had sold it and an acre of land to my parents in a quasi-legal transaction—the neighborhood was zoned for much larger parcels.

After the three-car garage and its two rooms were built and we moved in, my father raised the framed walls of the kitchen, one side of which was to be a huge cobblestone fireplace. The Little Guy and I watched as the unwieldy frame of the east wall started to dip and sag while Mother tried to help hold it up. We giggled; it looked like a TV cartoon. A minute later, Mother screamed. The frame of studs and boards crashed to the ground. The next thing I remember was Mother sobbing as she lay in the cab of our father's battered pickup. Her legs looked like the bloody cutlets that Father brought home from work.

"You kids don't make a damned sound," Father barked in his Bostonian accent.

"Take shallow breaths so he won't hear us," I ordered my freckle-faced brother. If I was six, he must have been four. We stole glances at Mother through the truck's back window, an oval of thick glass rimmed by a black rubber seal. She wore Hawaiian shorts and a white sleeveless blouse. Waves of her dark hair stuck to her sweaty face. She balled her fists, unclenched, balled her fists again.

Couldn't my father hear her crying? "Shouldn't she go to the hospital?" I asked.

Outside the garage, my father swore and pounded the splintered wall frame with a hammer. "If I want your opinion, I'll ask for it."

From the beginning, I sensed that the neighbors didn't like us. Their homes sat camouflaged in wooded acreage walled by wrought-iron fences and stone gates with names carved into them: Dial House, the Pinnacles. From the back door of the garage house, I surveyed the neighbors' glorious lives. The children at Five Oaks had horses the same color as their palomino hair.

There were horses everywhere. Expensive horses. On Sunday mornings, a hunt club charged across the hay field beyond the neighbor's orchard while huntsmen blew mournful calls on brass horns. Hounds filled the sky with yelps called *giving tongue*—only the basest people called a hound a dog. When the neighbor who owned the stable across the road came over to complain that our dog had chased their priciest racehorse, Father retorted that no horse cost that much. On weekends equestrians streamed passed our house. Their voices carried: "What's going on here?" Most people thought the dream house had burned down and we were rebuilding it.

Window glass arrived, and the dream house had eyes but no doors, just gaping holes, like the hole where the walk-in fireplace was supposed to be. Mother wanted the cobblestones to be laid askew, not in straight lines. They experimented with methods of laying stone; one involved a platform of stone weights on a set of planks that bridged two ceiling beams above the hole in the roof where the chimney would rise.

As I stood on the special subfloor that would accommodate the marble tiles to be laid there, my mother pointed up at the intricate system of ropes and pulleys, wagged a manicured fingernail, and warned, "I don't want you kids—especially you," she emphasized, her hazel eyes narrowing at me—"to walk heavily across this floor or to speak loudly. The suspended weight up there might fall and kill you."

Staring at the bale of cobblestones above my head, I shivered.

At school, I was the little girl who lived in the garage. When classmates asked where we slept, I ignored them; everyone was curious. "Do you walk down the neighbor's driveway when you get off the school bus because you're ashamed you live in a garage?"

"They tease me all the time," I complained to Mother.

"Just rise above it." She sat at a card table in one of the tiny rooms, reading *House Beautiful*. "And for God's sake, don't cry! That just eggs them on."

Usually, I roped my brother into playing horse with me. On one occasion when I brought a friend home, she discovered that we kept our pots and pans in the broken washing machine and had a toilet in the kitchen. My classmate had never seen anything so hilarious and told the entire school.

The community had a free riding school taught by a former colonel in the Czarist army—a *white* Russian as opposed to the dreaded red variety, who were trying to beat America to the moon and destroy our way of life. Most of the riding-school horses were donated ponies that the sponsor's children had outgrown. Rattail, Ginger, Brown Sugar, and Panda were the center of my summer universe from ages eight to eleven. When Mother dropped me off at the gated entrance, I made my way to the line of neighborhood children waiting for their turn at a lesson, feeling shy but determined. The colonel's assistants were teenage girls. For me, there was nothing else imaginable that provided a sense of mastery over something strong and alive.

During my first lesson, one of the big girls took me double. I sat in the English saddle in front of her in order to get the feel of straddling a horse and to learn to hold the reins. Soon I was able to ride alone, then to post the trot. Up, down, the iambic rhythm invaded my dreams.

Five days a week, my father dropped me off at the riding school on his way to work. In my third summer, I was allowed to help groom the horses and then to cool them out when the day's lessons had finished. Though the riding school was supported by a generous sponsor, the other girls' parents contributed. Our family was exempt, Mother informed me.

When summer ended, so did riding. I felt marooned. According to my mother, the dream house would be ready to move into any day, then my life would be just like everyone else's. I could almost touch it: a heated bedroom, clothes that didn't come from the school rummage sale, an allowance, a horse, a horse, a horse.

The doors never arrived. The cobblestone chimney kept falling down, the studs and boards of the interior walls were never Sheetrocked in, the man who helped my father nail cedar shakes onto our roof kept asking for his awful money. Sometimes I felt that the dream house was cursed. At school we studied California Indians. Shamans put spells on their burial grounds; not even wolves dared dig up the Indian dead.

After my third summer of riding lessons, I was invited to take instruction with the colonel on Saturdays during the winter. I lived for those Saturdays. At the riding school, I had a place in the world; I had value. I was able to manage the lovely horses owned by the other girls, mounts not suitable for them but purchased for them nevertheless. I wasn't fearless, but I had a good seat and wasn't deterred by wild-eyed balking or snorting nostrils. To earn lesson money, I picked walnuts, husking and selling them at a roadside stand at the top of our driveway. The nuts stained my hands the color of creosote. When cracked open, many yielded something shriveled and black inside.

The next summer I advanced to big-girl status, grooming and saddling the horses in the early-morning fog. That was the year the other girls got braces. "I need my smile straightened," I told Mother. "This baby tooth never fell out, and the new one overlaps it."

"Stop sucking your finger, and you wouldn't have crooked teeth," she told me. It was a point of ridicule and shame. Sucking my finger was the only way I could fall asleep at night, if I fell asleep at all.

That fall the riding school started farming out horses for the winter. I don't know how the society matron who hosted the school at her stable convinced my parents to take a horse, build a corral, and buy three tons of hay and a tarp to keep it dry. I was never allowed to forget that I'd had a horse before the family had a house. After the horse arrived, Mother purchased a chandelier for the foyer. It sat under a tarp, looking like a tent from the Arabian Nights.

On Saturdays, I rode along the road for an hour to my lesson, when I could afford to take one. I babysat. I searched under the seat of my father's truck for coins. If all else failed, I robbed my mother's purse for quarters, which caused a terrible scene—every penny was accounted for. Winter came on. My horse had no shelter; the paddock, in full view of the road, filled with mud. People complained. The horse looked ribby and threadbare. I pleaded for a bag of oats for Christmas. Someone donated a waterproof turnout sheet. When the vet charged us for worming the horse, Mother was furious.

I scraped up the entry fees to summer horse shows, paying for the cost of the check my mother wrote for me and the stamp to mail the entry to the horse-show office, so that I would learn the value of money. Since I had no way of trailering my horse—a borrowed riding school mount—I rode for hours to and from the horse-show facility. Sometimes I won; usually, I didn't. Having to try harder than other people was a given.

The autumn I turned fifteen, the meatpacking plant closed, and my father transferred to the northwest office. "Of course, this is the end of riding for her," Mother told a high school friend who phoned to say good-bye. "She loves horses too much. It's not healthy."

The idea of a new start felt daunting, but as we drove away from the half-built house with the boggy horse paddock, my back straightened. I felt lighter. No matter what my parents said, I was hopeful of getting a horse of my own and of having a life where "the little girl who lived in the garage" wouldn't find me.

In Oregon it rained all the time. "Clouds don't bother me," Mother chirped. She bought a pair of après-ski glasses with yellow lenses.

Enrolling midyear in a new high school, I found that being from California carried a lot of cachet. I made horsey friends at school and got an unpaid job walking polo ponies between chukkers at the hunt club. Mother seemed unhappy that I wasn't being paid and cranky about driving me to the horse park twice a week. As soon as I earned my stripes as a hot walker, I'd be paid, I told her, the first of many deceptions—there was a long wait-list of girls willing to work for free.

If I went longer than a week without smelling a horse, I thought I would perish. I got unpaid jobs riding horses for girls whose busy social calendars didn't allow them to exercise their mounts. At almost sixteen, I had saved two hundred dollars that was supposed to go toward college. Secretly, I hoped to use my bank account to buy a horse. I started looking. Every horse at the hunt club cost thousands except for one, a little bay gelding saved by the club manager from the kill pen of the stockyards where my father worked.

I asked the resident professional rider to put Pepper over a course of jumps. My heart thumped wildly as I watched from the grandstands.

"Nice," I said, barely able to squeak. "How much?" When I was told the price, my heart sank.

"Whaddya think?" The manager's paunch boiled over his white polo breeches.

I didn't know what to say. "Too much, I guess," I finally replied.

"What?" His face reddened as if I'd insulted him, the man who'd allowed me the privilege of walking his polo ponies in the rain for the last four months.

Adept at reading the body language of angry adults, I added, "Too much for that horse. I think I want more of a mount."

The stable manager smiled. "I'll keep my eye open for something." Mother was right; I'd become an accomplished liar.

My parents didn't buy a house in the horsey suburb with the good school system where we had been renting a tiny apartment. They bought an estate in the hinterlands between two mill towns near the old Oregon Trail. The summer retreat of a World War I profiteer, the house appeared to be a city block long, three stories high, and white as a refrigerator. Located along a snaking river miles from anywhere, it was cantilevered from age over a river, but it had been built to bridge a tributary that spilled down a waterfall. The river ran right under the house. This frightened me, its wild eddies and whirlpools raging on the other side of the living room's picture windows.

There was a powder room and a laundry and ironing room with a drying closet. The house even had a walk-in freezer, which never worked, but the door could be padlocked, and Christmas cookies were secured there. Above the three-car garage and boat bay were servants' quarters. The entire property looked to be in disrepair, its sale forced by bankruptcy. Inside, dampness emanated from the walls; everything needed painting.

"Our real estate agent said that it's never flooded," Mother assured us, but the maroon feathered Depression-era wallpaper covering the sunken dining room was stained around the bottom as if by brown bathtub rings. We had no near neighbors. Most of our property lay across the road on a vertical cliff. It was no place for a horse, even if I had been able to buy one. I had no way to get anywhere. Not that there was anywhere to go. When they had the time and inclination, my parents chauffeured me; driving lessons were not essential. My eventual husband would teach me to drive.

The fact that I got no allowance puzzled my new classmates, who thought surely anyone living in a mansion was wealthy. I wanted to blend in, which was going to be difficult; my new school unnerved me almost as much as the cold brown river. Boys carried knives; girls wore white lipstick spread on as thick as cake frosting. Two boys in my graduating class would be sentenced to life in prison for committing a murder for hire.

I would have felt rudderless if one of the debutantes from the hunt club hadn't given me her horse, a tall copper Thoroughbred, Zorro. I worked for his board mucking stalls at the blacksmith's barn a long walk down the river road from my house. Like many gift horses, Zorro had serious problems, one being that he trotted chronically lame. But I couldn't believe my good fortune and thought him the handsomest mount in my new 4-H club. He shared a pasture with a quarter horse filly the same color, the two sometimes grazing so close together that it looked as if they were one.

Problems arose immediately. I had no money for a vet, so when Zorro got sick with colic, I was beside myself; horses can die from colic if they don't receive immediate treatment. The blacksmith called the vet even though my mother had vetoed it—diverting funds from the outfitting of the new house was regarded as stealing from the *family*.

"Your father said I could put you in foster care," my mother told me when the bill arrived. My father, who had a long commute, was generally gloomy in mood and now had a bad back that prevented him from walking upright. He returned home every night bent like a carpenter's square and went directly to bed.

At the end of my first summer on the river, Zorro and I didn't place well at the county fair even though the blacksmith was the judge. But clearly, I could ride, and people who wanted to sell the mounts their children had lost interest in asked me to show their horses. Instead of being the little girl who lived in the garage, I was considered a good influence, which floored me: Wasn't I the same person?

The horses I rode did well, especially one giant gray with whom I competed in the high-jump competition at the state fair, where horse-show events alternated with rodeo events. In the final round of the open high-jump competition, my ride, Gray Gander, balked at a multicolored oxer, stopped dead, and then flew over it. Completely unseated, I struggled to stay astride and sprawled sideways over the saddle. Gander galloped on. I had my hands on the reins, together with a huge clump of his braided mane. He didn't slow down so that I could right myself, and I'd be eliminated if my feet touched the ground. I felt done for. Aiming Gander at what turned out to be the next and final fence, I thought that the triple bar would stop him. He launched himself, cleared it, no rails down, no faults, a perfect round. When I stayed on and righted myself, the stadium crowd went wild. Cowboys catcalled, threw ten-gallon hats in the air, and made popping noises by stomping paper cups. My vision blurred, I thought I would faint or throw up. We'd won.

Gray Gander sold immediately. Soon after, the river rose up and hammered our house, washing away the road. People thought that surely the bridge would go next. Many grand old river mansions were demolished in that flood. In the end, our house stood, but with a fir tree rammed through the living room. Not all the plate glass had shattered, though the hardwood floors warped and were covered with silt, the walls buckled, and the kitchen appliances rusted beyond saving. We had no flood insurance.

We moved to the dingy servants' quarters above the garage. Even after the house was painstakingly resurrected, we ate our meals out there on an old picnic table, the main house's kitchen too good to use and protected in plastic. There was even more stress over money. Mother, who was always nervous about driving, grew phobic and blamed it on the fact that we couldn't afford auto insurance. I was afraid to ask her for rides to after-school activities except to see my horse. Even that was usually denied.

One day Zorro got sick, and by the time I could get to where he was stabled, he had died. I wandered around in a fog for weeks. In the mornings when I awoke, I felt fine until I remembered, and then I felt as if I'd been knocked down by the outgoing tide. The blacksmith let me ride Zorro's pasture mate, Goldico. I made friends with the river, where I swam my borrowed mare. I rode bareback, and we bobbed in the swift current as her massive shoulders paddled from sandbar to sandbar, her mane floating on the surface like sea grass. I spent entire days riding from swimming hole to swimming hole. Astride, I felt a part of a greater whole. Goldico had been put to a palomino stallion. I thought longingly of the following spring and her foal, dreamed of raising horses. At the end of the summer, the stockyards closed, and my father transferred to the Deep South with the rest of the family. I took the Greyhound bus to the university in Eugene.

I spent Christmas at the home of a 4-H friend back near my old high school and got to ride Goldico one more time before she was sold, but I never saw her foal.

I sometimes think of them: little horse and big horse, foal and mare, necks bent in the same arc, heads together grazing on a shaggy green hill near the end of the Oregon Trail.

NINE

As True Colors's belly grew, the grass greened, and my horse lust turned to foal lust, even foal envy. Driving through the valley below our farm, I noticed a new foal with its dam in the field at the horse farm by the bend in the river. The next day there was another. I couldn't wait for T.C. to foal.

But the idea of helping at the birth filled me with trepidation. Horses are not like humans: After a mare's water breaks, the foal has between five and ten minutes to exit into this world; otherwise, problems ensue. It's imperative that the owner be present to troubleshoot—to help the mare pass the fetus or to clear the foal's nasal passages—even though horses do survive on the range.

Dr. Darla seemed almost as excited as I was and gave me an amateur foaling video produced by one of her clients. Suddenly, we were fast friends. "I don't think the owner of the mare in the video needed to pull this one. He was too zealous," she told me in a measured voice. "It's best if the mare can push the baby out by herself, without assistance. That way less damage is done. And it's really important that the mare stay down for five minutes after the foal's born, so that the last nourishment can pass to baby before one of them gets up, breaking the cord."

All I heard was *pull it*. The rest of Darla's instructions vaporized. Pull the foal out of the mother? Oh my God! My stomach filled with wet sand.

According to my foaling books, the foal comes out front hooves first, in a diving position, with the snouty fish-shaped head bent between the forelegs. Amazingly, the hooves are equipped with little slippers, finger-shaped protoplasm attached to baby's feet to protect the mother. First the forelegs, then the head, and finally, the shoulders of the foal are passed (if the mare is lucky; if she is unlucky, a breech). While pushing the shoulders out, the mare sometimes gives up trying, and from here, I might have to pull the rest of the way. Mares like privacy. Most foalings take place at night, in a protected if not hidden place. I needed to allow True Colors to feel safe and at the same time be ready to assist.

"When her udder fills and she begins dripping milk, then you know she'll foal in the next twenty-four to forty-eight hours, and you can start sleeping in the barn," Darla instructed in a sober voice. "Some owners start sleeping in the barn before that, so the mare can get used to them being there." We stood in front of our foaling box. Mark had removed all the shavings used for bedding—wheelbarrow loads—and replaced them with straw, because straw was cleaner and produced less dust than shavings. And not just any straw—it had to be wheat straw. Oat straw had sharp edges and might lacerate the baby's eye, according to the foal literature I'd read, underlined, memorized, and stacked on my bedside table, the floor beside my bed, and the windowsill next to it. The Winter Palace was in chaos.

This place is a pigsty, shrieked Joan Crawford. *There's clutter everywhere.*

Mares start cycling (called estrus) right after the first of the year, when the days begin to lengthen; they cycle every twenty-one days, the same amount of time it takes a chicken egg to hatch. They're bred in the late spring and give birth the following year, approximately 340 days later. Because we didn't know True Colors's breeding date, we couldn't determine her foaling date. So we watched her for signs and let her changing body direct us.

On a gray morning in mid-April, when the cottonwood fluff on the trees by the pond blew as thick as snow, I saw the first sign: edema around True Colors's milk bag—her mammary glands, crowned by two tiny teats, located between her hind legs. I stood next her as she and Willie grazed in the front pasture. She kept a wary eye on me, a serious expression on her face. I wondered if it was a bad sign that her belly looked lopsided instead of centered. Later, when I reported it to Darla, she assured me that the situation was normal. I studied the white-flowering clover on which True Colors feasted, then glanced back at her abdomen. *What's this?* I ran to the house for a pair of reading glasses. Something that looked like granules of sugar powdered her udders. Another sign.

I put True Colors in a paddock by herself. If T.C. took it upon herself to lie down and have her foal in the early morning, as some mares did (and T.C. might do this, I reasoned, since barns were new to her), she needed to be alone, without the worry of another horse harming her baby. Willie eyed me woefully as if being punished for he knew not what, then he ambled over to the fence that separated him from his girlfriend. The gangly bay lowered his long neck and huge head, staring mournfully at her through the boards. When he nickered, she didn't answer or even raise her head. That evening Willie was so distressed at being pushed out of True Colors's heart that he wouldn't eat his grain.

"Don't colic on me," I told the big bay at his late-night feeding. "I just couldn't cope." His sad eyes looked like bottomless pools of peat water.

"None of you colic or throw a shoe or get hurt until this foal is born, understand?" Ms. Piggy and Kermit didn't interrupt their eating. Alazan pushed his copper head and lightning-lash blaze over his stall door, looking for a carrot.

Signs of colic, I reminded myself—a horse going off its feed, not drinking, pawing, glancing anxiously at its sides, lying down, then getting up and acting uncomfortable—were also the signs of stage one of equine labor. I looked at True Colors standing in the darkest corner of her stall, ignoring her hay (she still felt shy about eating in front of me). Occasionally, she glanced at her sides, per usual. She always acted uncomfortable, so it would be hard for me to know when she went into labor.

Willie didn't colic that night, but he didn't eat or drink much, either—never a good sign in a horse. The next day, when I pried myself away from True Colors to check on the others, I glanced first at Willie's paddock. Where was he? An electrical charge ran down my neck. He lay in an unnatural position next to the fence where it turned a corner.

Oh, words of one syllable! Gripping either side of my head, I considered the situation: I was alone on the farm. Mark was an hour away in his lab. I didn't have friendly horse neighbors here in the Cascade foothills, as I'd had in New Jersey. When I had a cast horse (one that's down and can't get up) in the Sourlands, help was a phone call away: Within minutes the entire population of retired horsemen was at my door, along with the hired help—brawny youths who worked the soybean fields.

Running to the barn, I grabbed a yard-long dressage whip out of the tack room, then squeezed through the fence rails and ran out to where Willie lay with his legs uphill from his neck and torso. The *clomp, clomp* of my feet would have startled any horse, but Willie didn't move. After a minute, he raised his head slightly, regarded me, then put his head down again, the disc of his jaw resting on the grass. He wore a light green blanket called a New Zealand rug, waterproof tarp on the outside, a thin layer of wool felt on the inside. It buckled across his chest on the tightest notch, and I could see that when he moved his shoulders to try to raise his feet underneath himself, he came against the restriction of the blanket, stopped trying, and then lay down again. Most horses panicked when they found themselves in such a fix. In panicking, they would find they could get up. Not Willie, who seemed to have lost the will to live. Horses usually sleep standing up; if they're down for longer than a few hours, their weight begins crushing their vital organs. How to get him on his feet?

"Silly horse." He was stoic to a fault.

I approached his huge prone body, staring at the cowlicks on his stomach and at the midline, where the hair growing down one side of his barrel met the hair growing down the other. Slowly, I unfastened his blanket straps—first the buckle across his chest (for a minute I thought I'd need a knife to cut it off of him), then the leather strap, or surcingle, and finally, the two leather hind leg straps—a little tricky because he lay so close to the fence, jammed into the corner of the paddock.

"You're free now, big guy. You can get up." I clapped my hands above my head.

He followed the motion of my arms with one huge watery eye but only raised his muzzle into the air for an instant, then slammed it down, refusing to try to raise himself.

My heart pitched. I'd hung a long cotton rope in the aisle of the barn. While I might be able to finagle the rope under his shoulders, there was no way I could raise him by myself.

Feeling totally alone and defeated, I sat down on the ground and started to cry. Ms. Piggy and Kermit came to the fence on one side, Alazan in his paddock on the other. The hand that fed them was behaving oddly; they eyed me with concern. True Colors continued to graze, undaunted by me or by Willie's situation. After a minute, I gathered my courage, picked up the whip, got on my feet, and walked backward until I was about ten feet away from the downed horse. Then I began shouting and hooting and beating the ground violently with the whip.

The big bay horse jerked as if struck by a cattle prod, then jumped to his feet, shedding his blanket and lunging at me, teeth bared. It's not uncommon for a horse that's been cast to strike at the nearest target—often his liberator—when freed.

I dodged his bite as he sprang at me and then ducked when his hind hooves shot out as he spun around bucking, overjoyed by his freedom. The foals looked alarmed but didn't move. Alazan took off at a lope for a few strides. Then every horse's head jerked up, ears pricked in the direction of the pounding of hooves.

Startled, I looked around, catching the blur of True Colors as she flew into the trees at the far end of the back pasture, moving faster than Secretariat; the extra two hundred pounds she carried hadn't the slightest effect on her.

I closed my eyes as a bad thought stuck its talons into me. An abrupt fright could cause a mare to drop her foal—a serious concern, since premature equine neonates do not survive. I held my head in my hands. To come all this way with her and then have her lose her foal over a fluke; how could I have been so stupid? Why hadn't I put all the horses in the barn before I tried to scare Willie into getting up? If I'd taken his friends away, he might have gotten up without all the hoopla. Now I'd have to coax a very nervous T.C. back inside.

Bringing True Colors in that afternoon wasn't easy. The other horses had eaten their grain before they noticed that she was missing. Willie was the first to begin to call frantically, and the others followed in an ear-jarring cacophony. Finally, True Colors emerged from the woods but wouldn't approach the gate. While I stood at the fence waiting for her, I took comfort in the smell of lilacs—the white ones on gnarled shrubs, the dusty lavender hedges, and the tree-tall bushes so deep purple that they looked navy blue.

Eventually, I had to walk out and get her. Plodding to the gate—that suspicious break in the fence that was sometimes there and sometimes not—I sneezed. T.C. stopped dead. Every muscle in her athletic body tensed. In the next second she would probably pull away from me and be gone. Instead, she stood rock-still. Her eyes widened until I saw the wildfire color of her irises feathering into the white of the sclera. I stared at her heaving rib cage and huge belly.

"I'm so, so sorry," I told her, but she wouldn't look at me.

*   *   *

For several days, I held my breath, fearing that she'd abort. The white dogwoods came into bloom, then leafed out. On the day when our pink dogwood burst its coral blossoms, I saw that the flesh around True Colors's tailbone appeared to have dropped away, and her backbone stuck up like that of a starved dog. When I brought her in that afternoon, she seemed an inch more trusting of me. When I sneezed, her head jerked up, but she kept plodding after me, and I couldn't read any intention to take flight in her eyes. Her thoughts were elsewhere.

"Her milk bag was swollen this morning, and the edema didn't go down after I turned her out. In fact, it looked larger this afternoon," I told Darla over the phone.

"Won't be long now," she replied. I sensed that her husband was annoyed with my telephoning their home in the evenings to report each development, so I'd resorted to phoning during her afternoon rounds. Annoyed receptionists I could cope with.

Meanwhile, True Colors wasn't taking her situation seriously and continued to fly across the pasture at the least provocation, even when the Gang of Ten—a familiar flock of Canada geese nesting near our pond—landed next to her and began eating bugs from the grass, honking and snaking their necks.

And what was this—butterball Ms. Piggy looked like she was starting to cycle at the age of one year! Her vulva winked as she raised her tail and squatted, squirting urine. On the other side of the fence, a very intrigued Alazan reached his neck delicately over the hot wire that ringed the paddock and bit Filly's neck. She squealed with delight, her dark eyes widening. Kermit came up behind her, pressing his chest into her rump, trying to remember how to mount her, then gave up and went back to chasing blue dragonflies. We'd had Darla castrate him just after New Year's when, one day as the frozen mud near the paddock gates flaked like pie crust, the eight-hundred-pound yearling began mounting everything, fences, trees, but mostly Filly, and not always from the rear—he'd given her a watermelon-sized hematoma on her chest when he'd tried to mount her head. Both yearlings were graying; flecked with white on their coal-black rumps, they looked dappled with snow.

That night when I went down to the barn before bed for a late-night mare check, I walked out the front door onto the porch and tripped over a pair of bare legs.

"Ouch, that hurt," said a child's voice. It was Angel.

"What are you doing here?" I asked, stunned. It had to be at least eleven o'clock. "Why aren't you home in bed? Where's your friend Vicki? Is she here?"

"Don't mention her name," said Angel. "I'm not speaking to her."

"Why not? What are you doing here?"

"She's trying to steal my boyfriend. I just came to see how the mare was doing. Has she had her foal?"

"No," I said, pulling Angel to her feet. She was not even five feet tall but weighed about as much as I did. "Aren't you cold?" She wore cutoff jeans and no jacket.

"No." She shook her strawberry roan hair.

"Want a ride home?" One morning the week before, Angel had called and asked me to take her to school, which I did; she'd missed the bus, and her mother had gone to work.

"No," she answered as I dragged her with me in the direction of the barn. "Can I walk home through your back pasture?"

"Sure," I said. Her house was below our property, and I supposed that was how she'd gotten here, climbed the fence and walked up the slope. "I'll call you when T.C. foals," I assured her. How long had Angel been sitting on my porch? She didn't even carry a flashlight. "You sure you're all right?" I asked.

"Fine," she said gaily. Pulling away from my grip, she walked into the night.

By now the broodmares at the quarter horse farm next to the state high-way at the bend in the river had produced countless foals. Grazing in pairs, they made the landscape look timeless. The honey smell of the locust trees by the pond drifted in an open window in the Winter Pal-ace, where I intermittently stopped typing to watch T.C. out the win-dow through a pair of binoculars. At the end of April, the clearest sign happened. One morning I took a flake of hay into True Colors's stall and checked her udders: What looked like drops of clear wax dotted the ends of her nipples.

That night Mark and I moved a foam mattress down to the barn. First we made our bed in the tack room, but we were too far away. We needed to be able to see what was going on in the stall, so I made our bed on the rubber mat in the aisle opposite the feed room. We crawled into our sleeping bags fully clothed, our pull-on shoes, a watch with a second hand, and a flashlight at the ready.

Nobody slept. The idea that we were on the barn floor excited the horses, except for True Colors, who looked on edge, her lily-shaped ears flicking back and forth. Kermit and Ms. Piggy craned their necks over their stall doors, thinking our presence was some kind of a game. Alazan circled his stall, jutting his head out. Finally, they calmed and commenced a guttural snoring so loud that human sleep was impossible. Occasionally, I threw off my sleeping bag, stood up, and when my eyes accustomed to the dark, stared over the door into True Colors's stall. She lay on her side, her huge belly looming above her like a load of laundry, her legs stretched out stiff as if rigor mortis had set in.

Darla didn't know what to say when I reported this development to her the following morning. "Call me when the minute she foals. No matter what hour."

"Really?" I asked. "Your husband won't mind?"

"He's been a vet for years. Of course he won't mind."

I doubted that. He was the gatekeeper, always answering their home phone. "Who's this?" he'd bellow, when by now he must recognize my voice. Even the many receptionists at the vet clinic recognized my voice.

The huge Easter egg–colored rhododendrons in front of our house started to bud. Wax continued to form on T.C.'s nipples, first a little, then so much it dripped on her hind legs, leaving them sticky. The wax attracted pollen and dirt. Days passed. I turned a page on the wall calendar. The horses were now used to us sleeping in the barn and seemed happy to see us at night. We, on the other hand, were bleary-eyed and sleep-deprived. Nothing snores as loud as a horse, and there were five of them.

After the sun went down, I walked through the mist and rain every half hour until bedtime to check on T.C. At about ten, Mark and I crawled into our sleeping bags to try to sleep. When I heard T.C. lie down, I checked my watch with a penlight. Every evening I readied our foaling kit, kept on a bale of straw in front of the True Colors's stall: sterilized towels, sterilized lab coats, a bottle of livestock-strength iodine, a sterile piece of string, sterile gloves, sterile cotton, a stopwatch, a thermometer, a sterilized blade, an industrial-strength thirty-nine-gallon garbage bag with a string tie.

Every night before going to bed in the barn, we showered and put on clean clothes. Cleanliness was important; a foal is born without an immune system, and its survival rides on the care it receives the first few hours after birth. As the nights dragged on, I lay on my back, staring into the dark, listening to my heart pound, waiting for the restless noises of the first stage of labor.

After sleeping in the barn for two weeks, Mark and I were exhausted. I almost dozed off while driving to the grocery store to buy the enemas I would need for the foal after it was born. Mark nearly hit an apple tree when he nodded off while mowing on our tractor. We decided to take turns sleeping in the barn. That way at least one of us could get a night's rest.

The day the lipstick-red rhododendrons burst into flower, T.C. came in from the pasture dripping milk. Standing in the foaling stall, my feet rustling the foot-deep straw every time I took a step, I watched white pearls form on the ends of her nipples, then fall to the ground or splash on her legs. True Colors regarded me with suspicion until I left the building; only then would she approach her hay. She hardly touched her grain, although broodmares are supposed to be ravenous.

"She's uncomfortable because of the way the baby's positioned," said Darla. I was on the phone to her immediately after seeing the dripping milk. "She'll have it tonight for sure."

That night it was my turn to keep vigil, and I slept in my running shoes, thinking that I would dash up to the house for Mark when T.C. dropped to the floor, gripped by the second stage of labor. But where was stage one? True Colors stood inert, her left hind hoof cocked. Finally, at about eleven, I heard her walk over to her timothy and begin to pick through it.

The next morning, the drip had increased. True Colors's hind legs were stained white. I felt deeply troubled. Foals gain their immunity by sucking their mother's first milk, called colostrum. After about three days, the colostrum level starts to diminish. At this rate, there'd be nothing left for the foal.

I called Darla the minute her clinic's office started taking calls at nine A.M.

"Her bag's the size of a football this morning. Shouldn't I be collecting this milk?"

"Oh, she's going to have plenty of milk," chirped Darla. "She'll go any minute now." She sounded unusually cheery. It was a warm morning, and all the rhododendrons were in full flower, making the landscape feel tropical. Bright nuggets of dandelion studded our pastures. The air was filled with insects, little swarms of gnats clotted together by the fence around the old hand-dug well. Flies lit in the corners of the horses' eyes: time to bring out the squirt bottle of fly repellent. I'd accustomed Ms. Piggy and Kermit to the noise of the squirt bottle last fall; it took only a brief refresher for them to allow me to spray their bellies and chests before I turned them out to graze. I'd bought yearling-sized fly masks and fitted the mesh contraptions over their ears, Velcroing the masks at their throats.

I knew better than to get near T.C. with a spray bottle. The tiny noise, an almost silent *whoosh*, when I sprayed Willy in the next stall unsettled her so much that she looked as if she wanted to take flight. And when I tried to Velcro a standard horse-sized fly mask over her face after putting on her halter, she threw her head violently, her whiskery muzzle swatting me across the right cheekbone; a bruise rouged my eye. Lucky thing I didn't get the fly mask on her. The noise of Velcro tearing when I removed it would have launched her.

I asked Darla again whether I should be trying to save T.C.'s first milk. Somewhere I'd heard or read that horsemen did this so the foal would be assured early immunity.

"We know where we can lay our hands on some if we need it. I think she'll be fine." There was a lot of chatter in the background as the vet clinic opened the doors for dog and cat business. "Don't leave her alone," Darla instructed. "Keep an eye on her even in turnout."

"Okay," I said tentatively. Who was *we*?

All morning I resisted the impulse to call Darla back and query her about the mysterious supply of colostrum. By noon I'd worn a trail from the front door out to the gate of the front pasture, where True Colors ate grass so green it looked neon. Even from where I stood, I could see her milk dripping; sometimes it sprayed out of her nipples. Then I remembered: I'd heard about collecting a mare's first milk from Kath.

I tracked her down at a horse show in Calgary but didn't get her return call until late afternoon. After I apologized for being out of touch (all the while thinking I should ask if she was all right herself; she had a history of depression) and then explained the situation to her, Kath didn't skip a beat.

"Get that milk," she directed before I'd finished. "Large breeding farms keep a supply of it. They might give it or trade it to another breeding farm, but they don't know you."

"Okay." My stomach flip-flopped. "So what do I do?" I asked in a small voice.

"You've got some canning jars?" she asked.

"Yes," I said. "Mark went wild making blackberry jam last summer."

"Sterilize about half a dozen quart jars and about a dozen half-quart jars. Put on a sterile glove, if you have it, and if you don't, buy some. Take a sterile jar and let her milk drip into it for as long as you can—as long as she'll stand still and let you collect it." Kath paused as if to catch her breath from having done this more than once herself. No one responded faster than Kath did. I was so comforted by her friendship.

"Oh, before you start *milking*, take a damp sterile towel and wipe the udder free of dirt. If you get some funky stuff in the milk, a little is okay—it's not a perfect world. When you have about a third of a quart jar, transfer it to a half-quart jar. You're just using the quart jar because it has a bigger mouth—easier to capture the milk."

"Should I actually milk her like a cow?" I asked. My heart rose into my throat. I didn't know how to milk, and I was certain True Colors would never let me if I did.

"No, no. No actual milking," Kath commanded. "You don't want to stimulate those udders any more than they already are. Capture as much milk as you can tonight. If she doesn't foal, insist that your vet come have a look at her tomorrow."

"I'm on the phone to her day and night. She says not to worry."

"*Insist* that she come out," Kath said. "It could be just the rich grass that has brought her milk on early."

"Do you think something's wrong?"

There was a brief hesitation on the other end of the line. A horse-show announcer called something over a loudspeaker. "Hmm . . . The foal could be positioned wrong."

"What do I do with the milk?" I asked. "Keep it refrigerated?"

Kath continued, "No, put a sterile lid on it and put it in the freezer. When the foal is born, take it out and thaw it slowly. Do *not* put it in the microwave; that'll kill the colostrum. When it's room temperature, add a little hot water, one part water to three parts milk, so that the milk is about a hundred degrees, similar temp as the milk coming out of Mom. Then take a syringe full and slowly squirt it into the foal's mouth. About sixty milliliters every half hour, until you've used it all up and before the foal is twenty-four hours old."

"I think I better write this down." My hand was shaking so hard that I couldn't read what I'd scribbled on the notepad. "Thank you a thousand times," I told her.

I pulled out the huge sterilizing kettle from the storage cupboard under the stove and filled it with water, then collected our empty canning jars. When Mark got home, we took a quart jar down to the barn. Slowly, I eased the nose band of the halter over True Colors's muzzle, then in short movements, I brought the crown piece over her neck. She didn't flinch the way she usually did, and I couldn't help but wonder: Was she getting trained, or did this mark a change in her attitude?

We took turns, one holding the lead rope to keep her from moving around while the other one positioned the mouth of the jar under her dripping—sometimes squirting—nipples. My hand ached, my back hurt from bending over. True Colors's belly seemed as large as a planet. It felt as if we were her moons.

"Look there," Mark said as her sides moved.

"That's a good sign," I said. "At least we know the foal is still alive."

After a while, I felt safe enough to get down on my knees, holding the jar up to one nipple and then the other. True Colors's feet remained rooted.

I felt grateful when Mark volunteered to sleep in the barn that night. I had coffee nerves; my brain felt dim. If the foal came, I'd be useless. Even in my own bed, I hardly slept. When I heard the front door bang shut at five in the morning, I sat bolt upright, sure that Baby was coming. But no, Mark had just returned from his vigil.

By now True Colors was streaming milk. Before we turned the horses out, and while True Colors chewed her flake of morning hay, we collected more milk for the freezer. Sometimes pearl droplets splattered on my hands and I tasted it—sweet, buttery, a little like hard sauce. It must have an amazing fat content. Some cultures make cheese out of mare's milk, as well as a fermented drink. Milk from the dam was the only meat product an equine ever consumed. After weaning, he was herba-ceous for life.

It was May, and all the foals at the quarter horse farm at the bend in the river were romping in their grassy pasture, straying away from Mom and playing with each other. If ever there was a watched pot, it was True Colors. I studied her as she grazed that morning, her behavior nothing out of the ordinary. She didn't lie down or search out a secluded spot. She visited over the fence with the yearlings but ignored Willie, who stood forlornly, his bones inhabiting his large body as if he were an aged beast with one foot in the grave, though he was the same age as his girl-friend.

The minute the vet office started taking calls, I contacted Darla and insisted that she come out before the end of the day. "There's not much I can do," she pleaded.

"I'm afraid the foal is positioned wrong," I told her. "This mare is lit-erally gushing milk. There couldn't be any colostrum left for the foal."

"I told you not to worry about that." But reluctantly, she agreed to come the following day. "If True Colors doesn't foal tonight," she added with certainty.

One thing I knew for sure: There was nothing certain about this horse. Nothing about True Colors went by the book. When I called Kath to report my progress on all fronts, there was an exasperated silence on her end of the line. She was in her hotel room, near the grounds of the famous Calgary Stampede, and I hoped that her silence was because she was preoccupied by getting situated.

"Anything like this ever happen to you?" I asked.

"Yeah," she said, clipping her word with a paring knife. Silence. And then: "The foal died in the mother. It had been dead about two weeks before we discovered it."

I didn't know what to say. After a moment, I helped her out with "I take it that things went downhill from there."

"They bloody well did." I heard her suck in her breath. "Rose of Sha-ron, the world's most perfect mare. I've never found another one like her . . ." Her sentence trailed off into what sounded like a thread of wind.

I lay my head down on the kitchen table, clutching the receiver to my ear.

"So if this is the scenario," she said, regaining her voice, "you want to get the foal out of the mare before it rigors." She cleared her throat. "I'm not saying that's what's happening. If this were my mare," she went on, brightening a shade, "I'd keep collecting that milk."

I left my head on the table for a good five minutes after I said good-bye. What part of the world had I moved to, a surreal place where people over a thousand miles away could diagnose my equine health problems? I felt helpless and frustrated but counted my blessings, starting with Kath's friendship.

It was an unusually hot day for May, so warm that all my beautiful rhododendron flowers wilted. They would probably shrivel and brown tomorrow. But as I walked out the front door and across the porch on my way to bring the horses in from pasture, I noticed that the bubble-gum-pink rose at the back of the house had burst into flower, its hopeful perfume filling the air.

I stayed with True Colors most of the afternoon, brushing her, cap-turing her flowing milk in sterilized jars, which I dated and sealed. Then I tried to familiarize her with the hiss of the spray bottle so that I could apply fly repellent to her neck and chest. Her ebony mane shone, as did her sienna coat and pencil-straight tail, which now touched the ground. With a damp cloth, I dusted the dead skin off the scars on her face, studying their patterns of white hairs and bald black skin. As I worked, T.C. stood halterless in her stall; she always exhibited her best behavior when there were no restraints. Her milk made faint pinging noises as it dripped into the pale yellow straw or onto her hind legs. I bent over, trying to remove the thick sticky globs from the black fur of her cannon bones with a cloth dabbed in rubbing alcohol. Alas, the smell of isopro-pyl distressed her, and she sprang to a corner of her foaling box, her eyes wide but not angry—she never showed anger or even a hint of temper. Stubbornness, yes—she was very stubborn—but there was no meanness in this horse.

Strangely, later in the afternoon she didn't mind when I rubbed her chest with a rag soaked in citronella. I closed the barn's south-facing door, making it dark enough so that the burgeoning fly crop avoided the stalls. Again I groomed her gleaming coat. She stood stationary, now and then shifting her weight uneasily from one hind hoof to another. I waited for the foal to move but never saw the mare's sides jump. When I took hold of her tail, the bone felt as if it had come loose from her spine, and I could easily rotate it to the side to check her vulva, which looked more elongated and swollen than yesterday.

As I left to go up to the house for a quick dinner, I took in the other horses. All heads jutted over the stall doors, begging attention: Alazan's happy energy, Willie's silent imploring, Ms. Piggy's heart-shaped snout, Kermit's shy eyes. I had given them hardly a minute of my time that day. As they called after me, I identified each one's whinny by the timbre: Kermit's foghorn, Ms. Piggy's bell, Alazan's trumpet, Willie's bassoon. True Colors remained mute. I wondered if I knew what her voice sounded like, though I was sure I'd heard it. If she died foaling, how would I remember her whinny?

I hadn't seen livestock lying dead in roadside pastures until I moved to western Washington. Since landing here, I'd seen too many, one a bay draft mare with a bay foal. Both carcasses lay there for so many days that I had to remember to take a different road to town. Now, when I closed my eyes, I tried not to see my bay mare lying on her side, bloated, her legs stretched out stiff as fence posts.

True Colors didn't foal that night. I got almost no sleep listening to the other horses snore. For most of the morning I walked around in an insomniac fog.

"I can't see anything alarming about how she's carrying the foal," Darla said when she arrived before noon.

"But she's been dripping milk for a week. There must be something wrong."

"Sometimes that's how these things go," she said, trying to soothe me. We stood in front of True Colors's stall. Darla wore a blue-green surgical jumpsuit and eye shadow in a matching shade. That morning when I looked in the mirror, Joan Crawford had shrieked: *You look like the wrath of God!* Even though I was unconvinced that True Colors was all right, I was glad to have Darla's company.

"It's possible that the way she's carrying the foal is putting pressure on the milk bag. We do sometimes induce labor, but that can have a detrimental effect on the foal. It can't get up to nurse, which upsets the owner."

"You don't want to do a rectal on her and see if the foal is still okay?" I asked.

Darla fumbled with the penlight in her breast pocket. "Ah . . . I'd have to sedate her, and sedation could have an adverse reaction on the foal," she said.

"How adverse?" I asked.

"It could stop its heart," she replied.

I opened my mouth, but no words came out.

"I'm sure that your mare'll be fine, but I'm not so sure about you! Call me the minute she foals, and in the meantime, get some rest."

When True Colors didn't foal that day or the next, I gave up collecting milk. It was a warm night with a strawberry moon—one that shines brightly enough to pick berries. As I walked down to the barn, I studied the eerie shadows made by the fence posts. Inside, I didn't need a flashlight and could even read my watch as I lay down on the unleveled floor. Crawling inside my sleeping bag and adjusting my pillow, I glanced at the bale where yet again I'd laid out the foaling kit. Yesterday I'd resterilized my stack of towels. If sleeping on the floor was supposed to be good for one's back, why did every part of my body hurt?

True Colors methodically chewed hay. In the din, I made out her dark whale-sized body; she seemed perfectly at ease. By now all the horses were so used to one of us sleeping with them that they waited for us to come down for the night before they settled in, lowering their heads in their unique standing-up sleeping position. It gave me a warm feeling to think that they perceived us as part of their little herd.

I dozed off and had no idea what woke me. True Colors stood with her head bent in the corner where I always threw her a flake of hay. I strained but couldn't hear her chewing. There was a long silence; then she rustled the timothy with her nose, tossing some of it to one side. She took a chew and stopped. When I heard a rush of water, as if someone had turned on a high-powered hose full blast, I sat bolt upright. Grabbing my pull-on shoes, I glanced at my watch: 11:03. Out of my peripheral vision, I saw True Colors's tail fly straight up to the ceiling in an unnatural position. She turned, took a few steps, and in the next second plummeted to the floor as if she'd been shot, her legs stretched out. As she lay dead center in the stall, I grabbed my white lab coat. Trying to pull one arm through a sleeve, I got my hand caught and turned away. When I turned back, a white bubble protruded from between the hams of the mare's haunches.

What had happened to the hour or two of discomfort, the first stage of labor?

Tearing off the lab coat, I bolted for the house, my feet pounding the gravel drive in time with my heart. Bursting through the front door, I started screaming for Mark. Taking the stairs to the Winter Palace in two strides, I saw him hurriedly climb from bed. His shoes thudded on the floor. "Hurry," I entreated. He bounded past me down to the mudroom, where he pulled a jacket off the clothes tree. Flicking on the kitchen light, I grabbed the phone.

"What are you doing?" He brushed by me; the door slammed behind him.

"Telephoning Darla," I called after him. I couldn't dispel the sick feeling that something was amiss and that I would need her help.

Darla's home phone rang once before her husband answered. "Who is this?" he demanded. "She's indisposed."

I gave him my name and ran back to the barn.

The overhead lights were on, and the other horses were straining their necks over their stall doors, tossing their heads in apprehension. Mark wore sterile gloves and his white lab coat and was in the stall with T.C., who was still down, her tailbone bent back, a long black switch of hair stretching out behind her. Mark positioned himself at the mare's rump just as the foal began to emerge, forefeet first in the diving position, its snout and one pointy little hoof having broken through the white caul. I bent over the foal. Its beaky head bobbed like some kind of amphibian.

"Towels," Mark commanded.

I'd left the stall door open and ducked out into the aisle, grabbing a face towel and handing it to Mark, who dabbed the foal's nostrils, clearing them of blood-streaked mucus. He gave back the towel, then bent over and grabbed the strange-looking wet creature behind the shoulders, easing the hips and back legs out of the mother. There was a loud gurgle; when the foal's hind hooves came out, so did the giant watery placenta. The foal, the stall floor, and the fronts of our lab coats were soaked. True Colors raised her head, bending around to stare at her baby, the umbilical still attached.

Quietly, we walked outside the box, closed the door, and looked in. The foal sat up on its shoulders, its head like a just-hatched bird's. It didn't look like a horse but more like something prehistoric: a wet, dark baby pterodactyl. Its bobblehead nodded unsteadily on a pencil-thin neck. The pterodactyl struggled to move its forelegs underneath itself.

True Colors nickered to it, and when it squawked, the other horses went wild, bucking in their stalls. The yearlings' eyes filled with amazement and alarm. Ms. Piggy pawed the floor as Kermit repeatedly struck a front hoof against the wall. Willie's eyes widened, and he looked as if he wanted to climb over his door to protect the others. A strange new presence was in the barn: How had it gotten here? Where had it come from? All the horses wanted to see it. Willie bugled frantically.

True Colors twitched nervously, bringing her front hooves under her chest as if to rise. Mark and I darted back into her stall, hoping to reassure her. She needed to stay down for a few more minutes, and then we would break the umbilical. I went to her shoulders and stroked her several times, and then both of us started toweling the foal. Its head wobbled and its front legs flailed while the hind end remained inert.

When True Colors nickered again, the foal squawked more loudly. It had long floppy ears and pulled them back in a fit of temper when we tried to dry them.

"It seems healthy," I said.

"It keeps wanting to get up," Mark observed.

When True Colors heaved herself forward, I pushed back on her shoulders. *Stay down. Please.* It occurred to me that she was being unusually reasonable. Carefully, Mark held the umbilical cord in both hands and bent it so that it broke a few inches away from the foal's belly. We dabbed the stump with 9 percent iodine to help cauterize it, hopefully preventing bacteria from creeping into the foal's body.

The foal tried to rise but slipped on the afterbirth, which Mark cleared away. I gathered together the afterbirth—it looked like a tent made of animal tissue—and stuffed it in a black garbage sack for the vet to inspect later. If all the pieces weren't there, if True Colors hadn't expelled all of it, she would have to be given hormone injections to make her do so. Otherwise, she could founder—a condition that makes horses' feet heat up, the coffin bones rotate, and, in the worst-case scenario, the hooves fall off.

True Colors climbed to her feet and stood next to us, touching her baby with her nose, hovering over the foal and licking its face. The foal arched its spindly neck into the pressure of its mother's tongue, reveling in her touch.

"Time to get it up so it can nurse," I said. "To get any colostrum that's left." True Colors had been dripping milk for two weeks. Chances were slim that the baby would get an immune system from its mother.

I put my arms around the foal's shoulders. Mark took hold of the inert hind end. True Colors stayed right next to us, intent on her baby, ready to protect it from harm.

"It feels like we're trying to get a wire clothes hanger to stand up," I said, pausing to catch my breath after repeated attempts.

The foal's front end seemed strong and vital, but the hind legs didn't want to engage; its rump looked as airless and deflated as an old bicycle tire. Again and again, the foal slid down on the floor. Mark and I stepped back, studying the foal's haunches. True Colors hovered over it and continued to lick its shiny neck. Her milk bag streamed milk as the foal's toothless pink mouth made loud sucking noises.

"Something isn't right," I said. The taste of panic rose in my throat. I waited for Mark to speak, but he didn't.

The foal's hindquarters—sacrum, hips, hocks, cannon bones—were bent like two bowed legs that arced in the same direction, the line from hip to hoof making almost a half circle. Even with two of us helping, I couldn't see how it would be able to stand; the space behind its ribs looked oddly wasp-waisted and deformed.

Another fifteen minutes passed. The foal couldn't stand up by itself, and nothing we did could raise it.

"What should we do?" I implored, feeling on the edge of panic.

The three of us hovered over the baby, Mark and I and True Colors. While Mark and I continued to rub the foal with a towel, hoping to stimulate its nervous system, True Colors licked its ears and the top of its tiny head, much like a mother cat would clean a kitten. That was when I realized the complete change in her. We stood so close to the mare that Mark rubbed shoulders with her on one side and I rubbed shoulders with her on the other. As the head of the baby pterodactyl bobbed and sucked, True Colors planted herself above it, unshakable as granite.

TEN

"That foal has absolutely no white on it," Darla's husband remarked in a tone somewhere between anger and surprise. It was the first thing he said when he and Darla walked into our barn at a little after midnight.

Darla was all smiles, dressed in a just-pressed jumpsuit, her makeup freshly applied. Her husband wore a Carhartt jacket, his salt-and-pepper hair cut military-short. Darla didn't introduce him, and he said not one word of greeting other than to remark on our long-awaited newborn's lack of markings: no star, blaze, front or hind stockings. I wondered, was no white some kind of omen? Later, Darla told me that her husband had mistaken our white lab coats for butchers' smocks and thought we were readying ourselves for an autopsy.

Darla cooed to True Colors, who continued to stand rock-still above her baby with Mark and me on either side of her. Clearly, she treasured her foal.

"So what have we got?" Darla asked. "A filly or a colt?"

Mark and I exchanged glances. "Don't know." I flushed with embarrassment. "We've been too busy trying to get Baby up to check."

The two entered the stall with us and bent over the foal, who pinned its donkey ears flat against its neck. True Colors dropped her nose to the top of the foal's head as if to block the newcomers. *You may admire, but don't touch,* the mare's expression said.

Darla crooned, "Good girl. Just look how friendly and sensible this mare is!" She turned to me. "Can you believe her transformation?"

The husband-and-wife veterinary team lifted the foal's hind leg. "It's a little girl," squealed Darla. "What a pretty face." Foal showed her rosy gums in a fit of sucking.

"Little? How much do you think she weighs?" Mark asked. I could tell that his back hurt from our many attempts to raise True Colors's new baby.

"About a hundred and twenty-five pounds," replied Darla's husband matter-of-factly.

"Huge!" chimed Darla as she examined the foal's umbilical stump.

Careful, said the mare, wedging her nose between the visitors.

"How did that huge baby fit inside you?" asked Darla. We all wondered that. "What color is she?"

Baby looked a mottled black to me and would probably gray, like her siblings.

True Colors's nose followed Darla's stethoscope as the vet checked Baby's heart and lungs, then followed the instrument in Darla's hand as she checked Baby's eyes.

"One, two, three," said Darla. Suddenly, the vets' arms and legs were of one body; somehow they got Filly up. Mark and I took the front end, one of us on either side, with the vets steadying the rear. True Colors angled in close to me and stood at Baby's side, seeming to hold her breath.

We all had the same thought: *My God, Baby's tall!* Her bird head was almost up to my shoulder. She continued to suck, her lower lip already feathered with fine little chin whiskers. As she stood with her front legs splayed for balance, the vets inspected her froglike hind end. Her narrow hips looked as if they were made of pipe cleaners.

That was when I noticed the rubbery slippers on her tiny perfect hooves.

"Why do her ears flop?" Mark's expression clouded.

"That's normal," said Darla. "Her muscles don't have any tone yet." She didn't look at either of us when she spoke but continued, along with her husband, to inspect the foal's rear end. Would our foal survive long enough to get tone in her ear muscles? My heart filled with sadness at the thought that she might not.

The foal sucked on my wrist. What a curious little thing. Her toothless gums grabbed my sleeve. Though her head looked like a halibut, her eyes were bright. Could she see yet? She started smelling as much of me as she could reach, not shy at all, which surprised me. True Colors stood with her head above Baby's, warming both our faces with her breath. We were all huddled close together. I forgot what a cool night it was.

"Windswept to the right," said Darla's husband. The two continued to hold up the foal's hind end, which first swayed one way, with its weight on one hoof, and then swung in the other direction, the rear weight shifting to the opposite hoof.

My face was a question mark, I knew.

"That's what her leg deviation is called," explained Darla. The filly's legs did look exactly like the limbs of a gale-pruned tree on a coastal foothill.

Darla's husband carefully inserted a thermometer in the foal's rectum. Shame on us, we'd forgotten to take Baby's temperature. The pterodactyl flailed her legs in discomfort. At first it seemed as though she would cave in behind, but the flailing seemed to help her gain control of her stick legs. She was so crooked that she could not rest both hind hooves on the ground at the same time.

True Colors homed in on Darla's husband's hand as he held the thermometer in place. *Careful, don't hurt my baby,* her eyes pleaded.

"This foal's got a good willingness to thrive," said Darla. "Her temp's normal."

I haltered True Colors, and for the first time, she didn't flinch. While I held the mare, Mark operated the front end of the filly, and the two vets supported her rear end. All three adults guided the foal in her first awkward steps toward her mother's shiny black udder. True Colors stood anchored to the floor. She bent her neck, licking the foal's rear end. To encourage Baby, she give a nip at the base of her whisk broom of a tail.

Combing T.C.'s mane with my fingers, I grabbed for breath after each halting step the baby took. Not only was the foal's rear end deformed-looking, her brain seemed not to control her hind limbs. Though moving a few feet had tired Baby noticeably, she stretched her bird neck and touched the udder first with her upper lip and then her toothless pink gums. *Zappo!* She glommed onto a nipple and nursed with the noise of a hundred-pound suction cup, throwing her weight forward so eagerly that she almost toppled to the floor, even with three people holding her up.

True Colors's eyes went soft: No doubt the filly's relieving the pressure of her udder brought great relief. The foal dropped one teat, telescoped her neck forward an inch, crooked her head, and attached herself to the other teat. All of us watched her swallow each mouthful in golf ball–sized gulps that rolled down her throat. She let go of the second teat, went back to the first, then dropped her head, milk dripping from her nose and covering her chin. Slowly, the handlers lowered her exhausted body to the floor. As she slept curled in what horsemen call the jumbo-shrimp position, she looked to be all legs. True Colors bent over Baby, resting her muzzle on the foal's curly black mane, then moved her nose across the foal's rib cage back to her stump of a tail. *All here, all right.* She sighed.

While Baby slept, Darla pulled the huge slimy afterbirth from the garbage sack and stretched it out in the aisle. Her husband took True Colors's temperature with a rectal thermometer. She minded not at all; I was amazed. He inspected her vulva for tearing. "Everything normal," he reported in an almost friendly voice.

"She expelled it all," said Darla, stretching the two horns of the torn blood-streaked placenta over the rubber mat on the barn floor where Mark and I had slept for so many weeks. Luckily, I'd thrown our bedding into the tack room before the vets arrived.

"Why is the foal shaking like that?" I asked.

"She shouldn't shiver," said Darla, her frown lines showing.

Darla and I rubbed the sleeping foal with a towel to warm her while Mark busied himself hooking up an infrared heat light on a ceiling rafter above one end of the stall. Its glow turned the straw bedding pink. Foal, who'd stopped shivering, stirred and made sucking noises. I held T.C. while our team helped raise and steady Baby, again propelling her to the milk source. Her progress amazed me. I began to hope that she might survive.

During Baby's next twenty-minute nap, Darla and her husband reexamined the foal's umbilical, reapplying iodine, which made Baby flinch.

"Stings." Darla stroked the foal's ribs. Her face clouded. "She's got a small umbilical hernia two fingers wide." She held up her index and middle fingers as a measurement.

"What does that mean?" I asked, trying to read Darla's body language for clues.

The foal lay flat out, stretching her forelegs in front of her, her hind legs sprawled behind. Darla continued to stroke the bumpy washboard of the foal's rib cage. "It'll probably close on its own; most of them do. If not, it's a simple surgery. In the meantime, you want to make sure that her intestines aren't falling through the hole. Otherwise, they could torque."

I cringed. Blocked intestines meant a violent, painful death.

"Whenever you can, when she's lying or standing"—Darla moved her two fingers behind the umbilical and inserted them into the foal's belly—"push her abdominal wall in like this."

"Do you think she'll be able to nurse on her own?" I asked, fearing the answer. A foal is viable only if it can stand and nurse.

Baby stirred, pulling her bowed hind legs underneath her barrel, almost raising herself—a good thing, because she'd gained weight before our very eyes. This time after she nursed, the vets let her legs crumple under her so that she got the hang of lying down on her own.

"Stay with her a while," instructed Darla, "to make sure she can get up. I'll be back in the late afternoon to draw blood for an IgG." Filly's immunoglobulin count would indicate how much immunity she had received from her mother.

It was about two in the morning when they left. Mark and I stayed with the new pair for another hour to help Baby get up or down when she wanted a meal. Then I remembered my canning jars of frozen milk, one of which waited on the kitchen counter up at the house. I filled a syringe the way Kath had prescribed and at about three-fifteen gave Filly two syringes full when she was down but conscious. She happily swallowed the warmed milk, clapping her jaws together with delight. True Colors stood placidly above us, intently interested in what I was doing to her foal.

The other horses were still excited about the new presence, as well as the unusual hubbub of night visitors; they showed no sign of calming. I threw each a flake of hay, hoping to distract them, as their fervor disturbed True Colors. At about five in the morning, just after the fat white moon set and the predawn light crept over the foothills, Baby was able to raise and lower herself. Mark and I went up to the house for some sleep.

"Do you think she'll ever be normal?" I asked. I felt like begging any higher power to make her right.

He shrugged. "She's only a few hours old, and look how much she's straightened out." He had an objective scientist's attitude and fell asleep before his head hit the pillow. I could count on him for an honest, impartial observation, but I wanted comfort or reassurance that my long-awaited, hard-fought-for foal was going to survive and also be beautiful—as handsome as Kermit. Mark snored.

When I returned to the barn at seven-thirty that morning, the foal was up, able to walk a few steps before swaying to one side, tripping on herself, and falling. Then she was up again, smelling True Colors's front hooves and otherwise exploring her enormous mother. Immediately, I inspected T.C.'s udders: The nipples were deflated and the bag had shrunk, indications that the foal had nursed steadily during our absence.

True Colors was clearly elated by her possession. She hovered over Baby, too distracted to eat the chopped carrots that I'd brought her. When Baby nursed, there was a tranquil look in T.C.'s eye that I had never seen. When Baby slept, True Colors stood directly above her, sometimes touching Baby's head with her muzzle, sometimes licking her offspring's poll, where her head joined her neck. I thanked the organizing principle that the foal's hind end looked like someone had pumped air into her haunches. Baby's hips were unlevel, her left flank sucked in, her right flank bulging out, and her legs curved in a semicircle like two barrel staves. But praise be, now she could place both hind hooves on the floor at the same time.

What a friendly little mite! Her clear doe eyes looked to me for a syringe of milk before she went to her mother. This morning Baby had morphed from a flightless prehistoric bird into something more fawnlike. Had she grown taller in the last few hours? When she tried to bound to the far end of the stall, where I'd just turned off the heat light, True Colors immediately followed, her long neck always covering Baby's back like a shield. In the adjacent boxes, the other horses banged their water buckets. Ms. Piggy picked up her rubber feed dish and flung it over the stall door into the aisle. Quickly, I fed them and turned them out in their paddocks, returning to watch our newest addition. Like True Colors, I couldn't take my eyes off her and sat down in their stall, watching the sun angle through the narrow window at the base of the roofline. Soon light ignited the straw. Alone in the barn with her baby, True Colors closed her eyes.

Mark appeared. Just out of bed and a little fog-brained, he came into the nursing stall with a manure fork and muck bucket, intent on removing T.C.'s poop. A postpartum mare that manures easily is cause for celebration. But what about the foal? As Baby napped—new foals usually suckle every twenty minutes and sleep like the dead in between—I crawled around on my hands and knees, sorting through the straw looking for Baby's first feces, which, according to my foaling manual, would be small and dark and hard: the almost fossilized waste collected in the foal's gut during gestation. It was difficult for a foal to expel, and if the neonate gave up trying, an enema was needed.

"According to my literature, it's a red-letter hour when the foal learns to shit on her own," I told Mark.

"Ha!" He laughed, watching me crawling around. "Manure Mountain is a testament to that. We've had nothing but red-letter days."

I found no black pearls or anything that looked like rabbit turds, but since Baby showed no signs of straining to defecate, I'd put off giving an enema until Darla arrived. A black thought hung in the back of my mind: Maybe foal couldn't poop. Maybe her gut was twisted, like her legs.

"What're we going to call her?" Mark scattered fresh straw around the nursery box.

"Something that starts with C," I answered. Did we name horses that might not survive? Would giving Baby a name be a jinx? We horse people are superstitious.

With Mark helping to keep Foal down, I administered another syringe of milk. With amazing strength, Foal sprang up, knocking me to the floor as she launched herself toward the milk wagon. The fact that her hind legs and hooves twisted counterclockwise beneath her daunted her not at all. Reaching her dam's haunches, she maneuvered despite her affliction, zeroing in on Mom's udders like a compass to magnetic north.

"True Colors has hardly eaten," I said with concern. "She's never liked grain, but she hasn't touched her timothy, not even the alfalfa." A flake of hay weighed approximately four pounds; an adult horse consumed up to twenty pounds a day. T.C. hadn't eaten a fraction of that.

True Colors stood quietly as Foal nursed, the muscles of her abdomen flexing into her barrel. She closed her eyes again.

Mark carried a clean muck bucket and a scythe to the top of the front pasture near the hundred-year-old Douglas fir, the girth of it so wide that the fence made a jog around it. Soon I heard the *zik-zik* of the ancient implement as he slew a pile of green and brought it back for our broodmare. While T.C. nosed through it, picking out pieces of clover, Foal was up nibbling on strands of her mother's tail.

I asked Mark, "Could you give me a hand here?"

"Sure," he said, positioning himself on Baby's left and taking hold of the foal in the ballroom-dancing position: Facing Foal's middle, he grasped her around the chest and under the neck with his left arm, his right hand on top of the stub of a tail. Foal's back stood as high as my waist; when she stretched her head up, she was almost as tall as I was, nearly five-seven—the perfect height for a dance partner. For a few minutes they tangoed around the stall, but when Foal calmed—what a good brain she had!—and while Mark held her as if to begin a waltz, I was able to inject more of T.C.'s early milk into the corner of her mouth. She chewed and slurped, enjoying it immensely. We had gotten two quart jars' worth down her before she learned to get up so easily.

When Darla arrived just before dinner, Foal was up and exploring the crannies of her box, licking spiderwebs and chewing nubbins of hay and straw, utterly delighted with a purple clover flower she'd found in the pile of grass that Mark had scythed. Darla stood outside the stall observing Foal, who watched entranced as Mom raised her tail and manure fell out of her body. When True Colors peed, gushing a long stream of yellow liquid, Foal went ballistic with excitement, trying to kick and buck but instead crashing to the ground, hips angling in one direction, shoulders another. True Colors walked over to her baby, nuzzling her as if to say, *Pipe down, now.*

"Wow!" said Darla, noticeably awed. "She's really straightened out! What an alert little thing. And she must be at least ten hands tall!" Again we all wondered how she had fit inside her mother.

Mark and I thanked Darla profusely for coming out in the middle of the night. We hadn't showered and looked disheveled. Darla, as usual, looked as if she'd leaped from a magazine spread of Princess Diana look-alikes.

With Mark holding Baby in their newly learned dance position, Darla took her temperature, then drew some blood out of her neck. I held on to True Colors's lead rope; the mare seemed anxious about these procedures. Last, the vet administered an enema after warming it in a bucket of hot water. By now Baby's patience had worn thin. Darla compressed the bladder of the plastic bottle into Foal's rectum just as she gathered all her strength and exploded out of Mark's grip.

"Not even twenty-four hours old!" I said in amazement. Already she was stronger than her handlers and knew it.

Within moments, Foal stopped midstride, a look in her eye intensifying into wild surprise. When she lifted her bottlebrush tail, black pellets shot out of her like BBs from a pellet gun.

"She's looking good, and so is Mom," Darla said after we had taken T.C.'s temperature, a normal 99.8. The idea of having three people work on her, sticking instruments into her rear end, had been unthinkable just yesterday afternoon. "I'll call as soon as I get the foal's IgG count."

"Should I keep giving Baby her mother's early milk?" I asked.

"Not necessary." Darla climbed into the driver's side of her veterinary tuck.

I disregarded her advice. What could it hurt? Besides, the foal was so easy to work on. I felt like a kid playing with a life-sized stuffed animal, the same way I'd felt with Ms. Piggy when she first arrived. Returning to the foaling box, I went in and sat on the floor. When she finished nursing, Filly worked her toothless mouth, her face plastered with the smuggest look I'd ever seen. She pushed noses with her mother, then walked to her mother's rear and gnawed on her hock (the hind leg joint that compares to a human ankle but looks like an elbow) before moving on to sniff at a pile of Mom's manure, though her neck wasn't long enough to reach it. Foal sighed at all this effort, drew her long insect legs underneath her, and lowered herself onto a pillow of straw next to me. My smell had been on the syringes of milk she'd happily swallowed, so she associated me with nurturance. As True Colors bent down, touching her baby's back with her muzzle, I could feel the broodmare's warm grass-scented breath and the protection of her immense furry body. We were about the same size, the foal and I. The giant mother, about ten times our weight, stood over us, her summer coat the color of polished amber, her long black mane and tail the color of eternity. The foal dozed; my eyelids felt heavy. I had never felt such peace.

A cheerless sky pelted rain the next morning, Baby's second day of life, and when I got back from barn chores, Darla had left a phone message: Foal's immunoglobulin level was only 150 when, ideally, it should be 2,000. "I'll be out late afternoon with some serum," the recording blared.

Couldn't Darla get here sooner? All day Mark and I stayed glued to the nursing stall, as if keeping our foal in sight would ensure her survival.

"We have to give her a name," Mark insisted. "She's made it past Baby C."

"Maybe," I said gloomily, then self-corrected: "Okay, think positive." I'd ravaged all my "what to name your baby" books, as well as the encyclopedia, the *Oxford Unabridged*, and my library shelves. "How about . . . Colette?" One of my favorite authors. Colette—also sometimes called Coco, Coconut, Coke, Cokie, Coco Chanel—she became.

We scythed True Colors's muck buckets full of grass wet with rain, picked the manure out of her stall, fluffed her straw, practically living with her. I changed her water buckets, removed her uneaten hay, and brought her two fresh flakes, one of timothy and another of alfalfa. Though her grain was untouched, I refreshed that also, but she wouldn't have anything to do with it, not even when I held the rubber grain dish under her nose. Her large eyes looked at it, at me; she turned her head. Meanwhile, Baby came over and gummed a few nuggets of molasses-covered oats and corn. Just-cut new grass was the only thing True Colors ate with vigor.

What a tightrope it was balancing Foal's needs against those of the all-important mother. True Colors walked to the far end of her stall, clearly in need of stretching her legs. Colette, however, couldn't be turned out until she was three days old, when her eyes could focus. Her first day of turnout should be warm and dry; an old adage dictated that nothing fall on Baby for the first three weeks of life: not snow, hail, or rain. There was a more basic problem: Could this foal walk as far as the turnout?

Colette slept, guzzled milk, exchanged smug looks with her mother, skidded across her stall floor with more and more agility. She was terribly crooked behind, her limbs as thin as the legs of a Shaker chair. And it frustrated her to no end that her neck wasn't long enough to reach the ground. She could gum shreds of hay and grass only if I piled them up for her. True Colors stood placidly over her foal as Baby pawed through her mother's midday meal, then peed on it.

When I brought the other horses into the barn from their paddocks, I walked them past the nursing stall, letting each turn his head and have a peek at Baby. They were all intensely nosy, especially the riding horses. But God forbid one of them should get too close to the nursery stall door! True Colors lunged with fury, ears pinned and yellow teeth bared. I'd never seen such fierceness in her. Poor Willie nearly fell down when his girlfriend flew at him in rage. Initially, Baby pricked her ears forward—they looked less donkey-like today—curious about these other equines. But the ensuing fracas, the mare's forward rush, shoulders crashing against the stall door, confused and frightened Colette. She latched on to her mother's udder, shifting her weight from one bent hind leg to the other as she sucked. Watching the tableau, I thought, *I know that feeling: When in doubt, eat!*

When Darla arrived, Mark held Foal as the vet inserted a clear plastic tube into one nostril, pushing it down the throat. I held a bladder of white plasma over my head, stretching my arm as high as I could. Darla pumped the contents into Colette's stomach. Normally, this kind of thing would have sent True Colors bolting into the back pasture, but she stood quietly next to us, unhaltered and unheld, though visibly on edge.

"Who would've thought you'd be so good," Darla sang to her as she waited for the last drops of serum to flow through the plastic tube. The mare fixed her eyes on her offspring; almost resting her muzzle on Colette's back, she breathed warm air over her. Foal struggled—the tube was uncomfortable—but Mark held fast. "I'll be back tomorrow to get another IgG count," said Darla. "If it's a nice day, we can turn them out. Time to start thinking about the mare. Exercise will help her void her uterus."

"True Colors still hasn't had an appetite," I told the vet.

"All the more reason to get them outside tomorrow," said Darla.

But what about the foal? I wondered. *She can't run around, she's too crooked.*

I continued giving Colette syringes of her mother's early milk. She loved it, raising her tiny whiskered muzzle into the air as she lay in the straw while sitting up on her chest. Her forehead had a little dome to it, and the fur that stretched across it rippled like disquieted water, moving into the swirl of a cowlick above her eyes. I stroked Colette's neck and back, massaging her loose skin in a circular motion. She had long shiny dark bay fur with weedy tufts of curly black mane. Her shoulder blades looked too large for the rest of her; I could fit half the width of my hand into the sharp groove where her forearms joined the trunk of her body. Her eyes were amazing; they weren't brown, like those of an adult horse, but a blue that intensified when she drew her hooves under her in preparation for standing. Sometimes it seemed to take all her energy to raise herself. I admired her endless determination. She climbed to her feet, balanced herself, then heaved a long sigh before aiming her nose at Mom's udder.

* * *

When the receptionist at Darla's vet clinic telephoned to say that the serum raised Colette's immunoglobulin level only fifty points up to two hundred, Mark and I were stymied. We had hoped—hadn't we been told?—that it would raise the level to nearly two thousand. Darla would be out tomorrow morning with another dose, the receptionist said in a chatty voice.

The neighbor girls telephoned, asking if they could ride their ponies over to look at the foal. "No," I told Angel emphatically, feeling like the Wicked Witch of the West. "No visitors until she's two weeks old. She hasn't got an immune system yet."

"Can I come swim in your pond?" she whined.

"Okay," I relented. "But your mother or some adult has to come with you. And don't bring your pony."

"But he's not sick," she countered.

"It doesn't matter. He could be a carrier. I had to cancel my black-smith's appointment for fear Red might bring some disease from another farm."

"My pony only carries me. No one else can ride him," she said defensively.

Darla arrived late due to a colic emergency. Our other horses had been brought into the barn early because of flies. It had been a foggy morning, so I hadn't fly-sprayed them or put on their fly masks. Now the sun shone and the dewy grass sprinkled with diamonds, the sky studded with puffs of white. In the east, the snowy peaks parted to make way for a day so clear that we could almost see through the mountain pass.

"True Colors *still* has no appetite," I complained to the vet, who nodded and pursed her lips in concern.

After Darla administered a second dose of immunoglobulin, we decided it was the right time for Baby's first turnout. Mark slid the front door of the barn all the way back on its trolley. I haltered T.C., who put her head over the stall door, pressing her chest against it, eager to get Baby away from the inquisitiveness of the other horses. Colette was up and looking a little anxious; eyes alert and brow knitted, she stood behind her mother. Positioning himself on her left side, Mark took hold of Colette in the ballroom-dancing position. When he gave the word, Darla opened the stall door, and I cautiously led True Colors

135

out into the aisle, heading for daylight. T.C. immediately turned frantic. Where was Baby? Was she following? The other horses were straining their necks and calling out. True Colors began to trot around me. Baby struggled, tap-dancing on the rubber mat, then lunging forward. Mark tripped, fell, and she cantered off in a pegleg gait. Darla herded her in the direction of her mother. Once outside, we headed for the foal pen. True Colors reared, calling frantically to her baby, who squawked in response. Foal's antics reminded me of that nursery rhyme "There Was a Crooked Man." Out of the blue, Darla started to recite it.

"Been reading Mother Goose?" I asked.

"As a matter of fact . . ." Darla nodded and smiled mysteriously but didn't explain.

Meanwhile, Mark had recaptured Foal. True Colors crow-hopped and sidestepped to the pen along with Baby. Darla closed the gate behind them.

Now for the big moment. Mark and Darla held on to Colette, on opposite sides. Slowly, I unhooked the lead rope from True Colors's halter, my shoulders tightening as I braced myself for fireworks. Surely she would explode and run pell-mell to the other end of the turnout. Instead, she stood next to me as if we were attached. I held my breath. True Colors didn't move. Foal began to struggle, churning her front legs, straining to be free. True Colors stepped to the side as if waiting for Darla and Mark to release Colette, but they were afraid to do that. The danger was that after a mare had been confined for three days with her new baby, she might go berserk during her first turnout and inadvertently kick Baby, possibly dealing the little mite a fatal blow. True Colors moved not one hoof; she didn't even put her head down to graze.

"Jeez," said Mark when the struggling foal struck his nose with her head, almost escaping from his grasp. Darla stood firm but couldn't restrain the foal by herself.

"Let's try this." I snapped the lead back onto True Colors's halter and tried to get the mare to put her head down to graze. When that didn't work, I led her forward. Darla and Mark released their grip, and Colette toddled toward her mother, who put her nose to the grass and began to graze hungrily, almost pulling the blades up by their roots. She was famished. Why didn't she eat in her stall?

Colette tried to reach the grass. Her neck wouldn't stretch down far enough, even when she placed a foreleg well in front of herself. She began cavorting, romping and bucking in a cartoonish style. True Colors grazed on. Colette stopped at a daisy as if to smell it; a dandelion flower caught her eye. She ran tight rings around her mother, her face emblazoned with determination. She stumbled, went partway down, but pulled herself up. Foal appeared to be made of clothespins and clothes hangers.

"Think I should let Mom go?" I asked. Darla nodded solemnly. I unhooked the lead and stepped back. True Colors grazed until the foal homed in for a suck. By the time I'd walked back to the gate with the others, Colette was down for a nap in the jumbo-shrimp position, and True Colors was munching grass next to her tiny head.

"Amazing," said Darla.

"Do you think she'll ever be right?" I asked with trepidation. Surely by now Foal had an adequate immune system.

After a pause, Darla told me, "You probably won't be able to ride her."

"She could be a broodmare, couldn't she?" I asked, looking for a silver lining.

The sun caught in Darla's hair, turning it the color of candle flame. "Absolutely," she said.

True Colors
and Colette
on Colette's first
day of turnout.
Mark Bothwell

ELEVEN

Colette orbited her mother like an atomic particle buzzing its nucleus, as if attached by an invisible string. What defined the radius of that orbit? Did it have to do with Baby's vision? Or smell? During her first hours of turnout, Colette's hind end strengthened—we could almost see it happen. Baby's legs weren't actually crooked, just bent from the way she's been positioned in the mother. To my astonishment, she began to look less ridiculous behind. And she had a lovely head, even better-looking than Kermit's.

When I led True Colors back into the barn, the sun was high, warming the clover-covered ground. The grass smelled like honey. By now Foal knew how to follow, so Mark didn't have to waltz her home. My heart swelled. She moved with more agility and straightness—straightness is everything in a riding horse.

But once in the barn, Foal's blue eyes had difficulty adjusting to the dark. She pivoted on her wobbly pipe-cleaner behind, backing into the daylight. True Colors's head jerked away from me in alarm. Mom—as we now called her—whinnied frantically. The other horses mimicked her anxious neigh. Mark quickly grabbed Colette and tangoed her back into their stall. "Ouch," he screamed as her pogo-stick hooves danced on his size-thirteen boots.

Their plank door locked against the prying eyes of the other horses, True Colors bent her head into her hay and finally ate hungrily. Colette took a quick tug on Mom's udders and, reassured by familiar surroundings, collapsed on the straw and slept, lying so flat that she looked like a shadow.

When I brought True Colors a tub of sweet feed that I'd mixed with bran and warm water, she put her head into it, pushed some of the pieces of corn from one side of the tub to the other, took a bite, chewed, took another bite, then lost interest. Even a crisp night didn't whet her appetite for grain. Because our ribby foal had absolutely no fat on her, we kept the heat light on after dark. Both Mom and Baby gravitated to its fiery glow and slept haloed in pink light.

When Darla telephoned with the results of the foal's latest IgG test, I stared at the ceiling in disbelief. Colette's immunoglobulin level was only two hundred when it should be ten times that. It would take the foal sixty days to build her own immune system, and in the meantime, no new horses were to come near our barn. "Keep her as isolated as you can," Darla instructed. Two doses of serum had raised Colette's level by only fifty points? Mark and I couldn't figure out what had gone wrong.

"Maybe the serum's old," Mark theorized.

I remembered Kath's warning. "Maybe a technician thawed it in a microwave."

Had it had been the syringes of True Colors's early milk that had gotten Colette to her present immune level? We didn't know what to think. The next day, when a vet bill landed in our mailbox, we got another shock: The charges for the serum were astronomical.

Daily, I checked Colette's umbilical hernia to make sure her intestines hadn't fallen through the abdominal wall. I checked her umbilical stump to see that it was dry and not weepy. I checked her nose to make sure there was no discharge and then listened to her heart and lungs, though I had no idea what I was listening for. I took her temperature; she was a good patient, especially when napping.

On day five, Foal's ears started to prick forward. On day six, we were ready to turn the mare and the foal out at the same time as the other horses. I led T.C. while Mark guided Colette to their small safe pen. From the beginning, I read the worry written on True Colors's face. Once a schedule is established, a horse becomes attuned to it. Immediately, she noticed that I was turning her and Baby out right after their breakfast hay at regular turnout time; she knew the other horses would follow. Her overly eager stablemates would be a few feet away with just a board fence between them. Nervous, True Colors stood in the center of her pen, showing no interest in grazing. Colette, who still looked like a clothes hanger of a horse, rocketed from an ox-eyed daisy to a jewel weed to a fairy rose, her legs churning like egg beaters. I didn't understand how she didn't turn an ankle or crack a rib; it was as if she were made of rubber.

Positioning myself outside their pen, I was ready to run interference.

The yearlings trotted over to the fence and reached their necks over as far as the hot wire would allow them. In his excitement, Kermit struck the lowest board with his hoof. Both yearlings' dark eyes widened at the sight of their half sister. *What is it,* their expression asked, *an extraterrestrial spider?*

True Colors snaked her mahogany neck at the pair: *Stand back.* Both yearlings stood rooted. Then Mom did an amazing thing: Jigging the fenceline with Foal bounding after her, she paraded her new baby for the others to admire. *Look but don't touch,* her occasionally pinned ears told her stablemates. Her black mane and tail flew after her. T.C. made wild circling motions with her muzzle, directed first at Baby, encouraging her to come along, then warding off the equine onlookers, who stood absolutely transfixed. True Colors's expression turned to something I had never seen on her, and I'll never forget it—a look of pride and accomplishment. It was as if she were saying to the other horses: *Look at my baby, my pretty little girl. Look, but not too close, now.*

Colette didn't approach her siblings; instead, she stood almost under her mother, peaking through Mom's long tail with a worried expression. After a while the others quieted, and everyone, including T.C., went about the business of spring grass.

Everyone except Foal. Even if she'd had teeth, Colette's neck still wasn't long enough to graze, which was normal. She could, however, grab hold of a ball of Mom's manure, which she gobbled with relish. Sounds like mental-patient behavior, but this is how a foal acquires the enzymes needed for digestion.

Daily I went down my checklist: Foal's umbilical stump was healing; her umbilical hernia felt a little smaller; as each hour passed, she gained immunities; and with every turnout, her hindquarters visibly straightened, especially her sacrum and hips.

When Angel rode over on her pony to see the new foal, she looked heartbroken when I wouldn't allow her near the barn. "You're so mean." She pouted, her lower lip doubling in size. "I thought you were different than other grown-ups."

I tried to placate her. "You two girls can swim in my pond if you bring an adult with you."

Angel wore shorts and no shoes. "You mean Vicki?" She tossed her roan head. "Eldon turned her against me."

"Who's Eldon?" I asked.

"Vicki's boyfriend, but he used to be my boyfriend. I knew him from my brother's dirt-bike gang. He stole Vicki's mother's diet pills and tried to blame me." She sucked in her sausage lip and looked as if she might break into tears.

"Maybe not such great boyfriend material?" I asked. "You can swim in my pond, but take your pony home and bring your mom back with you. Okay?" I felt a pang of guilt. I got the impression that adults often wanted Angel gone.

"My mom's busy with Lido," she said, toying with her rawhide reins. The pony stood inert and reminded me of a four-post bed.

"Lido?"

"He's been paying her a lot of attention at the Sidewinder Tavern. My mom's going to turn me in to the police because of the diet pills," she said with a sober expression. "They must have fallen out of Eldon's pocket when he and Vicki came over. My mom found some of them when she was vacuuming. Eldon told her that I'd stolen them from Vicki's mother."

I wasn't up to worrying about the lives of the neighbor kids. "Your sister's visiting; she's a grown-up, right? She can come with you to swim at the pond."

Angel slumped. "My big sister don't swim in ponds," she said dejectedly. "The last time she swam in a pond, she got leeches stuck to her legs."

"Ick," I said. "What pond was that?"

"Yours," Angel said.

At one week, Colette flew around her turnout like a popcorn ball. She'd grown at least an inch in height, and I wondered how she bent her neck down and then crooked it to the side at such an odd angle in order to nurse as often as she did. A foal's nursing position looks like a cartoon rendition of whiplash. Though she seemed to thrive, we weren't out of the woods. Next we had to worry about the scours brought on by True Colors's foal heat.

When a mare cycles, it causes her foal to scour an endless stream of diarrhea, which has to be monitored. Uncontrolled scours is one of the major causes of foal mortality. A mare comes into heat ten days after her foal is born, and this is usually when horse farms rebreed their mares. I couldn't imagine shipping T.C. and even a healthy ten-day-old shadow of herself off to a breeding farm: too much opportunity for disaster. With True Colors's new attitude, rebreeding her next spring wouldn't be a problem.

Colette never scoured. Oh, what a good mother she had! Within two weeks of life, Coco had two adorable milk teeth breaking through the gums on her upper jaw. When she could almost reach the taller tufts of grass, we started turning the pair out in the back pasture, where T.C. had ten acres all to herself. Foal continued to orbit her mother, never straying. Nurse, sleep, nurse, sleep. True Colors devoured grass but barely ate her oats and corn. I had to throw away her rations or give them to another horse.

"She won't eat her grain," I complained to Darla.

"She probably eats it when you're not there," the vet told me.

"She spills it out by upending her dish, or the foal pees in it."

"She must be eating it off the floor, then," said Darla. Her voice had an edge to it, and I sensed that my concern was an annoyance. "Broodmares are ravenous," she added, as if repeating this saying were proof of her words.

The days lengthened, the temperatures rose, and the grass grew up to Colette's knees. She no longer had to telescope her neck out as far as she could and then angle a foreleg in front of herself, almost doing splits in order to reach a taste of green. Even more miraculous, she straightened behind. Now her back was flat as a desktop. Only a small dent remained in her left flank, with a slight leeward bend in her legs. Her wooly foal coat began to shed, first around her eyes and ears, and then gradually, down to the base of her neck; a sleek black velvet emerged. The dome on her forehead flattened, and her ears began to look like lilies. Running in ever larger circles around the mother planet, she grew broad in the chest and fattened, her ribs no longer visible. Within two months of life, she'd doubled her weight. One brilliant July morning, a UPS truck drove up and delivered a tiny pink foal halter with brass fittings—a gift from Kath.

If True Colors was living on anything except grass and hay, I didn't know what it was, though her weight was good; her coat dappled, unusual for a blood bay, especially one that was lactating. She always had enough milk for ravenous Colette, who by now had developed Olympic-level sucking skills. Gingerly, we led Baby to pasture, always careful to unhook the lead if she balked, so as not to put any pressure on her fragile neck, which daily grew thicker and more arched and looked not at all fragile. A very agreeable little thing, Colette learned to lead at age two months.

"She needs a friend," I told Mark as we watched her cavort in the field. "Kermit and Ms. Piggy had each other to play with." Thinking ahead, I asked, "How will we wean her? Colette and T.C. are insepa-rable." Their bond seemed unbreakable.

Finally, in late summer, when the grass dried, True Colors's grain started to disappear. We'd mowed the back field—Mark was mad for making hay—and most of what was left was stubble. Foal now weighed three hundred pounds. I started giving Colette a few cups of grain in a dog-sized feeding dish. Remembering Darla's instructions, I placed it about ten feet away from T.C. "so that Mom won't eat all of Baby's grain," Darla emphasized.

"But Mom doesn't even eat her own grain!"

Injecting paste wormer into the back of Colette's mouth every thirty days, we hoped to avoid the parasite infestation that our first foals had suffered. When Darla arrived to give Colette vaccinations—tetanus and flu—the vet inspected the foal's navel, which had dried and healed.

"Her hernia's closed a little," said Darla thoughtfully. Standing in the giant double stall, she and I and True Colors hovered over Colette as she napped. "She may not need surgery." She took the stethoscope out of her ears. "Heart sounds good."

I bent down over Colette. True Colors lowered her head and touched Baby's neck where her once wavy black mane had straightened and grown several inches. The mare's eyes shifted from me to Darla. Colette seemed not to notice when the veterinarian pulled two injections from her pocket and stuck her first in the neck and then in the flank.

"I can't believe how much she's straightened," Darla said with awe.

It was hot in the barn; the giant doors were open, as were the vents above the hay loft. Chilly nights and rainy days were in the past. We'd put away the heat light and changed the bedding from straw to shavings.

The following week, when Red shod the riding horses, he was able to walk right into the mare and foal's stall, nippers and rasp in hand, with-out True Colors flying into a panic. The broodmare hovered protectively over Baby while Red picked up each foal foot, snipping off her pointy toes. The mare didn't even flinch at the sound of the nippers. Colette wore her hind hooves unevenly due to her crookedness. Red leveled them off, and she stood straighter—what a little miracle!

"Even seen a foal this crooked?" I asked him. He stood next to True Colors, stroking her long sloping shoulder as the morning sun streamed through the barn window, setting the bedding alight.

"Good girl," he soothed in a voice he reserved for the most difficult of horses. Picking up one of her front hooves, he cupped it in one hand and, with the other, pared it with his hickory-handled farrier's knife. "This is amazing," he said of T.C.'s equanimity.

Answering me, he said, "Oh yeah, I've worked on 'em crookeder than your little one."

"Did they straighten out?" I braced myself for the answer.

"Sure," he said. "You'd be surprised how bent up some of 'em come out when they're born. The kind of crookedness that don't straighten is when it's in the front, when they got a clubfoot or turned knee."

I took a long sigh of relief and dared to hope that Colette would come right.

"The wife and I really got into it last night," Red said, apropos of nothing. "I told her that it was okay with me if the po-lice impound her vehicle should they find the tiniest little bit of dope in it. She sasses me right back with: *No, it ain't 'okay.*'" Red clanked his rasp and nippers together for emphasis.

True Colors whisked her tail, the sting of it catching me on the arm, where a welt began to rise. T.C.—all the horses, even the foal now—stood calmly during Red's animated monologues.

The next day T.C. began to eat her grain. "That giant foal is milking her dry; I've increased T.C.'s feed," I told Mark. Colette belonged to the clean-plate club, gobbling anything I put in front of her; obviously, she hadn't inherited Mom's fussy eating habits.

By September, there was nothing left of Colette's crookedness. *There is a god,* I thought, watching her and her mother graze on back pasture stubble. Colette could walk, trot, and canter like a normal horse. She was getting way too fat, so I'd been trying to find her a friend—another foal her age, just weaned and in need of the comfort of a pal.

The foals nearby either belonged to people who let their animals self-wean (something I had considered, but I'd concluded that T.C. would never deny Colette anything) or they belonged to the quarter horse farm down in the valley. There, the manager weaned all foals on the same day, cold turkey, removing the babies from their mothers. The new weanlings were left in the field and the mares stalled out of sight in the huge red barn. When the wind blew in the right direction, I could hear the foals—there must have been twenty of them—screaming from three miles away. What plaintive cries. The noise made both Colette's and True Colors's ears rotate nervously. Colette would run to her mother for a suck, and True Colors's eyes would go inward. The big quarter horse farm didn't need a companion for one of their foals, and they weren't at all interested in lending me a foal unless I wanted to buy it.

If being friendless bothered Colette, she didn't show it. She had a happy life. And True Colors was such an amenable mother that she shared her grain with her offspring, an unheard-of act of equine generosity.

One day during the first week of September, the sun so bright it looked wedding white, I drove up the grade to the farm, steering the Honda Civic into the hairpin turn. When the barn and front pasture came into view, I glanced at Colette grazing in her paddock. What was she doing, some sort of a silly walk with one of her hind legs? After pulling into the garage, I ran down to her corral in my street clothes. The foal, enormous now, had finished her grain and walked over to her mother's untouched rubber dish and started gobbling True Colors's sweet feed. The bay mare stood by passively and watched—a very odd occurrence. Usually, a hungry broodmare would run her foal off.

"No wonder you're so fat! Your mother lets you eat all her food!" I shooed Colette away, but she didn't frighten easily. I watched the movement of the ankle and pastern on her right hind leg. It looked as if she were double-jointed, the joint knuckling forward when she walked. When I got close, I heard a clicking sound in her leg. Something wasn't right here.

I telephoned Darla, who came out and diagnosed a condition called contracted tendons: Colette's bones were growing faster than her soft tissue. Very common, Darla assured me; Colette would grow out of it.

"True Colors lets her eat all her food," I reiterated.

A look of incredulity bordering on contempt crawled across Darla's face.

Colette's condition improved, but only before it got worse. Better, worse, then worse still. The only time Colette looked to be completely coming out of it was right after the blacksmith trimmed her feet. A week after her trim, she looked double-jointed again, her ankle clicking even louder. I needed a specialist.

When I telephoned Dr. Vogel, it seemed that I'd caught him during lunch hour. He chewed and spoke at the same time. A television blared in the background as he professed never to practice in my town—too "out of the way," though his private clinic in an upscale suburb was but five miles farther than Darla's clinic. After I'd agreed to pay a higher fee, he granted me a onetime consultation. The new vet arrived in a late-model white Mercedes, his hair professionally coiffed. He wore a Ralph Lauren shirt and khakis without one speck of dirt. Dr. Vogel assessed the situation right away and wasn't put off by my warnings about True Colors being a tad flighty. "You've got to get this foal weaned," he told me. "The problem is in the feeding. Too much rich feed. The sooner they're separated, the better."

Mare and foal didn't want to be parted, and it hurt our hearts to even think about pulling them asunder. Still, though Colette and her mother were bound by the strongest adhesive known to nature, it had to be done. That night Mark reluctantly turned the foaling box into two stalls. When I put T.C. into one stall and Mark herded Colette into the other, panic ensued, and the foal tried to jump the partition. After treating Colette's scrapes, we went back to square one, this time separating Mom and Baby for an hour a day during feeding time. When I put them back together, you'd think they'd been separated for decades. What nickering and mewing. Colette glommed on to Mom's udder as if she hadn't eaten in weeks.

Finally, we got them separated for the night, with the partition low enough so that True Colors could touch noses with Baby but tall enough so Colette couldn't jump over it. The next morning, their reunion looked like a new rodeo event. Foal ran to her mother, butting her head against the mare's flank, then crooking her neck and grabbing for a tit on Mom's swollen udder. After she'd had a good long suck, I led T.C. to the field, and Colette followed. In the afternoon, it was a major production to separate the pair for the night. After almost three months, they spent an entire day apart—each in a paddock where they could see each other but not touch. T.C. stood by the fence closest to her offspring, showing no interest in grazing; Colette bleated piteously.

The very hour that T.C.'s milk started to dry up, I could see the feral in her return. Without Colette at her side, the slightest movement of my arm was cause for flight. She did not want to be haltered even in her stall, and I resorted to herding her. With Colette at her side, she had let Mark lead her to pasture. Now she snorted every time he went into her stall to pick out the manure. True Colors had the agility of a panther, and it was difficult to guide her in any direction. The only thing that brought her in at night was the call of her herd, Willie's bassoon and Colette's pleading piccolo. When she was lactating, she would at least eat hay. Now she ate less than a flake at night, prefering to wait until she was put out to graze.

If I wanted to get near her, I again had to don my grubby barn jacket. The next time Red arrived to shoe the riding horses and trim Colette's hind hooves, he walked confidently into T.C.'s stall but wasn't able to pick up even one of her front feet. Her eyes flashed, she didn't appear to recognize him, and she certainly didn't trust me. Her irises were a many-layered deep chestnut, and when I looked into them I saw rock formations that reminded me of the Grand Tetons. Her body might have been in our barn, but her soul was running loose across the scablands of the high-desert range.

What had happened to all of my gentling and training, the many hours brushing her and sleeping next to her foal? Where had my giant, warm mother horse gone with her unconditional love?

TWELVE

Colette's hind legs straightened completely. In fact, they straightened too much and now resembled fence posts where they were supposed to sweep up in little crescents at the hock. Her tendons continued to look as if they were contracting. It hurt to listen to her walk across her paddock—the click echoed in my bones. After much pleading on my part, Dr. Vogel made another visit, prescribing stall rest, muscle relaxers, and a starvation diet.

"She's been overfed," he told me, his arms crossed in front of his well-pressed designer shirt. "It happens a lot in the Northwest—we've got year-round grazing and mild winters. Just look at all the killer grass you've got here."

"I hardly fed her anything," I protested. "Her mother let her eat all her grain."

"Huh." I could tell that he didn't believe me. "What breed's the dam? Nice-looking. Some kind of warmblood?" Dr. Vogel looked beyond Colette to the other side of the fence, where a calmed Willie grazed next to his beloved True Colors.

As if she could feel our eyes upon her, the mare walked away; Willie followed two steps behind. We'd had a break in the weather, and the pasture glistened. True Colors's "foal belly" had vanished and her winter coat shone like polished furniture.

"Racetrack Thoroughbred," I answered.

"Naw?" He put a stick of nicotine gum in his mouth. "Not with that rear end. Nice view." He looked around, and I felt him mentally calculating the value of our real estate. "We're going to have special shoes put on that weanling's hind feet."

"Shoes?" I asked, stunned. "On a foal?"

"They'll help stretch those tendons. Once they get put on, you won't be able to turn her out. She could hurt herself."

148

I put my head in my hands, feeling like I needed muscle relaxants myself.

Dr. Vogel telephoned Red, giving specific instructions for hand-forged baby clompers with extensions welded to the toes. They looked like fetish shoes for horses.

As Red shoed Colette, I found it hard to imagine the patience and skill it took to trim her hind feet, hammer out the objets d'art, burn them into the filly's hooves, then nail them on without sticking her in the quick. Red executed it all with Coco standing on three legs while he bent over double, working underneath her. If the gymnastics fazed him, he didn't let on.

"Hell," said Red, "there's not many things I love more than the wife." He stood up straight, then bent backward, taking a moment's rest as he counted on his fingers: hunting, fishing, his job, the three girls. "Up until now she never gave me a day's trouble, if ya don't count her drinking."

Unlike most young horses, Colette didn't mind someone pounding on the bottom of her hooves. She had started to gray on her lovely baroque neck, her appearance more refined than Ms. Piggy's or Kermit's. She'd inherited all of True Colors's lovely attributes.

Following Dr. Vogel's instructions, we kept Colette stalled for a month in the double box where she was born. Twice a day I hand-walked her for twenty minutes, leading her up the driveway, around the front pasture, trying not to run out of exciting places to go—Colette remained cooperative if she wasn't bored. I didn't want to think what would happen if she were to pull away from me and run at liberty with those deadly shoes nailed to her feet. If all this wasn't torture enough, we were supposed to be starving her. Too much protein had gotten her into this situation; in theory, low-calorie hay and no grain would put her right. How was I supposed to walk her around a grass pasture without her heading for a snack?

After a week, Colette began to thin, like a leggy string-bean adolescent with a snippy teenager attitude. As cold weather came on, she tired of being in the barn alone all day while the other horses roamed, but she contented herself watching spiders spin and our rescued Maine coon cat, Maxie, hunt wee beasties.

One brisk November day, as I walked Colette past the drooping limbs of the hundred-year-old fir, a yellow school bus passed. The high-pitched whine of compression brakes sent Filly into a fit of out-of-control cavorting. She reared and swung her butt, then *whack,* struck me with a hind hoof squarely on the hip. I shrieked, clutching my side with one hand, holding the lead with the other. As if to do penance, Coco leaped, whacking herself on the side of her knee.

I ordered her shoes removed and hung them on the barn wall as a reminder—of what, I wasn't certain, but they remain there to this day.

"Is there anything else I can do for you?" asked Dr. Vogel when I telephoned him that evening.

"Yes," I said. "She needs a friend."

"I have a killer idea," he said.

There is no other way to describe Byron: Everything about him was wrong. When he was unloaded from the van on a cloudy mid-November Monday, he was the ugliest weanling I'd ever seen—the color of wet cement, scrawny, hammerheaded, with marble eyes too narrowly spaced. No wonder his dam had kicked him in the mouth. There had been a wild gale at our farm the night before, so violent that falling trees had killed several pigeons. Recalling the terrible noise our Alaska spruce had made as it had split apart, I imagined that as the sound of Byron's jawbones breaking.

Byron had been sent to us from a Thoroughbred breeder near the Canadian border to recover from his fracture and to be a pasture mate to Colette. Horses mature better if they romp with youngsters their own age; old-timers call this "laying down bone."

Byron? Wherever did he get that name? I wondered as I led him to his box next to Colette's roomy nursery stall. For the most part, her sweet temper had returned with a regular turnout schedule. And her contracted tendons had vanished as suddenly and mysteriously as they had begun. She stared at the newcomer with her soulful walnut eyes, then put her head over the stall door and sniffed noses with him. A moment passed before she pinned her ears and turned her butt to the door. In equine body language, this maneuver said: *You have cooties.*

Horses have a keen sense of smell, and I chalked up Colette's adverse reaction as her ability to ferret out the odor of surgery that lingered on Byron's recently wired-together lower and upper mandibles.

An hour later, while on the phone to the barn manager at Magic

Meadow Racing Stables to get Byron's feeding and medication instructions, I asked how he got his name. "Default," the manager said. There was a chuckle in his voice as he explained: When Phillipa's Magic took offense at the gray colt's familiarity with her new foal, Phillipa's Pride, and kicked him in the head, the grooms had started calling him Bumsniffer. When his mother divvied out the same punishment a week later, the name stuck. The Jockey Club nixed naughty expressions, hence Byron's Song.

I had hoped to house both weanlings in the large nursery stall, but ten seconds after I led Byron into Colette's indoor run, the fur started to fly. My little gray filly hammered her hind hooves into the stall wall, kicking down several two-by-sixes. I quickly removed and stalled Byron two boxes away, which didn't seem to be far enough for Colette.

Turning the foals out together in a paddock the following day met with a little less friction, at least for the first five minutes, while the new friends were distracted by pigeon calls. The cries of birds for their lost mates cut into everyone's heart.

Colette had a large round behind, a short back, and a neck attached at the top of her withers, affecting the posture of a sea horse. Half her size, Byron resembled something between a charred chicken bone and one of the fallen tree limbs that littered the pasture. After the pigeons reorganized on the barn roof, things seemed uneventful for the length of time it took Colette to pick a corner of the corral and position herself with her rear end aimed at the center of the turnout and one hind foot cocked. She resembled a loaded cannon. Byron danced around, eager to light her fuse.

Two steps forward, one step back. I secured a lead rope to Byron's halter and moved him into an adjacent paddock.

The other horses eyed the newcomer suspiciously. When none would play "touch nose" with him through the fence rails, Byron began to fly around his turnout. Between bites of grass, Ms. Piggy and Kermit studied him sidelong. True Colors stared transfixed for several seconds, then, as if recognizing him as an indecorous associate from her past, fled into the woods. Not even the two riding geldings could be induced into running the fenceline. Alazan bucked in place, throwing a shoe. I grimaced, mouthing words of one syllable. Byron tried to entice Willie Africa into a biting match between the lowest rail and the ground. It looked as if the baby racehorse were comparing his saucer-sized feet to Willie's dinner-plate hooves.

Mark and I spent the day cleaning up after the freakish storm, collecting fallen limbs, repairing broken fences and downed gutters. During barn check that night, Byron's stall appeared as if the eighty-mile-an-hour gusts of two days before had blasted through it. He'd torn his grain bin off the wall, stepped on his salt block, defecated in his water bucket, and pawed a hole in the floor. His half-eaten hay rations had been trod upon. Watching Byron eat made me wince. The few milk teeth remaining in his mouth hit in a nerve-jarring *clap-clap*. Cracked corn dribbled out of his mouth, and no expression of discomfort crossed his face. He had Satan's willingness to thrive.

During morning feeding a few days later, I noticed a lone pigeon roosting in the rafters of Byron's stall. It was one of the birds that had lost his spouse in the storm. He was there again at night. Pigeons in our neck of the woods mate for life, and I felt a pang of sadness for the little gray bird that gleamed green in the early-winter sun, then I remembered: Messy pigeons were hardly welcome guests. When Byron, who had earned the barn name Nothing But Trouble (shortened to Nothing But), lay down, Pij swooped out of the rafters and began eating the molasses-soaked grain that had fallen from the weanling's mouth.

Was it loneliness or Pij's fog-colored feathers and the foal's mousy coat that bound them? In the week following, Pij moved from the barn beams to the top plank of the stall divider, gliding down to peck the manger floor free of corn right alongside Byron as the weanling ate his dinner rations. During daytime turnout, the riding horses and T.C. eyed Byron as if he were a green fly. Colette kept as far away as possible from his paddock fence.

As I carried Byron's noon hay rations to him in his turnout pen, he decided that I was someone to run with. Never, before or since, have I come so close to getting kicked in the head. He squealed joyfully as he bounded toward me, knocking the feed tub from my hands and then lashing out with a hind leg. Once I had scrambled to safety outside his paddock, I sat on the ground hugging myself until my heart rate slowed. Project Friend, as I called the acquisition of Byron, had indeed been a "killer" idea.

In his stall that night, however, Byron was sweetness and light as he and Pij ate grain together from the manger. I watched the foal gently butt the bird aside with his thimble-sized muzzle, then stand protectively over Pij, shielding him from Maxie Cat's lustful eyes.

The last morning of November was a day so clear that the glaciers on the side of Mount Whitehorse glowed pink in the rising sun. Leading Byron to his paddock, I noticed that Pij followed, perching on a gatepost. Then—I could not believe my eyes—Pij flew the fenceline as Byron galloped after him, up and back. A pigeon exercising a race colt? As Pij circled overhead, Byron began running circuits around the rectangular-shaped corral. His spidery legs blurred as he galloped into the corner, across the diagonal, around the far turn, down the home stretch, faster, fast enough to outfly a bird to the polelike water bucket of a finish line near the gate. None of the other horses paid this any mind except True Colors. She raised her swan neck to the sky and snorted like a dragon.

Just before Christmas, I began turning Byron out alone in the wooded back pasture. Each time the bird followed the grayling from his stall. Always Pij began to fly around the fenceline. Always Byron ignored the year-round grass and ran after the bird, galloping the racing oval bred into his genes. And always foal trailed bird, finally overtaking the gray-green wingspan. True Colors trotted to the fence and stared as if in recognition; whatever this mad running was, it was in her blood as well. I tried to read her expression. Concern? Fear? Was she staring down a telescope to her past, her earliest memories of life on a racetrack training farm?

Dr. Vogel telephoned periodically to check on Byron's jaw and Colette's developmental problems. "They're both doing great!" I reported with pride.

"Then get that filly back on full feed," he instructed. "Lots of high-protein hay, grain, good grass."

"But that's what got her in this mess!" Dumbfounded, I feared taking his advice.

When I reached Kath, who was in an ashram in India, she told me, "I'd take those instructions with a grain of salt."

On New Year's Day, according to Jockey Club rules, Byron officially became a yearling and True Colors turned ten. Byron's chest had broadened, and the muscles in his upper forelegs had gained definition. His hooves grew straight and strong. As horse and bird bolted into their morning workout and the other equines looked on, the flare of Byron's nostrils widened, turning the rose hew of a mountain sunrise.

By February, Byron's jaw had healed without scar or disfigurement. It was almost certain that by the time he turned two, his mouth would be able to tolerate a snaffle bit and he'd be able to begin his first thirty days of training. Come late spring, Ms. Piggy and Kermit would turn two, and come autumn, I'd have to start thinking about breaking each to saddle. Mark and I were excited about both of them and had decided not to sell either this year. I was undecided on whether to breed True Colors, which kept me awake at night. If I sent her to a breeding farm, would she get hurt? Might she injure someone?

On the Saturday after Valentine's Day, a sleek silver tractor-trailer pulled into our driveway. We loaded Byron onto the ten-horse van that would whisk him up the interstate, across the border, and back to the farm in the Kootenai where he'd been born.

As the van, empty except for Byron, pulled out onto the county road, we could hear him pawing madly and then scrambling to balance himself. The noise of his hooves made a *rat-a-tat-tat* like rifle fire inside the metal trailer, and he whinnied in a series of forlorn howls. As our horses nibbled hay in their stalls, none raised a head at the commotion except True Colors. Uncharacteristically, she stood pressing her chest against her stall door, trumpeting after Byron. Hadn't T.C. jumped out of a racehorse transport as a three-year-old, leaping from one fate to another? Maybe she had second sight and knew what might become of Byron— the destiny of many racehorses—if he wasn't careful and lucky. I'd never seen her distraught in this way. It took her until well after dark to settle.

The day Byron left, Pij vanished. I never saw either of them again. All these years later, I think of Byron's Song running the grassy turf of British Columbia race courses, a lithe grindstone-colored gelding leading the field as he chases a ruff-necked bird eight furlongs across the finish line into history.

THIRTEEN

It may have been Red who first called True Colors an anchor mare, or maybe it was Monte, the ex-jockey who came to the farm to break Kermit and Ms. Piggy. I'd kept asking myself: *What kind of a horse is this mare?* Not a boss or alpha mare, driving others from her territory using her arsenal. Once in a blue moon, T.C. might pin her ears over some infraction in herd etiquette, but that was the extent of any ire on her part now that she was not guarding a newborn.

Come the spring equinox, we decided not to rebreed her. "Next year for sure," I told Mark. The idea of trying to load True Colors in a trailer, then hauling her to a breeding farm to leave her in the hands of strangers, overwhelmed me, as did the price of board, stud fees, and breeding procedures. We had a staggering number of vet bills left over from Colette and were looking at the cost of breaking the two-year-olds. Darla had quit practicing in order to have a baby, and we couldn't afford Dr. Vogel's astronomical come-out fee, so for everyday needs, we started using Doc Short, an old-time farm vet right out of *All Creatures Great and Small*. Short, as he was called by everyone including himself, was about my height and had a head of home-barbered silver hair. He always arrived in a battered Japanese pickup, wearing a gray sweatshirt and Wellingtons, eager to trek out into the muck of a Northwest corral.

Though Short's specialty was horses, True Colors didn't cotton to him. She stared wild-eyed, her entire body tense as a tree trunk, then she flew backward into the corner of her stall with such force that I feared her next move would be to rear over the top of him.

"She's terrified of most men," I apologized. "She's warmed up to Mark a little, but she won't let him put a halter on her." Right from the get-go, it was clear that we'd have trouble getting even one vaccination into her, and in the end, no injections were given.

Undaunted, Doc decided to borrow a blowgun from a zoo vet. On his next visit, we began with the most important inoculation, tetanus. "Okay, troops," the vet instructed Mark and me, "swiftness is important here. No talking, no unnecessary movements." Clearly, he'd worked on other wild and feral animals.

Positioning himself in the next stall, Short stood on a mounting block. He pointed his blowgun—it looked like a six-foot length of copper pipe—over the stall partition and took aim as True Colors flew panic-stricken around her box. When she came to rest, head rammed into a corner, butt pointed at the center of the stall, he shot the needle into her thigh. She froze. Quickly, I entered her box and attached a rope to her halter. Just as quickly, Doc Short followed, attached a syringe to the needle, and pushed the plunger. Though the mare remained frozen, we knew she was a time bomb, her fuse almost spent.

As we regrouped outside her stall, I spoke up: "What would be the wisdom in giving her that one vaccination? Look at her, she's mortified." The three of us stared as the mare trembled. Though it was a cool day, the low sky as ash-colored as Doc Short's sweatshirt, I could see sweat bleeding through the mare's red fur. I felt bad for her. Everything we did to her seemed like a violation of the Geneva Convention.

Reluctantly, Doc Short agreed. "She's lived this long without being vaccinated. But if we ever have to give her more than one injection, remember that the first needle into her is a tranquilizer. I should have thought of that," he chided himself. "Can't leave on bad terms with her." Walking back into T.C.'s stall, he looked at the ground, inching toward her. Slowly, he raised his hand to touch her shoulder. True Colors leaned away from him and snorted but didn't move her feet. Doc scratched her. "You don't have any use for me, do you, honey cake?" he sang, as if lullabying a toddler.

Colette jutted her head over her door. Most vets came here to see her; why wasn't she getting any attention? her expression asked. She had a long but pretty face and a thick mane. Thankfully, she also had Kermit's temperament. After he'd gotten over his fright of humans, he'd turned out to be very forgiving.

"How's this one doing?" Doc asked. We were standing in the aisle again. He stroked Colette's gray velvet nose.

"Great," I told him, "as long as Red shows up once a month to trim her hind hooves. That seems to keep any signs of double-jointedness at bay."

"Getting to be a big girl." Doc smiled. Colette's sloe eyes, which had turned almost black, softened; she licked his hand the way a dog might.

"She's a yearling now," Mark said proudly. He and Coco had a special relationship. When he went in to pick out her manure, she acted as if she wanted Mark to embrace her in the ballroom-dancing position and waltz around the stall.

Dr. Short sometimes attended Mark's lectures at the university, and the two went off on a rant, my alphabet but not my language. Listening politely, I shifted my weight, eyeing T.C., who stood in the back of her stall, braced for another attack.

We had almost no spring that year, then in late summer, everything happened at once. Temperatures rose into the nineties. I had to make appointments to trim Colette more often. With each visit, Red seemed more agitated; there was no obvious reason why.

Today I wanted to ask him if he knew anyone who would come to our farm and break Kermit and Ms. Piggy. As soon as he got out of his truck, however, I could tell it would be a chore to keep Red's mind on his blacksmithing. I brought out Colette before he got going on one of his monologues.

"When I confronted the wife"—Red bent over Filly, paring down her hoof—"she turned into a different person."

Next I ushered Red into T.C.'s stall. After trimming her left front hoof and before moving around to her right, Red paused, took off his baseball cap, and ran his fingers through his ginger hair. "What is it about this horse?" he asked, as much of himself as of me. "She's different, but I just can't put my finger on why."

I brought out Kermit and held him in the aisle.

"Forget intervention therapy. All this talk about feelings is too much like work." As he whittled Kermit's left hind foot, crescent moons of hoof paring flew from his farrier's knife. Red stood up, dropped Kermit's hoof, and confronted me directly. "My father-in-law found us an affordable private detective to find out who her supplier is."

I was so distracted that I completely forgot to ask if he could recommend an itinerant horse breaker. A few weeks later, through the grapevine, I found Monte Gibbons, aka Monkey Gee. His girlfriend, Jewel, worked in the tack store I frequented, and her knowledge of horses and equipment impressed me. She'd been the one to suggest using Dr. Short. Her boyfriend, an ex-jockey, worked at the Longacres racetrack and broke horses during the off-season.

Monte arrived at our farm in his twenty-year-old black spit-shined Coupe de Ville the day after racing ended in mid-September. A fine-boned, diminutive man about my age, he had a head of rangy chocolate-colored hair, a freckled monkey face, and good teeth that I later found out were dentures. He chain-smoked Chesterfields and I suspected was addicted to painkillers. Monte had gotten his start breaking horses in rural Maryland, near where Mark and I had found Alazan. In fact, he'd jockeyed several of Al's relatives.

Popping open the Caddy's cavernous trunk, Monte pulled out a cold box of grapes and bananas. "Banana peels are my calling cards," he joked with an impish smile.

Over the phone a few weeks before, Monte had outlined his procedure and terms: He'd come out to our place six days a week for three weeks. Payment was due at the end of each week. He'd need one of us to be there to assist. "We'll use my equipment," he told me. "That way I know the leather 'n' stitching's safe. Them warmbloods are bigger than Thoroughbreds—bigger and dumber. They don't call 'em dumbbloods for nothin'. So you might have to buy a surcingle, if mine don't fit. We'll start midmonth. In the meantime, if you got them critters on grain, take 'em off of it. No high-protein feed that'll heat up their brains."

"Will both horses be broken to ride after three weeks of training?" I asked.

"Don't know," Monte replied. He had a clear mid-Atlantic accent. "In three weeks I gotta drive a friend's father to Vegas."

Jewel was eminently trustworthy, so I trusted Monte Gee, and in the end, it turned out to be the right thing to do—though believe me, I had my doubts at the time, especially after I learned that Monte always had a line on good BC bud, offering free samples if I knew anyone who was interested.

From the get-go, Monte—Monkey to his close associates—was a talkaholic and immensely entertaining. Like many people attracted to dangerous sports, he was also a walking definition of attention deficit disorder. More to the point, our horses loved him. Oddly, he didn't seem to be deeply fond of equines. "It's my job; horses are just the only thing I know. My dad dropped me off at Laurel Park when I was thirteen, told me to make myself useful." When I asked if he'd ever owned a horse, Monte replied, "God, no. I got better things to do with my money."

Monte had nicknames for all of our horses. Kermit and Ms. Piggy were Baby Orca One and Two, or just the Baby Orcas. When he walked past True Colors's stall, he stopped dead in his tracks. "Spitting image of Jewel's gelding, Charlemagne. Calls him Charlotte; I don't know why. Hunter champion many years running. Jewel's brother purchased him at an auction for a hundred dollars as a suckling. Some guy had bought his mother but didn't want the foal. Jewel's brother took him home in a station wagon." Then he asked, "What happened to her face?"

People who rescued cast-off horses and made them into champions were my kind of people, so I told Monte more about True Colors than he ever wanted to know.

"How ya doin,' Shy-lotte?" he said sympathetically. True Colors turned her head slowly to the side, her eye softening—a sign of submission. "You ride her?" he asked me.

"God, no," I said, imitating Monte's jargon without meaning to. "She's not broken. Like I said, she's terrified of people."

Opening her stall door, he went in with her. She stood rooted at the back of her stall. When he walked up and patted her shoulder, she didn't balk or even flinch. I was amazed. T.C. glanced at Monte thoughtfully. "She don't seem so terrified to me," he said.

"Maybe she's turned over a new leaf," I replied hopefully. I didn't say, *But you're not trying to do anything to her—give her an injection, trim her feet, catch her.*

Monte began by taking each Orca individually into the grooming stall and familiarizing him or her with the bridle and bit. After buckling a surcingle around the horse's barrel, he snapped a pair of long web reins to the bit, then pushed the reins through the rings on the surcingle. Next he stood in back of the horse and drove it around the arena from the ground. In this way, they learned the basics: go, stop, turn left and right. Later, he familiarized them with the saddle—Monte used a tiny racing saddle and an extra-long girth. As he line-drove each horse individually, the saddle's stirrups jostled, at first unsettling the youngster. Ms. Piggy was more undone by the stirrups banging against her sides than Kermit. Pretty soon it became obvious that Kermit was the more teachable. Pigster jumped at the slightest provocation, hot-blooded, like her racehorse mother.

"Mares is usually goosier," Monte explained.

He first attempted mounting in the grooming stall. To begin, he stood on an upended muck bucket and lay over the horse's back. Next he lay with his full weight on the horse. As he slowly inched a leg over Kermit's back, I held my breath. Finally, he sat up. Very slowly. Monte's weight was nothing to either Kermit or Ms. Piggy; they seemed not even to notice it. But their eyes bugged out in surprise when Monkey first sat up straight on top of them. It went against the order of the universe that his head should be above theirs. The handler belonged on the ground, what was he doing up there? Such events caused near panic. Heretofore only predators lodged above their heads—bobcats hiding in trees, for instance. In their expressions of shock and concern, their eyes widened, ringed with white, their gaze moving backward, trying to take in whatever it was that Monte was doing on their backs.

Next Monte ground-drove each horse with poundage—a special rucksack filled with bags of sand. After that, he drove them with poundage that bounced and made noise, to mimic a rider. As he handled the reins, calling out words of either encouragement or correction, he rambled on, spinning yarns about his past. His first job, he told me as he persuaded Ms. Piggy to circle to the right around him (which must have seemed wrong to her, because since day one, she'd been handled from the left), he was supposed to be earning money for his Catholic-school uniform.

"When the meet at Laurel Park ended, I got on as a muck boy at a Thoroughbred farm named . . . I forget . . . Three Oaks." He'd lied about his age and his ability to drive a car. The owner had just purchased a shiny blue New Holland tractor, which Monte was supposed to use to haul manure. Since he didn't know how to drive a car, let alone a tractor, he sneaked out at night to give himself a lesson. *Sneaked out* was perhaps not the correct term, since the owner was absent and the day help had gone, Monte lived rent-free in an apartment above the barn in return for working as a night watchman in addition to a muck boy. First he fortified himself with some courage he found in the liquor closet. The tractor was easy to start, he just turned the key, which was always kept in the ignition. Then he started playing with the controls. What kind of a contraption was this: The clutch and brake were the same pedal?

Suddenly, the New Holland headed for the pond like a runaway horse. Monte bailed. The tractor continued into the water, where it came to a gasping halt with only its exhaust pipe sticking out.

"I went to bed that night with a splitting headache," Monte told me. He was trying to get Kermit to trot so that the stirrups would bang against the two-year-old's sides. "I figured that in the morning, some excuse would come to me." That night torrential rains blew. The pond filled to overflowing, leaving no sign of Blue, as Monkey Gee called the tractor. The tractor's disappearance was a complete mystery until the following July, when the pond started to dry up and the exhaust pipe's smokestack broke the surface. By then Monte was gone, having been fired months before, after raiding the owner's liquor closet, getting drunk, and falling asleep while taking a shower in his upstairs living quarters. The shower overflowed onto the floor and drained into the room below, called the Great Hall, where the owner was entertaining his horse-buying clientele. On a completely cloudless night, it started raining on the farm's fete.

Sometimes Monte asked us to pay him in cash, but one week he was happy to take part of his payment in basil. It had been a long Indian summer, and we had rows of basil that would perish with the first frost. We could put up only so much pesto, so we were happy to trade herbs for horse training. In his off hours, Monkey Gee loved two things: Cajun cooking and big band music.

During the third week, Monte was able to get on both of the Orcas in the arena. My job was to clip a rope to one bit ring and lead either Kermit or Ms. Piggy along.

"I gotta drive my friend's father to Vegas," Monte told me.

"Why can't your friend drive his father?" I asked, sure the trip was some kind of subterfuge. I wanted my horses ridable and couldn't finish the job myself.

"Nils? Nils has gotta work. He's got horses at Bay Meadows. Embu and Kamba."

"Those don't sound like Thoroughbred names." Now I was really incredulous.

"African. Nils was in the Peace Corps. Nils is a different kinda guy."

I didn't know what to say. I'd never heard of a Thoroughbred-race-horse person who'd been in the Peace Corps.

"Time to give your critters a breather," said Monte, as if this were the normal course of events in horse training. And maybe it was. "How 'bout if I come back in a month or two and do another three weeks with 'em to get ya goin'?"

Monte and I stood next to Kermit in the grooming stall. "Tell ya what," he said encouragingly, "when I come back, I'll give ya a special deal on breakin' Shy-lotte."

"What?" I felt as if my lower jaw had come unhinged. When I found my voice, I asked, "Do you think she can be broken? She's so terrified of people." It had been a landmark day when I no longer needed my smelly barn jacket to get near True Colors. I was so delighted about this little piece of progress that I had wanted to call up Darla to tell her.

After we put Kermit back in his stall, Monte and I walked down the barn aisle and stopped in front of True Colors's door. She'd grown a winter coat, and though hers was thick, like the others', it was short and gleamed like burnished agate. "That there's an anchor mare, not a boss mare," Monte told me. "She's got a kind eye. Them two foals you got of hers"—he gestured at Kermit and Colette—"they got her temperament and looks. She refined the heck out of that draft stallion. Not every mare will do that."

"Thanks," I told him. Inside, I beamed. "You *really* think she could be ridden?" My heart leaped. True Colors was a fabulous mover with a long elevated trot and an uphill, high-stepping canter that looked as if she were climbing stairs when she galloped.

Monte shrugged. "Why not? This mare don't want to kill nobody. She don't even want to break your arm." He knitted his brow, and his small brown eyes shone the same color as his freckles. "You think I'd be wantin' to break her if I thought she was dangerous? No horse is worth my life."

I went back and forth. I could hardly wait, and then I was filled with trepidation: Breaking True Colors could go very wrong, very fast. While Monte was gone, I took first Kermit and then Ms. Piggy into the grooming stall, saddled and bridled them, and sat on them while they stood quietly in the crossties. I decided against taking them into the arena and stayed in the safety of the barn.

Colette was growing like a wildflower. The toes of her hind hooves seemed to lengthen overnight, and I started trying to rasp them off myself. Every time I called to make an appointment, Red's wife said that he was no longer servicing my area.

"But I only live ten miles away from you. Maybe eight." By rural standards, I was practically a neighbor.

"He's got to draw the line somewhere." Her voice was stern and manly.

"But Colette is a special case," I implored. "She's a yearling with developmental problems, and he's the only blacksmith who can help her."

"You'll have to call back and talk to him, then," she said, and hung up.

When I finally reached Red, he gave me an appointment, no questions asked. When he arrived, he seemed unusually quiet. No outbursts, just a professional posture. Maybe therapy had done some good. Maybe he and his wife had gone to a marriage counselor. Or perhaps his whole tribe had had family therapy.

"Ain't coming here no more," he told me after he finished shoeing and while he was putting his tools back in the rear of his battered truck. "I wanna tell you that I've enjoyed working here, but I just can't come no more."

I was stunned. "What are you talking about?" I asked. "What about Colette? She needs you." I felt so exasperated that I wanted to cry.

"Too far," he said. "I figure it this way: If I don't work any farther away than fifteen minutes from my house, then I can keep an eye on the wife. If I don't find out who her supplier is, it's gonna kill me."

Red didn't leave me without a blacksmith. He gave me the name of a brother farrier, Gordy, who was about ten years younger than Red. Gordy arrived exactly on time and looked like someone who had played pro football. Clearly, he had the strength needed, but when he walked into True Colors's stall, she became instantly alarmed. Every muscle trembled. "That mare's got stallion fitness." Gordy nervously clanked his nippers and rasp together. True Colors flew around to face the wall.

"She doesn't really need to be trimmed," I said. "Let's leave her until next time."

After Gordy left, the horses' hooves looked low in the heel and long in the toe. The next day Alazan could barely walk, and Colette was worse instead of better. In the end, Dr. Short telephoned Red and begged him to come back one more time to fix Colette while I searched for a replacement to whom I would give Red's written instructions. Red agreed, as long as I'd do all the writing.

When Monte returned to the farm after Christmas, I was still banging my head against the wall because of the blacksmith situation. After a quick refresher course, Monte was back on top of both Kermit and Ms. Piggy. Turn left, turn right, stop: They had that part of their training down pat. The cue to move forward without a leadoff from someone on the ground was more difficult. I would lead Kermit around the arena, then unhook the lead rope and walk beside him. Sometimes Monte would have to encourage Kermit with a tap of the jockey's bat on his massive black shoulder and, when that didn't work, on his flank. Ms. Piggy needed less encouragement. Eventually, both got the idea, and I got to sit on them and try. It was an awesome feeling to have known these two as foals untouched by human hands and then, two years later, to be on their backs steering them around a riding arena at the walk. Trotting was scarier. Both youngsters were uncertain about being in the arena without another horse. Baby steps built their confidence.

"Next time we'll start on Shy-lotte," Monte told me after he'd managed to trot both Kermit and Ms. Piggy around the arena.

"T.C. hasn't had her feet trimmed in months," I said, knowing that Monte was insistent about riding only horses with their feet in good condition. One of the worst accidents a rider can have is when his mount takes a fall.

Monkey Gee cross-tied True Colors in the grooming stall. She looked tentatively at him and braced herself against the ropes clipped on to either side of her halter. As he walked around her, studying her feet, she followed him with her eyes.

"Her hooves are okay," he said. "They're kinda ragged, but her toes ain't long. She wears 'em down herself."

"She trims her own feet?" I asked.

"Yeah. 'Course, it would look nice if someone could finish them off," said Monte. "Nils quit the track. Why don't you try him? Jewel told him that he should meet you, 'cause you're a poet, so he knows who you are. He brings his poems over for Jewel to read. I don't touch the stuff, myself. She told him, 'No wonder you're depressed all the time, Nils, writin' this kinda stuff.' Jewel said that he should stick with woodworking—Nils makes dishes outta hardwood."

"Nils, who was in the Peace Corps in Africa, is a blacksmith?"

"Yeah, he shod horses at Longacres before he quit. He might come out here if you got some interesting hardwoods he could pick up on."

"How about a fallen-down cherry tree? So why'd he quit the track?"

Monkey Gee shrugged. "Didn't say. That's just the kind of guy he is."

In the small-world department, Nils had grown up in California, a few miles from where I'd grown up, and attended a rival high school. He had a master's degree in anthropology. What did I have to lose?

Nils arrived in a battered gray van. He had unkempt hair and a ragged beard the same color as his Ford Econoline and looked years older than he was. Medium height and athletic, he turned out to be amazingly good with horses. True Colors wasn't in love with him, but she didn't snort dragon fire when he entered her stall.

"I won't bother with her hind hooves," Nils told me after he'd trimmed her fronts with no drama whatsoever. He had gunmetal eyes that looked like they wanted to be blue. "Her hinds are chipped, but she wears 'em perfect." Monte's well-being was at stake, and since Nils was one of Monte's best friends, I took his word for it. And those were almost the only words Nils spoke to me during his entire visit.

He must have had a back of steel and an acrobat's training. I'd never seen anyone able to get so well under a horse. The youngsters practically tap-danced on his back. Nils never swore at them or complained in any way. In fact, he seemed not to notice that these thousand-plus-pound critters were running races over the top of him.

Nils did speak once more during his visit. After he shoed Alazan and before he started on Willie, he said, "I'm vegetarian."

I have no idea why he revealed this. It seemed out of left field. Later, Nils would put his finger on exactly what it was about True Colors's character that set her apart from other horses.

Just after the New Year, Monte arrived to break T.C. She was much easier to handle with two people. Monte led her forward, and when that didn't work, I pushed from behind. She seemed disarmed by his nonthreatening manner; he never moved fast around horses—although once, when he sneezed, T.C. went into paroxysms of fright.

"You gotta get over this, Shy-lotte," he told her in a stern but kind voice and went on with what he was doing. Much to my surprise, she adjusted almost immediately to the bridle and bit. Monte had brought one of his own, called a dog bone, a straight bar with metal rings on either end and the bar covered with plastic, like a pacifier. When he put the surcingle around her barrel like the cinch on a saddle, she didn't flinch and showed no girthiness—some horses object to anything tight cinched around the middle and kick at the girth. True Colors was tense, her muscles wound like a clock about to chime, but this bothered Monte not at all.

"She's real fit. Just look at the delineation of those chest muscles," he said. "Always hard breaking a fit horse."

T.C. regarded Monte cautiously. She seemed to like the sound of his chatter.

During her ground work, True Colors shied a lot: at the wind rattling the trees, at a sudden downpour raining nails on the metal roof of the arena. As long as there were no fast movements or sudden changes in weather, she was a quick study. But when she shied, she did it so violently that I feared she'd get caught up in Monte's ground lines. I wondered what she'd be like under saddle when there were horses or people around who didn't know her foibles. But every time I saw her move at the trot or canter or even the walk, I knew that I wasn't completely foolish to try to break her.

Monte had been working with T.C. for about three weeks when Nils came for our next shoeing appointment. "I've finally figured it out about this mare," he said. He'd arrived two hours earlier and hadn't said anything since, so hearing his voice scratching into the cold air was a bit of a surprise. "I woke up in the middle of the night, and it came to me. She's unneedy. She don't need nobody. Most horses aren't like that. A horse is a dependent animal."

He was exactly right. And he was a rare human being who thought about his clients' horses in the middle of the night. His insight struck deep inside me.

"You could probably get away with never trimming her feet," he continued. "Don't know why I'm telling you that, since I'd be putting myself out of a job."

The day Monte put his jockey's saddle on True Colors and rode her around the arena, I thought my heart would explode, I was so filled with awe. From the expression in her eyes, I knew that she was extremely nervous about him being up there, his head above her head. She remained sensible, however, didn't panic and fly into a blind fury or run into an arena support post or duck under the railing. Eventually, Monte was able to trot her. Under saddle, she had a powerful engine. The first time I got up on her, I don't know who was more nervous, her or me. It took several minutes before I stopped shaking, and that was when I discovered that I loved the solid feel of her beneath me. Willie's dressage saddle fit True Colors perfectly. Jewel had helped me select a nice leather bridle for her, and eventually, she graduated from a dog-bone bit to a silver snaffle broken in the middle.

It was a late-April afternoon; the pale sky was streaked with foam. By the pond, the fluff from the cottonwoods piled up like snow, which made my hay fever kick in. Whenever I sneezed, T.C. jumped. As I walked her around the arena on the sand footing, I wondered if I could ever take her to a competition, with the flower boxes and waving flags and static from a loudspeaker.

I began our lesson with a long-strided walk and then shortened her strides. We sidestepped to the left and then the right, turned on the haunches. The slightest brush of my pant leg against her side quickened her walk, but I could not get her to trot. Monte's voice echoed in my ears. As I had sat on Kermit when we first started him, Monte had instructed: "Hit him on the butt with the bat. Now hit him again." Kermit had picked up the trot.

I aimed True Colors around the first turn on the short side of the arena, then around the second turn and across the diagonal. Her neck was set high and came out of her chest like a swan's, her head cascading off the end of it like a waterfall. Monte was right, she did have the presence of a stallion. I gave her a little leg, and she took one step of trot and went back to the walk. More leg, another step. More leg, she gave me nothing. I turned left, going counterclockwise around the arena. Trot, walk, trot, walk. In hindsight, I should have stopped there and taken up the task again on another day. But I was so close. I wanted just twelve meters of the trot. I wanted to feel that pure iambic beat. Moving the wrist of my right hand, which held the racing bat and the right rein, I tapped her shoulder. She jumped but didn't trot. When I tried again, her back tightened beneath my seat.

I turned across the diagonal again. *Tap-tap.* She trotted and stopped.

Putting my reins in one hand, I reached behind me, tapping her on the flank behind my leg, like I'd seen Monte do. Her neck arched, but she didn't trot. I touched her again, and the leather flap on the end of the jockey's bat made a *pop* when it hit her.

True Colors shot forward. Her spine arched upward, unseating me. All four of her feet flew off the ground with such power that I was thrown to one side. Her rear end fishtailed above her head, launching me from the saddle. In the air, I felt the film of my life go into a surreal slow motion. As my right boot scraped across the saddle, she freed herself of my weight. I hung in the air, taking in my surroundings—her upwardly curved back and downwardly thrust neck, the way she planted her feet in the sand as she landed—before I struck the ground.

The footing was four inches of sand on top of hardpan. As I hit the arena floor, my teeth vibrated in my jaw. My legs bounced, moving away from my torso. A salty ferrous taste filled my mouth. My hip dug through the sand into bedrock. I grabbed for breath. As I spat out blood, sand, and part of a tooth, I stared through True Colors's rear legs while she slid to a dead stop. Craning her neck, she regarded me not unkindly as I sprawled unmoving on the ground. I thought: *This horse needs a rider as much as she needs a rowboat.*

Hearing the clamor, the other horses began to neigh wildly from inside the barn, a cacophony of brass, cymbals, and the drumroll of hooves against stall doors. Panicked to be without their anchor, they felt unmoored on an uncharted tide.

FOURTEEN

If only I'd been a better rider and had more experience; if only I'd taken True Colors along more slowly.

After T.C. threw me, I lost most of my fillings and had to wear braces on my teeth for years. T.C.'s buck was so hard, and she was so physically fit and had been feral for so long that, regretfully, I decided that she should not be ridden. Forever after, every time a visitor to the farm would point to her and comment, "*That's* your best mover," I felt stabbed in the heart.

Come autumn, I took another bad fall. Ms. Piggy, now a steely anthracite color, had the mind of a Jaguar and the body of a Mack truck. She'd grown to be a roly-poly sixteen hands with no withers to help the saddle stay in place. As I trotted her around the arena, the saddle started to slip to one side, goosing her forward. Before hitting the ground, I whacked my shin against the support post of the arena that I'd spent much of my adult life saving money to build. Nothing broke, but I limped for months.

Shortly after, Ms. Piggy sent me to the emergency room, but not because I fell off her. She couldn't eat, couldn't open and close her mouth, couldn't even move her jaw. Had she gotten something stuck in her teeth? Fingers and palm as flat as a spatula, I inserted my hand vertically into the side of her mouth the way Kath had once shown me. Keeping well away from her teeth, I pushed up against the soft wet tissue of her cheek. Where was Kath when I needed her? I bemoaned her disappearance from my life. I had twelve inches of hand and arm in the side of Ms. Piggy's mouth when the three-year-old tossed her head. My hand was sucked toward her throat, and *squish* she chomped my thumb between her brontosaurus clappers. My nail was gone.

The pain felt heart-stopping. Blood gushed over both of us, covering Ms. Piggy's gray muzzle and my hair. My clothes stained, my fingers

169

stuck together. After I stumbled up to the house, I had trouble dialing the phone. I wasn't calling the ER but Doc Short, who came immediately. He unhitched the horse trailer from our GMC truck so that I could drive myself to the hospital while he diagnosed Ms. Piggy: She'd been bitten or stung by some kind of insect that had temporarily paralyzed her face. We all fully recovered.

I couldn't send my shy True Colors off to a breeding farm, where the management was sure to stall her 24/7. All the same, on cold, torrentially rainy days when it was too bone-chillingly windy to ride, I forced myself to search through copies of *Chronicle of the Horse* for a suitable stallion to breed to her via artificial insemination. I didn't want to think about the stocks that the farm staff would have to use in order to achieve it, or all the needles they would stab into her—breeding a horse required a vast array of drugs. And they might have to sedate her in order to palpate her. Maybe I should turn her loose in my back pasture for the rest of her life. Since spring was months away, I put T.C.'s future on hold again.

We hired Kolika to come to the farm to paint the interior.

"What are you cooking?" she asked, washing her brushes in the sink while I peeled carrots. The crescents of her fingernails were rimmed with white.

The aroma of latex made me light-headed. "Chicken soup. That's what we decided, didn't we?" I asked, trying to avoid a confrontation. At breakfast, we'd had a heated *discussion* over cooking oatmeal: no cooked raisins. "It's not the same if you add the raisins after the oatmeal is cooked," I'd complained.

"It's a matter of texture," she'd told me. "There's texture in paint, fabrics, food—texture's important to me as an artist. You're a poet, don't words have texture?"

"Yeah, but usually, I don't have to eat them." This made her laugh.

When she complained about the way I made soup, I left the sink for a time-out and sat down at the kitchen table, pretending to thumb through a horse magazine while I decompressed. There it was in front of me, a photo of the perfect stallion: a very refined black Percheron in Ohio.

Kolika finished painting at the end of January just before a Banana Express, an unseasonably warm wind and rain, blew in. The horses didn't mind being outside in it, all except T.C., who that day stood at the back gate. *There's something the matter with her,* I thought as I glanced down at the paddocks from my desk up in the Winter Palace. *She never wants to come in, even when she's the last horse left in the pasture.*

Rain beat against the window; pools of standing water dotted the ground like mirrors. I turned off my computer and went out to her. Her coat dripped, as did her mane and tail; such things had never bothered her. The horses had been out only an hour, so a routine change couldn't explain her strange behavior.

"What's a matter, girl?" She turned toward me with a sad expression. "Not feeling well?" Sometimes an abrupt change in the weather and barometric pressure brought on colic. She let me clip a rope to her halter and lead her out the gate into the barn. Inside her stall, I was shocked when she eagerly ate her grain, then tackled her hay with vigor. She wasn't colicky; colicky horses don't eat. I stayed with her, scraping the rainwater off her coat with a shedding blade. By this time Willie had noticed her absence and started bellowing. She answered him, when usually, she didn't; her whinny had an alarmed ring to it. The others began to neigh. I heard the pounding of hooves, and when I looked out, Willie was standing by the gate and Al was running. Colette, Kermit, and Ms. Piggy looked at me with long, imploring faces: *Bring me in.*

"Okay, okay," I said, dashing for the paddocks with ropes and halters in hand. I pulled the hood of my jacket over my head, but a stinging rain pelted me in the face. After getting the other horses in, I was completely soaked. Rain fell like a gray curtain. I started to worry about the river rising up over the highway at the bottom of our hill.

Unstrapping the horses' wet blankets, I hung each to dry on hooks Mark had welded from Willie's and Alazan's shoes. All but the very young and T.C. wore turnout rugs made of Gore-Tex with a layer of fiberfill; keeping our horses in weatherproof blankets was as pricy as outfitting a Girl Scout troop with winter tents.

All at once the wild tropical rain ceased; a peacefulness ensued. I listened to the noise of horses masticating as the light began to change. True Colors raised her head, her ears pricked. The sun came out, making me squint. I heard a faraway rumble, a heavy rolling sound down in the valley as if a train had derailed. Then the ground started to shake, and the horses wheeled in their stalls, nickering—all except True Colors, who stood with her head lowered as if bracing herself. With a loud *smack,* like a bat against a wall, the wind cracked into the south side of the barn, and the barn's huge sliding door bowed inward. It sounded as if the derailed train were heading up the ravine toward us.

A gate flew off its hinges, splintering as it hit the ground. Afraid to walk to the house, I took cover in the grooming stall, crouching in a corner, shielding my head with my arms. For an hour or more, we were pummeled by a ferocious gale; I learned later that gusts clocked at up to ninety miles an hour. Huge hundred-year-old trees fell, barn roofs were torn off like the tops of envelopes, houses pushed off their foundations. Down on the state highway, semis blew off the road. Tree limbs littered the landscape. Blue stars sparked from the writhing snakes of downed power lines. Our electricity was knocked out: no heat or light, no water. All roads closed.

Mark somehow made it home; he'd been almost to the farm when the storm hit. Suddenly, our entire existence revolved around keeping the horses fed and watered. Only one of our fences was down—a miracle. An ancient hemlock had fallen squarely on a hundred feet of it. We carried water from the pond in muck buckets set inside a wheelbarrow, pushing it through mud to the barn. Our living room fireplace wasn't much use—most of the warmth escaped up the chimney—but the woodstove upstairs saved us. The Winter Palace felt toasty. We could heat tea water on the woodstove as well as cook pizza from our rapidly defrosting freezer.

Pushing a wheelbarrow full of water through ever deepening muck was beast-of-burden work. Horses consume vast quantities of water, and they like it refreshed every twenty-four hours. Our phone went out and our flashlight batteries ran low. No one came to assist. The roads in the foothills remained covered with downed trees and sparking electrical lines. On the fifth night, the ground froze; in the early hours, a heavy snow blew in, blanketing the landscape. Remarkably, our pond froze. It seldom glazed over more than a few feet from shore. After seven days— still no electricity, had the Pacific Utility Department forgotten us?— the six inches of snow began to melt. Then temperatures plummeted into the teens: completely unheard of in this part of the world. All our pipes froze.

The pond ice measured inches thick. To get water, Mark had to hack through it with an ax. We hauled our wheelbarrow over a rough trail of broken snow, sometimes crawling hand over hand on ice. Most of the water sloshed out onto us and into our boots. It took all morning just to keep the horses watered. I hadn't bathed in a week; it was difficult even to wash my hands and face. We were out of clean clothes, and our house was cold no matter how the fires roared. There were fewer than eight hours of light in a winter day, and our batteries were dead. I'd never felt so physically miserable and ready to give up on farm life.

To make matters worse, it was too treacherous to turn the horses out, since the paddocks were a sheet of ice. From the beginning, it was apparent that True Colors was more adept at walking on frozen ground than the others. She was my canary in the mine. In the late morning, I haltered her—sometimes it still took me ten minutes to do this—and led her out the barn's south-facing door. If she balked, legs braced in front of her, refusing to go farther, she was telling me it was unsafe. Back we went into the barn. Ms. Piggy might be the horse with all the charm, but T.C. was the horse with all the sense. I depended on her with an almost mystical feeling.

Mark and I walked each horse individually up and down the barn aisle for ten minutes at a stretch several times a day, or turned them out in pairs in the arena, where the sand was frozen but not covered with ice. I was always the one who led True Colors to pasture. If I was gone and Mark had to do this, he herded her. But now, in the barn, she allowed Mark to lead her quietly up and down the aisle. "She's my on-again, off-again girlfriend," Mark said, guiding her into the grooming stall and turning her around.

At night, we began to see house lights below us in the valley. Day twelve: still no electricity. Life felt intolerable without bathing. The minute the roads opened, we drove forty minutes to Jewel's house for a shower, on back roads clogged with slow-moving cars. At first I thought people were evacuating, but these were sightseers touring the destruction: A dairy barn with a gambrel roof had blown down, a covered riding arena had collapsed, a fifty-acre stand of alder was completely leveled, like playing cards. The situation felt ghoulish. We shuddered. Our little farm was safe.

True Colors had known that a gale was about to strike—our valley's strongest wind since records had been kept. She'd heard it when the other horses had not. I often wondered what would have happened if I hadn't heeded her as she stood at the gate, begging me to bring her in. She had saved the herd.

In May we backed our truck up to our horse trailer and hitched it up. I put down the loading ramp and left a trail of alfalfa hay leading up into the box. True Colors wasn't fooled. After what seemed like hours, we got her loaded and drove off to Twin Tamaracks Farm, a breeding facility located in an upscale suburb at the top of a wooded knoll behind an endless expanse of white fence.

True Colors wore a resigned expression once we loaded back at our farm. It remained unchanged as she backed out of the trailer at Twin Tamaracks and didn't alter as the manager's petite young wife led her away. T.C. didn't even give a surprised glance at her new surroundings. She wouldn't meet my eye; she looked through me as if I weren't there.

"You'll be okay," I told her, pushing a carrot through the metal bars of her spacious box. The carrot fell into the straw bedding. She didn't move to pick it up. Nor did she walk over to the hay to inspect it. Head to the wall, she stood listlessly. When I went in to give her a good-bye pet, she gave no reaction.

"She don't look so spooky to me," the tall, pitchfork-thin manager told Mark and me as he smiled and waved good-bye.

"She'll fool you," I warned, lifting up the horse trailer's ramp and securing it. "No horse moves faster."

It started to rain as Mark maneuvered our truck down the curvy road. The empty trailer rattled behind us, and a damp emptiness crawled over me. I hadn't been parted from True Colors for three years, which seemed like the better part of my life. I felt like Judas, coaxing her into our trailer and then dumping her off with only a bag of carrots and a warning to her handlers: "Don't take her halter off."

The report from Dr. Vogel was that True Colors didn't "take" the first time they brought her into heat, ordered the semen, and inseminated her. Now he was going to try again and hoped to get her "settled." When I went to visit her, she looked moderately happy, a few more lights in her eyes than when I'd last seen her.

"She's sweet," said the pixie-faced stable girl. Much to my surprise, no one had a discouraging word about how much trouble she was. "She don't stall-walk, crib, or weave," said the stable girl, who must have been in her late teens. "She just stands in here and minds her own business, don't even cry when she's the only horse in the barn. We don't get many like that."

"She's just terribly frightened," said Dr. Vogel, who happened to be in residence that afternoon. He let me know in great detail that he was trying to transplant an embryo into a host mare that day. Dr. Vogel wore Italian shoes so new they squeaked.

A month later, True Colors was in foal, according to Dr. Vogel. The final report, however, was that she had lost the fetus by her twenty-five-day preg check. As I backed her down the ramp of the trailer at our farm, her head jerked up. Pushing her black nose into the air, she stared transfixed at . . . what? The absurd beauty of our view, white peaks now so pink in the sunset that they look painted? She began to bray wildly. You'd have thought the barn were on fire. The look that came over her was total surprise. Delightedly excited, she appeared to be in a state of disbelief. I realized that never before had she gotten into a trailer and returned to a familiar place. As I led her into the barn and down the aisle, the other horses thrust their heads over their doors with joy. I put her in her stall and decided then that she could be the farm babysitter. What difference did it make if T.C. wouldn't drop a foal next spring? Didn't we already have enough horses? And Kermit was progressing nicely; he'd be ready for his first dressage show in a year.

It made a tremendous difference, actually. How could we be a horse farm without a spring foal? I tried not to feel let down and avoided adding up all the vet charges. I'd never get the stud fee back, but I could try rebreeding her next year without having to pay a new fee—if that's what I decided to do. We already had two nice youngsters out of T.C. In fact, we'd scheduled Monte to come again in the fall to break Colette, who'd finally outgrown the contracted tendon problem in her hind legs. Even at sixteen hands, Colette was more refined than Kermit—her older brother wasn't just a man's horse but a large man's horse.

October: One neon day followed another. The deciduous trees—maples, alder, dogwood—ignited into burning color: pomegranate, chartreuse, pumpkin. Monte was driving Colette from the ground in the arena. He stood behind her while regaling me with a tale from his racetrack past: "I was workin' for this pinhooker. One day he was piss-mad at me for getting pinched back after the gate opened and losing the race . . ." Monte pulled Colette to a halt. Staring at True Colors, who stood dozing in a paddock below the arena, Monte said, "I thought you told me that Shy-lotte wasn't in foal."

I followed Monte's gaze. True Colors's coat shone in the sun as if it had been rubbed with lamp oil. I stared at her belly, which indeed had a suspicious bulge to it.

"You think?" I asked him.

"I'd say so," he replied. He picked up the long lines and shushed Colette forward. "You need to buy a stallion of your own," he told me.

Monte had just pushed one of my buttons. "I do *not* need a stallion!"

Keeping a stallion was like keeping a lion. Choosing not to be a stallion owner was probably the easiest decision I'd ever made. Now it was my turn to regale Monte: "Once when I was riding stirrup to stirrup next to a woman on a mare, I heard a giant *whump* from behind us. Two shod hooves flew through the air, and a roan stallion ridden by a capable professional mounted the mare. I thought we were all dead!"

"I didn't say that you should ride your stallion," Monte countered.

"How is this possible?" I asked Mark that evening. "How does True Colors hide these foals from veterinary scrutiny? The same thing happened with the last foal. Remember?"

Mark was preoccupied. I'd found him in the living room, standing on a stepladder, adjusting the skylight he'd installed last summer. It lifted our mood to be able to look up at the ceiling and see a mural of stars. The trouble with skylights is that they usually leak.

"So what are we going to name it?" Mark asked.

I shrugged. "Something that starts with D."

When Dr. Short arrived to give the horses their seasonal flu vaccinations, he, too, thought True Colors looked to be in foal. "Where're ya gonna put this new one?" His huge smile and narrow lips made his unshaved face look like a jack-o'-lantern.

All at once we had too many horses and decided to sell Alazan. With his basics in dressage and his jumping ability, he'd make a perfect pony-club mount. I put ads in the local equestrian newsletters, and Jewel put an ad up on the bulletin board of the tack store.

Winter wasn't the best time, but as spring came on, I got flocks of interested callers, just as True Colors's belly started to look enormous. It's always hard to sell a horse—a little like having a piece of flesh cut from your body—but the idea of a new arrival made parting with Alazan a touch easier. Again we were uncertain of T.C.'s due date. Was it 340 days from the first breeding or the second? We decided on the second. Dr. Vogel never returned Dr. Short's phone calls. I felt truly indebted to our everyday vet for trying to communicate with him, though Dr. Short wasn't without his eccentricities. He refused to talk to our blacksmith, Nils, for instance. But equine practitioners refusing to talk to their fellow practitioners isn't at all uncommon in the horse world.

Kolika sometimes came to the farm to keep me company—and to prepare to paint the exterior of our house. As the hours of light advanced at neck-breaking speed, the days lengthening at both ends, Kolika and I spent hours grooming True Colors, trying to exfoliate her winter coat. Carefully, we brushed and curried—no fast motions—then used a shedding blade. She stood patiently in her stall as we worked, hair filling the air like a sienna fog. Once T.C.'s barrel jumped right in front of where I was brushing her. It looked as if the foal had tried to stick a hoof out the side of her. Raising my arm up and over True Colors's back, I tried to put my ear to her side behind her ribs, but she shot away from me. Later that night, I was able to lean against her, arms at my sides, putting an ear to her gut. Warm against my cheek, her large body had a wholesome smell. She let me press against her only long enough for me to hear what sounded like a fish darting through water. Walking back to the house, I witnessed another natural wonder: the aurora borealis. Transfixed, I stared into what looked like a solar scream in the night sky.

We watched for the usual signs of impending labor. T.C.'s belly moved back, her abdomen dropped, milk veins bulged, udders filled, and nipples distended like two black cones. Nothing about her behavior gave her away. She didn't act needy, her hind legs didn't stock or swell up. She picked at her food as usual, and when she wasn't eating, she stood in the back of her stall. We turned her out in a pasture by herself, and of course, Willie pined after her and went off his feed. Then one morning there was wax, and by evening I saw white dots on the ends of her nipples. The next morning there were tiny drops of milk. *Here we go again,* I thought, dragging out my plastic storage crate of canning jars, which

Kolika offered to wash and sterilize for me, thank God. This time I'd do it right and start collecting colostrum the minute T.C.'s milk began to drip.

"I imagine that the neighbor girls will want to come see the foal." Kolika lifted a Mason jar out of the boiling pot with a pair of tongs.

I grimaced. "I don't think so." Our eyes met. "I didn't tell you what happened."

Kolika wiped her hands on her denim overalls, which she wore over a tropical-purple-and-orange tie-dyed T-shirt.

"Last fall," I said, "Angel showed up in a skimpy bikini. I mean, it was a warm day, but not *that* warm. So, picture this: white knit bathing suit, white translucent skin. And on her chest is this black—and I mean *black*—bruise in the shape of a hand."

"Like someone forced her down," said Kolika, who was street-smart.

"That was my thought. I mean, it took my breath away. I couldn't help it: 'What happened to you?' just fell out of my mouth. Angel didn't skip a beat. She said, 'Oh, it's from my underwear, all my bras are too tight.' And gave me a show-girl grin.

"What struck me," I told Kolika, "other than wondering if she'd been raped, was how easily she lied. It just took my breath away. I paced around, wondering if I should call Child Protective Services."

Kolika's eyes hardened. "So what happened?"

"Angel rode up on her pony a few days later. I asked her how she was and what she was doing. At this point I hadn't decided—school, sheriff, or social services. This isn't Berkeley, you can't call the Free Clinic and ask for advice. Anyway, Angel said that she was babysitting all week and gave me this woe-is-me smile. When I asked her why, she told me that it was her mother's birthday and her mother was going to party all week— and get this, even though someone from CPS was going to visit their house on Monday. Presumably, her mother wouldn't be there for the interview. So I asked why Child Protective Services was coming to visit, and Angel said very matter-of-factly that someone at school thought that her little half brother was being molested by a male in the home. She said this in the same tone she might tell me it was going to rain."

"I can guess how this washes out," said Kolika, removing jars from the cauldron.

"No, you can't," I told her.

Kolika shifted her weight onto one Birkenstock sandal. "They moved away."

"Did I already tell you this?"

"Happens all the time. If you get into trouble with the authorities in one county, move to a different county. Better yet, another state."

As we finished sterilizing the jars, neither of us spoke. I thought of how protective mother horses usually are. True Colors was certainly protective; her only crime was letting her foal eat her food.

"Sometimes mares have been known to savage their foals when they're first born," I told Kolika, who was drinking a mug of Postum. I took a sip of black tea. "There's a saying: The foal never rejects the mare."

Kolika smiled. "So why would a mare do that?"

"Nobody knows; vets think it's caused by hormonal imbalance. It's just one reason you need to be there when the mare foals."

"They might savage their foals, but I bet a mare wouldn't stand idly by while some other horse savaged her foal," Kolika remarked, punctuating her sentence with her earthenware mug. "You ever hear from her?"

"Angel? She decided to go live with her father and stepmonster."

That evening Kolika left to fly to California, where she was designing a trompe l'oeil of a garden in Tuscany for a wall in Santa Monica. I brought T.C. in from pasture a little later than I'd intended. She was indeed dripping milk, but not quite enough to catch in a jar.

After a long discussion, Mark and I decided that, given T.C.'s last delivery, we didn't need to start sleeping in the barn yet. The next morning, her bag looked large enough to burst. Dr. Short stopped by to have a look and told me that he didn't think she'd foal for a week or two. Same story as last time, he assured. Should I sleep in the barn tonight? I couldn't decide. I was sterilizing towels when the phone rang.

"Kath!" She was just over the international border in Vancouver during a layover and had some time to kill. I gave her a rundown on all my critters. After I'd gone through True Colors's latest foaling saga, there was a pause on her end of the line.

"I don't care what that vet says," Kath told me sternly. "That mare could foal any minute. Don't leave her alone."

I never argued with Kath. That afternoon, I got T.C.'s stall stripped and filled with straw—a big job, carting all the shavings in her double box up to the manure pile, more than five loads of it—and then laid out the foaling kit on a hay bale. The other horses thought it was fun that their people were again spending the night with them. *Party time,* they seemed to be saying to each other as they stomped hooves and looked over their doors to see if I was still there after lights out.

True Colors remained mouse-quiet, ate her hay, and stood in the back of her stall. It was a cool, rainless night with gauzy, low-hanging clouds wafting across a black ceiling of stars. I woke up at about four A.M., so stiff that it felt like my limbs were nailed to my body. The floor was lumpy and damp. Getting to my feet, I looked in at T.C. She stood quietly, her large belly dwarfing the rest of her. Her milk made pinging noises in the straw. "Time to start collecting," I said. But first I yawned, stretched, and decided to catch some Z's in my own bed.

Could I sleep? No, and not because Mark was snoring. He wasn't. Maybe I could drop off if I had my favorite pillow; I'd left it down at the barn. Pulling on my shoes and a jacket, I walked out the front door and unhooked the metal gate across the driveway. Hearing the chain clank, a horse nickered. "Not feeding time yet," I muttered. Opening the barn door and walking out of the sharp bite of dawn into the horse-warm air, I found all the horses jutting their necks over their doors.

"You're not due to be fed for hours!" Bending down, I snatched up my pillow. As I straightened and looked in at T.C., the pillow fell from my hand.

She stood quietly, head down, licking a tiny bay replica of herself. The memory of the Madonna's serene expression as portrayed by Botticelli, da Vinci, Raphael—those famous paintings hanging in the Uffizi—flew into my head.

True Colors had already cleaned "Daybreak" off, gotten the foal up—which severed the cord—let her nurse, and was now stroking Baby's forehead with her tongue. The placenta lay in a pile next to the sleeping foal, and what was left of the fetal membranes hung like a torn rag from between the mare's hind legs.

She'd done all the hard work.

FIFTEEN

The air was heavy with the smell of fire azaleas, the weather dry for late spring; we turned True Colors and her new foal out on Daybreak's second day of life. What a gorgeous bay filly, as square as a table, with two white stockings on her hind legs and an agreeable temperament. Soon, however, a dark cloud appeared in our blue sky: T.C. had a glazed look in her eyes and walked endlessly, tiring her foal.

Sunday: Vets didn't like to come out on weekends for nonemergencies. On Friday, Daybreak had passed her neonatal exam with flying colors. She'd gained immunity from her mother's first milk; she had a good heart rate, a strong pulse, clear eyes and lungs. T.C. passed her postpartum exam as well. So why was she pacing the boundary of her paddock? Her foal bobbed behind, bouncing like a flea at first, then pawing and making a whining bleat for Mom to wait up, to stop and nurse, to stop and rest. T.C. complied for a minute, then marched on with a thousand-yard stare.

I telephoned the vet, but the associate on call didn't think anything was wrong. I tried to call Kath but couldn't find her; sadly, I never heard from her again. To this day I mourn her disappearance from my life and have no idea why she stopped communicating with me. Kath was one of a string of what I call "horse geniuses" who fell into and out of my life— usually people without a lot of formal education or a professional degree who operated on the fringes. Chiropractors, masseuses, acupuncturists, blacksmiths, psychics, trainers, all had an amazing gift at communicating with equines.

By Monday, Daybreak was lively and had been fitted with the little pink halter that Kath had given to Colette, but the five-day-old foal's hind legs were alarmingly swollen. Nervously, I dialed Dr. Short, who came out and injected anti-inflammatories and antibiotics.

"Could be joint ill." Doc looked concerned. "Or too much exercise too soon."

When I explained that True Colors had been walking the fence aimlessly all weekend, Doc shrugged. "Though a horse has a brain as small as a baseball, we haven't been able to plumb it." He said this not unkindly, crossing his stubby arms in front of his chest.

Later, I learned what might have caused T.C.'s strange behavior, and it endeared her to me even more. Mares can feel crampy just after foaling, when the uterus contracts to expel the placenta; administering a painkiller is often necessary. I'd never had to do this with T.C., as she showed no signs of discomfort. In hindsight, she may have been so stoic that she hid it. I didn't know then that postpartum contractions could go on for days and be quite severe. Walking was True Colors's antidote, the only way she knew to save herself. By the time the vet arrived, her thousand-yard stare had vanished.

"You got a regular horse factory here," Monkey Gee said when he looked in at the new foal. He had come to the farm to help us practice loading Kermit into a trailer. "When are ya gonna buy a stallion?" he asked Mark. Mark looked interested.

"Stallions are no end of trouble," I told both of them.

Before loading Kermit, Mark and Monte sped off for a quick tour of the garden, with Mark rhapsodizing about his basil crop. Neither heard a word I said.

When they returned, Mark backed up the trailer into the barn. We lowered the tailgate, which doubled as a loading ramp. The idea was that Kermit could walk out of his stall, down the aisle, up the ramp, into the trailer.

"How many horses you got now?" asked Monte.

Ms. Piggy, Willie, T.C., and three of her foals: Kermit, Colette, and Daybreak. Alazan had sold to a pony-club family. I missed his teacup-sized muzzle and lightning-slash blaze and sometimes felt teary-eyed.

Kermit looked magnificent. It was hard to believe that one of our own foals was heading for a dressage education with Annabelle N., who'd just relocated here from Virginia. Annabelle had an aristocratic but sensible air and had known the mother of my New Jersey trainer, Dot, a pillar of the East Coast horse world. Annabelle warmed to Kermit's temperament and potential and quickly recognized True Colors's value as a broodmare. Her praise set my heart aglow and helped me weather the snags, detours, and setbacks of training the big gray gelding. Nils had recently nailed Kermit's first shoes on his front feet, but the usually gentle giant hadn't liked having his hooves banged on and violently pulled his foot away, injuring the blacksmith's hand.

Kermit was humongous. And timid. Right now he was terrified of the trailer. When he stepped on the ramp, it made a hollow sound, causing him to back up uncontrollably. As True Colors looked on, I wondered what she thought. At her side was Daybreak, sometimes called Daisy, who, at age two months, had just outgrown her pretty pink halter.

Eventually, we would have to sell some of the foals—that was the idea of a farm—but I couldn't think about that today. Today we were familiarizing Kermit with the sound of the trailer ramp, a little like the noise of a horse walking over a bridge. Kermit's eyes asked: *What evil troll lurks there?*

The following day, Monte couldn't visit, so Mark and I tried the same

True Colors and Daybreak the day Daybreak outgrew her little pink halter.
Mark Bothwell

drill on our own. Finally, we coaxed Kermit all the way into the trailer. We encouraged him to eat the alfalfa in the hay bin and to smell the scent of other horses who had ridden there. Reluctantly, he took a couple of chews of his favorite hay, but then . . . Sometimes you can look at a horse's eye and see him thinking, as if the neurons in his brain travel in slow motion, jumping from one synapse to another. Kermit's expression went inward. He started to scramble, his hooves made a terrible racket on the trailer floor, and the noise magnified, reverberating against the metal walls, which frightened him more. His eyes widened and he started to back out. We let him. He moved slowly, not trying to fly out in a fury. That got a "good boy" from us. As he carefully stepped backward down the ramp, his dark gray butt reminded me of that of an elephant. Mark and I stood on either side to help guide him. When Kermit stepped off the ramp onto terra firma, he tried to turn around, pinning Mark against the wall. Mark's shoulders compressed as he tried to flatten himself against the tack room door frame. Just as I reached for Kermit's lead rope to guide him back to his stall, I heard Mark gasp. His face turned white, and he stumbled. To steady himself, he grabbed at the sawhorse where we put saddles while tacking up. He started to breathe convulsively, his mouth open.

I was shaking. "I didn't see exactly what happened."

"I don't think I can continue with this." He spoke rationally between gasps, leaning over the sawhorse. Grasping it with both hands, he shuddered. "I heard a pop." Did you hear anything?" His face turned as bloodless as cotton.

Alarmed, I tried to remain sure-footed. Quickly returning Kermit to his stall, I noticed that True Colors had jutted her head over her door. When I reached out to put my hand to Mark's forehead, the mare flinched as if someone were about to strike her. Mark felt cold to my touch, and his hands were icicles. Though I couldn't tell if his pulse was normal or if he was in shock (he had a low heart rate inherited from his mother), something was very wrong. Up at the house, I unbuttoned his blue canvas work shirt. His sternum protruded at an odd angle, his collarbone stuck out, and the left side of his chest looked sunken.

What scared me most was how easily he agreed to go to the emergency room. Though he worked in one of the world's largest research hospitals, he was terrified of doctors.

As our neighbors often said, they don't call it "Death" Valley for nothing. After the admissions nurse took a family history (a grandfather had died of a heart attack at age seventy), the ER doctor diagnosed Mark as having a heart attack.

"What?" I said in disbelief. My healthy husband lay on a gurney attached to a heart monitor. After nitroglycerin was administered, his slow heart rate slowed further. "He had an accident with a horse! Look, his collarbone is sticking out."

"And," continued the physician, a humorless man with large teeth that looked as if they had been spray-painted white, "this isn't his first."

"If he'd had a heart attack before, wouldn't he know it?" I tried to remember how old Mark was.

"Not necessarily." The doctor was as calm as salt.

"We need to get him to the University Hospital," I said. The heart monitor registered twenty beats a minute. "Look!" I pointed at the falling numbers.

"You're upset." The MD's expression was deadpan as a nurse rushed to Mark.

"Upset? Why won't you understand? He got smashed by a horse!"

Valley General was unable to handle a heart attack as severe as Mark's, I was told as an attendant in scrubs prepared to load my husband into an ambulance that would speed him to the big county hospital. I pleaded with the ER to send Mark to the University Hospital. "He has colleagues there," I entreated. I was told that the ride would take too much time and paperwork, endangering Mark's life. The emergency lights flashed, and Medic One sped off into the warm Sunday afternoon. County General's cardiologist was golfing and it was three hours before he saw Mark. All I could think of was: *How will I sell this farm and find us a house closer to my husband's work so that he can take up the life of a heart patient?* At eleven P.M., after hearing nothing from the hospital, I called the admitting desk, demanding to speak to Mr. Bothwell. They told me he was sleeping peacefully.

I thought: *He's dead.* "You've killed him" was on the tip of my tongue.

The resident cardiologist at the county hospital found no sign of a heart attack or heart damage, present or past. Mark was discharged with no mention of the bone protruding from his chest. After he complained of severe pain whenever he moved, he was given Tylenol. The bill for all of this came to nearly ten thousand dollars, completely covered by our insurance.

Two hospitals, several specialists, no diagnosis—how is that possible in the United States of America? It was Mark's responsibility to "pursue the matter." The popping sound that he heard when Kermit stepped sideways off the trailer ramp, compressing his shoulders together, had been the tearing of the cartilage that attached his rib cage to his sternum. This had "freed" his sternum from one side of his rib cage, as well as his collarbone. As it turned out, the only treatment for the torn cartilage was for his chest to be bound up like a mummy. For weeks he needed help getting in and out of bed and in and out of the car. The good news, Mark told me with a smirk, was that he got out of barn chores—for months.

A year later, Kermit starred at his first dressage show in the outdoor sand arena of Bridle Trails State Park. It was the end of August, a dry day with the promise of a warm summer night. Kermit backed calmly out of our trailer wearing a size-87 navy and gray sheet to keep the dust off him, as well as Willie's navy and gray shipping boots. Mark held Kermit's lead rope while I saddled him up. Peeling off the oversize T-shirt and wraparound skirt I wore over my white breeches and white shirt, I pulled on my knee-high black boots, then shoved an arm through the sleeve of my black show jacket. Fastening the chin strap of my helmet, I mounted. Kermit lifted his muzzle, sniffed the scent of strange horses, and bellowed. His entire body shook.

"Where's your stock tie?" Mark carried a grooming cloth in his back pocket.

"It's a schooling show. No neckwear required." Thank God. By the time I got the square knot tied and pinned with my only piece of gold jewelry—an antique Tiffany stock pin given to me by a Princeton neighbor—my white cravat looked shopworn.

As we walked to the warm-up area, Kermit's step felt spring-loaded. After putting him through his paces, I left the glut of competitors and walked him around the outside of the white four-cornered dressage arena. The judge and her scribe sat in a gazebo-like shed on the other side of the low white fence behind the letter C. Before I entered the arena to complete my test, Mark had to lead us past the judge's box several times so that Kermit could get used to the noise of papers rustling inside.

When the judge rang her dinner bell, I entered at A, trotted down the center line, halted in the middle at X, and promptly dropped my whip.

"Can someone pick it up for me?" I asked the judge after I saluted her. If I dismounted to pick it up myself, I'd be disqualified.

"No," she replied. Her voice was without expression.

"No? But this is a schooling show," I implored.

She shook her head.

I wasn't sure Kermit was ridable without a whip and felt heartbroken to have struggled so hard to get this far and then been so nervous as to let the whip fall out of my hand. I trotted forward, turned left at C, and circled at E. At K, I asked Kermit to canter around the short end of the arena and down the long side. Kermit didn't notice that I didn't have a whip until I was nearly at the end of the test, which took about four minutes; by then he had his own momentum. He seemed to enjoy being alone in the arena and didn't shy at the spectators, who, bless them, remained as silent as statues, or at the flower boxes filled with plastic pansies. Even the scribe clapped for us at the end.

In her comments, the judge praised Kermit's potential: *a gentle giant,* her very words. For a moment, I blotted out the memory of Kermit backing down the trailer ramp, swinging his salt-and-pepper tail toward Mark and, with no malice whatsoever, smashing my husband against the barn wall like an insect.

Though Kermit took an enormous amount of energy to ride, he would advance up the levels. Willie seemed not to be able to advance at all. Since I planned to rebreed True Colors in the spring, and I couldn't bear to part with any of her babies—they felt like family—I regretfully decided to sell Willie. He had a lot of attributes, and I felt sure I could find him a good home: He was tall enough for a man to ride, he could jump, he had fox-hunted and competed in dressage shows. I tried to sell him by word of mouth and for a while got nowhere, which bothered me not at all. Mark, however, was eager to realize even a tiny bit of revenue. "I'll put an ad in *Chronicle of Horse* tomorrow," I told him.

Rebecca, a local dressage teacher with a training center named after her favorite children's book, Sunnybrook Farm, arrived with her husband and a student new to riding, Cornelia, to look at Willie for Rebecca's husband. When Cornelia saw him, her clear hazel eyes turned to saucers, like a cartoon character who'd just fallen in love. Cory, as she was called, had light brown hair cut into a perfect pageboy and worked as a techie for Boeing. She was blisteringly timid and mounted with trepidation. The few steps of trot she managed were almost her undoing. Willie took not one smidgen of advantage of this slight, frightened person.

"Sold," she said with sudden authority.

I felt shaken and sat down on the mounting block. Maybe I didn't want to sell Willie: It wasn't too late to back out. Maybe I should put a higher price on him. In the end, I did neither, as if I'd foreseen what a fortuitous pairing this was. Not only would Willie and Cornelia be inseparable for the rest of his very long life; they would become my neighbors and Cornelia my confidante and friend, my bulwark against things to come. When the black and red Sunnybrook Farm van pulled out of my driveway with Willie's long black tail flowing out the back end, I felt overcome. A good soul was leaving my stewardship. *My buddy,* I thought as the trailer disappeared. I felt as if someone had burned a cigarette hole in my heart.

Willie had been a loyal friend, and I felt bad, tearing him away from his companions and his home. Though he was not the perfect horse for me, I choked up as I thought of his lonesome whinny; after he was unloaded at his new destination, he would call for me ceaselessly as he was led by a strange person to a strange stall. I reassured myself: He was in good hands; Rebecca had a reputation as a good trainer. I could tell from the lights in her eyes that she thought he was the deal of the century. And clearly, Cornelia was in love with him.

Though a horse is considered property, selling one is different than selling a house or a car. Horses have souls. I always try to find a buyer who will invest a lot of time and concern in the new mount. Also, I ask that the buyer give me the right of first refusal should he decide to sell. Somehow the possibility of someday getting Willie back made his departure a fraction easier.

True Colors didn't have time to be upset that her pasture mate was gone, because we were busy trying to wean Daybreak. T.C. was never eager to be separated from her baby. If the little tyke wasn't in sight, T.C. reared and screamed, her entire body pleading: *Where is she? I need to see her right now!* I didn't have much time to mourn Willie's departure, either. The minute he was gone, out of the blue, Annabelle offered me her imported Dutch competition mare, Vera. Annabelle didn't own a stable of her own yet and was the mother of two preschoolers. The handsome white mare had been having mysterious lameness problems in her right hind. And Vera, who'd undergone lifesaving colic surgery the year before, was prone to bouts of abdominal pain. Trying to find a job for her mare, Annabelle had bred her, but that, too, had failed.

The seventeen-hand good-natured Vera arrived at High & Dry Farm a week after Willie left. All my stalls were filled now, but I couldn't say no to a horse that could piaffe (trot in place), passage (a slow elevated trot), and half-pass (moving sideways in a scissors step) like the Olympic horse Annabelle had hoped Vera would become. Like many upper-level dressage horses, Vera had been kept in a stall without turnout so that she wouldn't hurt herself frolicking in the field. I had Nils remove her hind shoes the very day she arrived, and we turned Vera out in a small corral next to T.C. It was immediately apparent that the two mares were soulmates. They trotted toward each other, sniffed noses over the fence, and ever after were never more than a few feet apart.

At first Vera walked in a twelve-foot-by-twelve-foot square, as if she were still in a stall and couldn't walk in any other configuration. Over time, the squares got larger and the two mares roamed the back pasture, standing so close that their shadows fused. With a long warmblood head about twice the size of T.C.'s, her neck attached high on her chest, Vera had had one foal years ago, and I liked to think that motherhood was what bonded them. Monte called her Snow White. She was a welcome addition and a blast to ride—no riding horse was more surefooted. After she had been allowed to roam free for a few months, her hind lameness was barely noticeable, and eventually, I was able to show the lovely, well-trained horse. What an enormous piece of luck she was.

The bad news came the following spring, when we shipped T.C. off to be bred to a fancy Canadian warmblood. At the same time, we tried to breed Vera via artificial insemination at home—she was used to veterinary intervention, and we could handle her ourselves. Vera failed to breed. T.C. didn't "take," either, and was returned "empty."

"You gotta buy your own stallion. Horses breed easier the old-fashioned way," Monte told us. "At least go to the bloodstock auction at the racetrack and take a look." He'd come to the farm to gentle Daybreak. We had a good crop of basil this year and were happy to trade for his services.

"I do not want a stallion. They're a wealth of trouble," I told him. Twelve hundred pounds of hard-hoofed, testosterone-filled muscle and bone was usually impossible to reason with, if *reason* were the correct word. Striking, biting, kicking, charging. But Mark, who was not as experienced with horses—though certainly not one to throw good money after bad—thought it was a fine idea.

I told Monte, "I don't want to get involved with hobbles and tranquilizers and steroids. It's too overwhelming. And dangerous."

Monte stood in the grooming stall, a brush in one hand and a mane-and-tail comb in the other. Positioned in front of Daybreak's square shoulder, he vigorously combed and pulled in order to get her black cockscomb of a mane to fall on one side of her neck. The yearling turned, regarding him cautiously as he began braiding. "Gonna tame this crow's nest, darlin'," he said, admiring his first plait. "Shy-lotte ran with a herd, didn't she?" he asked, referring to True Colors. "She's pasture-bred before, she can do it again."

"No kidding?" Mark's face lit up.

"I've been meaning to ask you, Monte," I said. "What's this little warty thing on Daybreak's stomach here, back by her udders?"

"Don't change the subject." Monte's expression turned stern. "That's a silly little sarcoid that'll go away in time."

That night I told Mark that keeping a stallion would require a special fence, six feet high, constructed of railroad-tie posts, two-by-six rails, and heavy stable-mesh wire. I thought the idea of having to build the colossus of corrals would detour him. It didn't.

"If you buy a stallion, your husband will divorce you," Jewel told me when I went to the tack store for a pair of extra-large bell boots to protect Kermit's front hooves. Jewel had dark brows and a perfect helmet of brown hair.

"Mark is threatening to divorce me if I don't buy a stallion," I said. No one believed me. I couldn't believe the situation I was now in.

Deciding to purchase a stallion felt like jumping off a boat dock into the unknown depths of Lake Michigan, not knowing the temperature of the water, whether I'd ever hit bottom, or what I'd find there. As the auction approached, I braced myself for the metaphorical sting I'd feel as my toes cut the water and a cold shock zapped up my spine.

The winter mixed sale was held on the first weekend in December. The catalog arrived in the mail, perfect-bound and almost an inch thick: 340 yearlings, 107 broodmares, 47 weanlings, 40 horses of racing age. According to Monte, our best bet was to buy a yearling colt—in under a month, by Jockey Club rules, he'd be a two-year-old and able to breed come spring.

The yearlings would be auctioned in the racetrack sales pavilion on Saturday starting at noon. Horses were required to be on the grounds by Friday for viewing. Each horse had an oval-shaped yellow and black number epoxied to his left hip; yearlings wore hip numbers 1 through 340 and came on the block in numerical order.

I dived into the sale book, studying the information. Each sale horse had its own page. At the top in the outside margin was the horse's hip number; in the center, the name of the horse's owner or the bloodstock agent to whom the horse was consigned. The horse's registered name appeared in boldface; below was its foaling date and pedigree going back three generations. Under the pedigree was the black type, or racing history of its ancestors. The more black type, the more expensive the horse. We weren't looking for racing bloodline, but a good dressage progenitor.

According to Jewel, many a stellar riding mount had been picked up at a good price at this auction. I looked for the sires of well-known show horses in the pedigrees of the yearling colts and tagged them. Jewel knew the sires that sometimes produced foals with neurological conditions and had X'd across those pages. If a horse had a vice such as cribbing (sucking air, which then has to work its way through the system and can cause digestive disturbances), weaving (swinging the neck back and forth), or stall-walking (endlessly pacing back and forth), I drew X's across those pages. I didn't want my future stallion to have any of True Colors's relatives on either side—inbreeding in horses is as disastrous as inbreeding with anything else. More X's.

I whittled my selection list down to twenty yearlings. Mailing in my letter of credit, I received a buyer's number and a note: *All sales final and in cash.* How does that work when a horse is sold for tens of thousands?

Nothing that I had to worry about; in the racing world, I was small change.

On Friday we stopped at our local bank. Mark stuffed the stack of hundred-dollar bills in his wallet, then wedged it into his hip pocket. We arrived at the old Seattle racetrack at noon on a chilly overcast day with our sale book in hand and headed to the shed rows where the yearlings were housed. The low buildings looked like barracks, the weathered siding freshly painted industrial green. The stalls were small and dark and filled with fresh straw; their Dutch doors faced the outside, the aisleway in front of the stalls protected by a wide overhang of eave. I counted twenty stalls to a shed row, ten on either side, then scanned the crowd: Where was Monte? Jewel had to work but would be here to advise us tomorrow. Mark headed for the business office next to the cafeteria, and the smell of grilling burgers, to look for Monte, who'd agreed to conduct what he called a "ball check." Often a horse listed as a colt in the sale book was castrated by the time he came to auction. There were other concerns: A male horse's testicles didn't always descend; such colts were called *ridglings*. Sometimes it was obvious that both testicles had descended, sometimes not. Double or single ridglings would be unsuitable for breeding. Mark's notepad listed the numbers of horses we might be able to afford.

I tried to go through my book methodically, number by number, but the horses weren't stabled the way they were organized in the sale book. I felt overwhelmed but impressed. All equines, weanlings included, had their manes plaited and their coats polished to a metallic sheen. The handlers wore spit-shined paddock boots and baseball hats in their stable's racing colors, the logo embroidered in the center. Some bloodstock agents put out cloth-covered tables offering coffee and Danish. At the request of a potential buyer, handlers—called *lads*—marched their horses up and down the green between shed rows, both horse and lad strutting with military precision.

I heard not one curse word, not even when a fractious weaning stepped on a handler's foot. There was a litany of *yes, sirs* in between one horse calling to another and an occasional anxious beast striking his stall door, as if asking to be taken out and shown off to the public. The few female grooms seemed to be daughters or girlfriends of the people involved. Otherwise, the agents, handlers, buyers, and officials were predominantly male and an "old boys' club" atmosphere prevailed, in sharp contrast to the dressage population in America, which is about 90 percent female.

After watching other potential buyers, I started methodically going down the shed rows and looking in at each yearling, asking the handler to take one of my prospective choices out and walk him on the green. I was impressed with how well behaved these youngsters were, how easily they led and halted and stood squarely while several people converged on them, picking up a hoof, watching them walk to see if they dragged a toe or paddled (a conformational defect causing the lower part of the front leg to swing out during locomotion) or had a deviated knee. The horse was only required to walk; no other gaits were allowed. Of course, a horse might spook and exhibit a few steps of trot, the gait at which lameness is most often detected. I kept my eyes glued in case one of them trotted and also to see whom I might be bidding against.

In the margins of my book, I made furious notes. *Check right eye, kind, smart, catlike—second choice, pigeon-toed, clubfooted, huge, sweet— first choice.* At the Reiner Bloodstock barn, which was decked out in blue and yellow streamers with matching tack trunks, I spotted Mark and Monte. Or rather, I heard Monte talking to a handler, his voice and mile-a-minute manner of speaking carrying above the chatter.

We exchanged glances. "They've all passed so far," Mark said with a conspiratorial smile. He looked the part of a buyer in his tweed driving hat, bomber jacket, and Tony Lama cowboy boots.

My faculties began to fade, and all the bay yearlings looked alike. I sat down at the coffee station of Blue Ribbon Racing Stables and X'ed out several chestnut colts with white legs and white horned feet, fearing a repetition of Alazan's problems.

At the end of the day, there were five favorites that Mark and I agreed on. We returned home and went to bed that night completely played out. In the morning, Mark hitched our trailer to our pickup, and we drove down the interstate. The racetrack parking lot was clogged with vans and shiny semis used to transport horses across the country. We got the last spot. The number of prospective buyers milling among the shed rows had increased tenfold over the day before. A number of women had Dolly Parton hair and wore mink jackets and diamond earrings. One man with dark hair who conversed in French as he gestured with a ruby-studded hand wore a full-length fur coat, his shirt open at the neck to reveal a king's ransom in gold chains. Clearly not from around here, where fur doesn't fare well in the rain and the asphalt skies spit intermittently.

Latching on to Jewel, I guided her to the shed rows. Inspecting the first horse, she drew a Virginia Slim from her Coach bag. "This one's got different-sized front hooves," she whispered, rolling her eyes. I couldn't see the defect. "His feet are trimmed to hide it," she added. The horse with a cloudy eye probably had a cataract.

"This bay has a big trot with good elevation," I told her as we stood in front of the stall door of 184, Kells. "I saw him moving around yesterday when someone accidentally knocked over a folding chair." He was one of the few horses handled by a woman.

"Nice." Jewel looked at the compact bay's wide chest as the groom led him out. "Bold Ruler's in his pedigree. Sired lots of show champions. He'd be my choice."

The handler was in her early twenties, with dark curly hair. Instead of wearing English paddock boots, she dressed like a cowgirl and seemed eager to march Kells up and down the green for us. "He's a happy puppy," she drawled. "I teached him some tricks." She smiled fondly at him and scratched his ear.

"Do you think that he and T.C. would be a good nick?" I asked Jewel.

"Definitely. And you could put him to Ms. Piggy."

"I already bred Ms. Piggy. To the stallion that I tried to breed to True Colors. Otherwise I'd have lost my stud fee. It turned into a fiasco. Pigster got a uterine infection, and they had to clean her up and try again." Inwardly, I cringed at the huge vet bills we'd incurred to save the stud fee, which was at least as much as a mortgage payment.

"In-ter-est-ing," Jewel said. I tried to read her expression. When I pressed her, she added, "Lots of mares get infected at breed farms. That's one reason I never bred any of my horses. Sometimes they never get rid of the infection."

A loud noise like a hammer hitting a saw blade sounded over the loudspeaker. Jewel and I headed for the sales pavilion.

The amphitheater had descending rows of seats upholstered in red velvet, sloping down to a stage where the horses were lead out one by one and auctioned off by a professional who stood behind a podium draped in purple velvet and trimmed in gold braid. To the right was a bank of phones manned by young men in business suits, their job to handle call-in bidders. I couldn't count the people in the audience, hundreds, and it seemed that everyone smoked. No one removed his hat.

"Who's the guy in the fur coat?" I asked Jewel, gesturing at the front row of seats.

"From Dubai." She arched her brows meaningfully. "Always buys yearlings."

A buzzer sounded. The auction began, the hypnotic ring of the auctioneer's call filling the room. I held my breath. Mark appeared, taking the seat I'd saved for him. When I asked where Monte was, he shrugged. Sitting between Jewel and Mark, I alternately clutched one or the other of them. Nobody bid on the first horse, a filly—I didn't know that could happen. The second horse didn't sell; its minimum wasn't reached. I hadn't known a horse could have a minimum, and I began to feel foolish. Then yearlings started selling hard and fast, the auctioneer's trill like a yodel. The horse with the cataract sold for a pile of money to the fur coat from Dubai, the bidding done mostly by the well-dressed men in the front row and the suits manning the phone bank. None of them looked like they'd ever come near a horse.

The first colt I'd circled was led out. Mark made the opening bid, and then the bids went up out of sight. Next was a horse with contracted tendons, a condition I had firsthand experience with. That colt went for twenty thousand. The next horse, a gray filly, didn't sell. The owner had withdrawn the following horse. The auctioneer seemed to know or recognize the men bidding. Were there any women buyers? Mark recognized a familiar face from the medical center when he bid on a fancy colt. "A doc who invented some kind of heart valve," Mark whispered.

I couldn't believe how calmly the yearlings walked down the runway and stood patiently onstage in front of the crowd, like contestants in a beauty contest. "Probably had a preshow cocktail," said Jewel, "a little ace," short for acepromazine.

Everyone looked emotionless, as if they were playing poker. No one sat on the edge of a seat but me. All the same, the adrenaline in the room became palpable. When the auctioner called, "Sold," and slammed his gavel on the podium, then pointed the handle end of his mallet at the buyer, the horse was led off the stage and back to the shed rows. "Good journey," Jewel and I whispered after them.

Our second choice was led out. This time Mark let someone else open, then raised his hand on the third bid. The two men who had bid previously glanced at each other and a bidding war ensued. We reached our limit and Mark dropped out. A gentleman in a black western shirt standing in the back of the theater by the exit door made a surprise tie-breaking bid. Who were these people buying horses they had not even seen trot? No X-rays. No thorough vet inspection. Who could afford to risk this kind of money?

Our last choice came out, number 184. Mark turned to me. "You do the bidding."

"What?" I wasn't prepared and heard my heart thud.

"What horse is this?" asked Jewel, fumbling with my sale book.

"Kells," I whispered. "Your favorite."

I let someone else open. It turned out to be the groom who worked for the bloodstock agent to whom Kells had been consigned. Someone else made a second bid. I made the third, just ahead of the first bidder, who looked perplexed.

The auctioneer looked to the first bidder, then the second. I looked at Kells. He had a lovely arch to his neck, made more visible by his plaited mane. His neck was set high on his chest, like Vera's. He had a well-developed rump, like T.C. And he did have a cute head, with widely spaced eyes and small ears like the buds of just-opening roses.

"I love that tiny white star in the middle of his forehead," said Jewel.

I stared at him and held my breath. He had no other white on him. Black horned hooves and straight legs. Lovely, though a little on the short side.

Jewel nudged me. I raised my hand. The auctioneer's head nodded in the direction of the other bidders. The young woman handler looked tearful, her face reddening.

"Going once," called the auctioneer into his microphone. "Any other bids?"

I tried to breathe. Would this be the sire of True Colors's next foal?

"Going . . ." He scanned the semicircle of audience, then took in the clot of men standing by the exit doors.

"Sold!"

SIXTEEN

"You let Shy-lotte teach your stallion how to do his job," Monte advised as we loaded Kells into our trailer after the auction. The sky opened, and rain was hammering the top of our rig when the ex-jockey appeared to help us coax our newest equine into the trailer. I was already sweet on this horse—his small fuzzy ears warmed my wet hand as I stroked them.

That had been four months ago, and it was now early spring. The pussy willows had finished furring, and the purple crocuses were up. By the pond, several bald eagles perched in the crags of an old cottonwood. Below, on the new bridge that Mark had built to the island, a great blue heron stood on impossibly thin legs, scanning the cattails.

During Kells's first few weeks here, I turned him out in a paddock next to Kermit before putting the two young horses together. Now they played in the front pasture like puppies. The mares were less welcoming. When we'd arrived at the farm with Kells, I'd wanted him to stretch his legs before we got him settled in his stall—riding in a trailer is difficult for a horse, as he has to work at keeping his balance. Mark led him into our new stallion corral—a remodel of the old foal pen. Kells put his nose to the ground and started to graze as if he'd lived here all his life. At the time, Vera, True Colors, and the other girls—Ms. Piggy, Daybreak, and Colette—were grazing in the back pasture. They'd wandered over the brow of the hill to get out of the flogging wind that spiraled down off the glaciers. The mares didn't know that we'd returned with a new horse.

Ms. Piggy was the first to amble up the slope toward the gate. Her precise inner clock told her it was five minutes unto mealtime. Was it her unborn foal that caused the pooch in her barrel or her efficient metabolism storing fat for all her winters to come? The other horses followed. Kells raised his dainty head, pricking his ears. When he nickered, Ms. Piggy stopped dead in her tracks. Even from where I stood, I could

197

see her reel backward and snort. Then, like a runaway locomotive, she hurled herself in the opposite direction with such force that she tore off a shoe, pitching it in Kells's direction. The other mares galloped after her, True Colors taking the lead. Kells bleated, staring at the spot between two bare maples where the band had vanished.

By night, most of the mares began to settle into the idea of having a new presence in the barn. Ms. Piggy remained wary and on her guard, worried that another mouth to feed might reduce the size of her meals. Walking down the aisle to check on the well-being of each before lights out, I listened to the peaceful noise of equines munching hay. All our horses were colored bay or gray, and I made a chant out of naming their colors as I walked along.

Flicking off the barn lights, I wondered about the color of Ms. Piggy's unborn foal. I had a lot of anxiety over the impending parturition. True Colors had successfully borne her first on the range by herself, but it seemed unlikely that Pigster was cut from the same cloth. This would be our first foal born to a mare other than T.C., and I had doubts about Ms. Piggy's maternal instincts. Would Pigster reject her foal or, worse, savage the poor little termite if he got within reach of her grain dish? My foaling literature told me that first-time mothers were none too keen on letting their neonates nurse. I'd have to take measures to prevent the new mom from kicking her hours-old foal and dealing it a fatal blow. It came home to me that True Colors wasn't just a good broodmare but one of the world's best—so good, in fact, that I worried that she might try to steal Ms. Piggy's baby.

I think it was Kath who told me that she once had a really maternal mare too old to breed who always tried to appropriate the other mares' foals. I'd remembered this story last summer when our college-age horsesitter had boarded her white Arab dressage horse for a few weeks. True Colors had immediately formed an unusually fond attachment to Chantilly Lace, guarding the pony-sized mare as if she were her own offspring.

I closed the barn door against the elements, pulled the hood of my old parka over my head, and walked up the gravel drive to the house. Something else nagged at me. When Ms. Piggy's foal arrived, there would be eight horses and seven stalls. I'd have to sell one or even more of True Colors's foals.

* * *

Integrating Kells into the herd was going fine until right after New Year's, when I made a serious mistake. It was getting on in the afternoon, close to feeding time. In the west, the clouds had turned fuchsia. I'd led True Colors out of her stall into the front pasture and started to pick the manure piles out of her box, then I got distracted. We were in need of a second barn cat; small beasties scurried everywhere, leaving their calling cards. I had nightmares about hantavirus. All our barn cats were house cats at heart, and I was trying to encourage my latest found feline, a long-haired tortoiseshell named Hillary Clinton, to take up residence in the hay loft. I got so involved with trying to entice Hillary C. up the ladder (why was it that I thought I needed to teach a cat to climb?) that I forgot True Colors was in the front pasture. I finished picking out her stall and went on to Kells's box. Putting his halter on, I led him from his stall, opened the sliding doors, and turned him out in the front pasture, now bathed in the light of a smoky lavender sunset. He had the habit of dunking his hay in his water bucket before eating it, so I straightened his feed area. Picking up a pile of manure with the new red plastic manure fork I'd gotten for Christmas, I listened to him trot up the gravel drive toward the gate. Odd. He usually started inhaling grass—the front pasture was filled with winter clover. Then I remembered.

Ohmygod! I grabbed Kells's lead rope off its hook and dived into the feed room for carrots. Sliding open the huge door, I was almost afraid to look outside. When turned out together, Kells and Kermit played rough; Kelly had no paddock manners whatsoever. Surely he would torment T.C. What punishment would she divvy out to him?

He had already located the bay mare grazing by the fence at the turn in the road and was trotting enthusiastically around her, tail raised like a bolt of black crepe. True Colors stood firmly in one spot, every sinew tensed and her neck arched, like an equestrian statue. First she faced him, fending him off with teeth that flashed in the setting sun. Pivoting around, she turned her butt toward him and kicked high into the air with both hind hooves—less dangerous to another horse than kicking low at the knees. Kells failed to take even this warning. Ramming his nose in her face, he snorted like a bull. True Colors never moved from her tiny piece of real estate, instinctively knowing not to run; casting herself as prey would incite him further. She kicked again, this time striking Kells squarely at the base of the neck. Her message screamed, *Stay back.* She swung around and struck out at him with a foreleg, snaking her neck and brandishing her teeth. Oblivious, Kells continued to dog the mare but didn't try to mount her. Finally, after he'd stepped on her heels one too many times, she walloped him squarely in the chest with a hind hoof. The blow knocked the wind out of him. He staggered, and I thought he would fall. She stood firm, haunches pulled under her like the cocked hammer of a gun. He reeled from side to side, took a step, shook himself, then bent down, taking a bite of grass. True Colors tossed her head with a stern expression. Then she, too, put her head down to graze. Nothing more transpired. They grazed peacefully within feet of each other as if they were old friends. After a while, I walked out, attached a lead rope to Kells's halter, and brought him in. Much to my surprise, True Colors followed as if this were the ordained order of the herd.

The hard fruit had set in our little orchard; it looked as if we'd have a bumper crop of Gravenstein apples and Bose pears. Despite Kelly and True Colors's meeting, I wasn't ready for his first breeding season. In fact, I was a nervous wreck. Ms. Piggy, once my adorable stuffed toy of a baby horse and now a monstrous gray killer whale, was due to foal any day, after which we were going to pasture-breed T.C. to Kells and then try to rebreed Vera via artificial insemination. Though True Colors had thrown four offspring, she looked as sleek-bodied as a maiden. As summer approached, her bay coat dappled like sumac. As T.C. streaked across the back pasture alongside the white, high-necked Vera, her mane and black flag of a tail flew in the wind of her gallop.

True Colors's foal, the full-grown Kermit, was headed to his first recognized dressage competition. I bit my nails, worried that I'd make a fool of myself in front of the entire equestrian population.

Ms. Piggy foaled after dinner one night during the first week in June. Her parturition went by the book, almost. Mark and I happened to be in the barn, trying to entice Hillary Clinton into taking up permanent residence in the loft instead of on our bed in the Winter Place. Mark had built her an eating station above T.C.'s stall, as True Colors was the only horse who didn't mind Hillary climbing up her door and then jumping into the loft.

We were in the loft, building the cat bed and watching Pigster eating her hay when, without warning, her water broke. Spellbound, we stared. For a few minutes, she chewed as if nothing had happened, then she fell as if slain, lying rigored, though still masticating. A white sack emerged, and the foal's dowel-like legs broke through the caul. Midchew, Ms. Piggy heaved a huge sigh.

Luckily, I had laid out our foaling kit. We tugged on our lab coats and gloves, and Mark went first into the foaling box. It appeared that Pigster had given up pushing. Bending over and reaching inside the birth canal, Mark pulled the foal's shoulders free. Ms. Piggy continued chewing, unconcerned about what was happening to her hindquarters. I went in with a flake of hay and laid it in front of her nose, hoping she'd remain down. She stayed in place.

The foal looked dark bay. From the very beginning, this baby had a knock-down, drag-out willingness to thrive. As long as there was food in front of her, Ms. Piggy was happy to stay down, though occasionally, she glanced at her midsection as if she'd experienced a twinge of colic. Quickly, we toweled the foal dry—what a tiger. The foal's head bobbed as it drew up its front legs, trying to raise itself even before getting out of the sack. We couldn't tell if the tyke didn't like us rubbing him or if he wanted to tussle with us. Somehow I knew before we broke the cord and got him up that this warrior was male.

He was on his feet before his mother was. When Ms. Piggy got to the end of her hay, she rose, and only then did she turn to inspect the fracas going on down by her tail. Her expression was mystified when she saw that there was something small and furry and damp in the stall with her. At first she looked stricken. Then Pigster ran to her foal, thrusting her neck protectively over Baby's back, sniffing his tail. The froth of her gray forelock and mane swirled around her as she shook her head with excitement. When Baby tried to take a step, she followed; she wouldn't permit him to go anywhere on his own without hovering over him. It was as if she'd found buried treasure.

The hard thing was getting him to nurse, though he had the best sucking reflexes I'd ever seen. He was a giant—150 pounds. Piggy's udders dripped at first, then the volume turned up to a continuous spray. It wasn't that her udders were sensitive, she just didn't want him to move away from where she could nuzzle and groom him with her upper lip.

She wanted him right in front of her and whirligigged around whenever we tried to guide Baby past her shoulder toward her udders. Finally, we put a halter and rope on her and backed her into a corner. I distracted her with a bucket of apples while Mark grabbed the foal and rumbaed him toward Mom's hind end. Never has a foal attached itself faster or with more barnacle-like force. The minute he began to suck, a film rolled over Ms. Piggy's eyes. She pulled her head from the apple bucket and whipped her neck around, pressing her muzzle into Baby's rump as if the smell of him were heaven.

The other horses were out of their minds with inquisitiveness, all except T.C. She had thrust her head over her stall door and stared transfixed in the direction of the nursery stall, not moving a hair since the new foal was born. I offered her one of Ms. Piggy's Fuji apples, but she refused to eat commercially grown fruit. "Don't get any ideas about absconding with Ms. Piggy's baby," I told her kindly. "She seems fond of it."

Dr. Vogel came for the neonatal exam. "Be careful of this one," he said, dusting himself off and examining the stain on his khakis after Baby had tipped him onto the floor of the stall. "He'll nibble your hand like a fawn and, when your back is turned, jump you down!"

On mare and foal's first day of turnout, a flock of tiny yellow goldfinches flitted from post to post. Ms. Piggy paraded her colt along the fenceline so that the others could admire but not get too close to her treasure. He was the only thing that had ever taken precedence over eating for her. True Colors stood on the other side of the fence in the back pasture, watching like a proud auntie. When the foal shot toward a chirping finch, his mother scurried after him, and True Colors's gaze followed. When he lay down for a nap after a long tug on Ms. Piggy's udders, his mother stood over him, lowering her muzzle to his sleeping body. True Colors continued to watch the pair, never moving from her post, seldom shifting her weight or bending down for a nibble of grass. During his nap, both True Colors and Ms. Piggy watched Baby's breathing as if he were a little god. T.C.'s expression wasn't covetous—as I so often observed, there was no meanness in this mare. On the foal's second day of turnout, I saw True Colors steal long looks at the new mom and baby. When all the hoopla died down, I turned the new pair out in the back pasture with T.C. and Vera; the two mature mares watched Baby but never approached. He orbited at breakneck speed around his gargantuan mother like an atomically charged particle. This foal named himself: Electron.

Ms. Piggy with Electron
at a few days old.
Mark Bothwell

Now we could move on to next year's foal crop: the hair-raising job of pasture-breeding True Colors to Kells and then trying yet again to get Vera to conceive to a fancy warmblood sire via artificial insemination. Pasture breeding was an art. If I only slightly miscalculated T.C.'s heat cycle, she might wield Kells a blow that could end his life. She wasn't cycling in January, when I'd accidentally turned the two out together in the front pasture. Now estrus had come on full tilt, and T.C. was, for lack of a better word, moody. The ups and downs of human sexuality don't hold a candle to that of mares and their wildly vacillating attitudes toward procreating. In order for one plus one to equal three horses, a study of these girls' bad-hair days would be vital.

Each day we paraded the mares individually past Kells's stall with him secured safely inside. If True Colors stopped in front of his door and the two exchanged congenial hellos, we let them sniff each other further and then watched how things progressed. If T.C. squealed, struck out murderously with a foreleg, pinning her ears and lunging at the stallion with Dracula teeth, we returned her to her stall. Obviously, she had not started to come into heat.

If T.C. didn't pin her ears but looked slightly interested in touching noses with Kells, this reaction told us that a follicle was building in one of her ovaries. We were looking for the day when she didn't discourage him from stretching his head over the stall door and biting her neck, the day when she would let Kelly chew on her amorously and when she might even try to chew on him. Day one would probably be the next day, the day she lowered her rump and squirted urine into his face. The smell of mare musk sent Kells spinning around his stall, fleering—raising his upper lip and turning it inside out. He might even trumpet and make the most godforsaken guttural noises before attempting to jump over the stall door. But we wanted to breed her on day three and then again on day five. Breeding a horse this way is called *live cover*, and it's the only way a Thoroughbred foal can be registered with the American Jockey Club.

I barely slept during the next two nights. The thought of witnessing an accident or of losing one of my beloved horses brought on cold sweats. Though I tried, I couldn't find any knowledgeable person to help us. On day three, T.C. squirted a pond of urine in front of Kells's stall and then bent her entire body amorously into his overtures. He chewed on her neck so lasciviously, she looked as if she'd just come in from a tropical rain. At noon, I turned her out in the back pasture.

After Kells calmed down enough for us to handle him, I put my arms around his neck and buried my face in his short satiny coat; he had the clean healthy smell of a young animal. I scratched his ear and kissed his lovely head as I fed him carrots before leading him to the back pasture, where T.C. grazed a good distance from the gate. The sun wasn't hot, the air cooled by a bridal veil of high clouds. Leaving Kells's halter on so I could catch him more easily if things went wrong, I opened the gate, walked him out into the field, and unhitched his lead rope. "Good journey," I whispered, patting his flank as he walked briskly past me.

Mark and I stood on the gravel path in front of the paddocks, looking south into the wide expanse of sky. Kells spotted T.C. and trotted energetically toward her. When she saw him, the blood bay spread her forelegs in a defensive stance.

Covering my eyes with one hand, I grabbed Mark with the other. Kells immediately reared in excitement and mounted T.C., not from behind but on her neck, just in front of her shoulder. True Colors stood her ground, biting him on the elbow. Kells shrieked; he stumbled, falling halfway to the ground. T.C. turned and ran a few meters, then twirled to face the younger bay. He limped toward her, his limp disappearing as he walked. They met head to head, and after a few minutes, he started nibbling her neck. For a time she let him before wheeling around and walloping him with her hind hooves in the chest, the neck, the rib cage. This dance went on for so long that I stopped counting the blows she dished out. Had I misread T.C. about being receptive enough to breed? Kells must have had the wind knocked out of him, because he could no longer keep up with her when she ran off. Finally, when he looked completely deflated, she presented her hind end, squirting a stream of milky urine. He mounted her. We left them together for an hour. When it was clear that T.C. had become weary of Kells's advances and he was showing no sign of letting up, we went out and brought the pair in.

"Kells looks as if he's run an eight-furlong race twice," I told Mark. The poor guy couldn't hold up his neck and hung his head level with his back. We examined him for injuries, but nowhere was the skin broken. In his stall, he walked to his water bucket and sank his muzzle into it. True Colors hadn't a scratch on her, either. Clearly, she was the more fit of the two. She eyed me skeptically, then stood calmly in the back of her stall, waiting for me to leave the barn so she could eat in solitude.

The next day, Kells was so muscle-sore that he could hardly trot as he patrolled the front pasture, ridding it of the gang of ten Canada geese, which had multiplied to thirty. Occasionally, he called to the other horses inside the barn. No one answered. Now that he was a breeding stallion, we no longer turned him out with Kermit and were afraid to turn him out when the mares weren't safely locked in their stalls. Two days later, on day five of T.C.'s heat cycle, Kells was still sore. Neither of us had the heart to put the pair together again.

* * *

We took a few days off from horse breeding before turning our attention to Vera. It was the big weekend of Kermit's first recognized show. The smell of popcorn and the sight of fluttering red and blue triangle flags put Kermit on edge. He brought his knees excitedly up to his chest as he did a passage-like trot to his stall in one of the horse barns at the state fairgrounds, huge industrial buildings that I imagined had been built by an agribusiness contractor. Inside, the stalls looked like metal cages. The presence of other horses reassured Kermit, and when we brought him his hay, he settled in.

Quickly, Mark and I unloaded our gear. My classes weren't until tomorrow; today was Kermit's day to get accustomed to the activity, especially the strange noises: the public address system, the trucks shifting gears on the highway, airplanes taking off and landing. The trainer across the aisle from us had brought a string of horses; her stalls were decorated in her stable colors, green and white. She'd purchased an empty stall to use as a tack room and had it tricked out like a suite at the Ritz. We had one horse and his one stall and used the aisle for our equipment.

When Kermit had finished half a bag of carrots, I haltered him and took him for a walk past the outdoor competition arena to the warm-up area. It was a bright day, and all the freshly painted white fences sparkled. We stood at the rail and watched exhibitors riding imported horses. Everyone looked so polished and well turned out. How, I wondered, did the Faye Dunaway look-alike keep her maroon fingernails so long and ride so well? These people must not care for their own horses, much less raise them from foals. If they did, they had help—lots of it.

During lunch intermission, it was permissible to walk Kermit around the outdoor competition arena. When a plane came in for a landing at the airfield across the road, the noise didn't frighten him, but the shadow did; he nearly splayed himself on the ground. Mark, who had run to retrieve my number in the horse show office, found us.

"You want me to stand in the judges' box and rustle whatever papers are in there?" he asked.

"Oh, please!"

I coaxed Kermit back and forth in front of the white gazebo so he could get used to sounds coming out of it. Next we led him to the huge indoor arena that looked like the Cow Palace. Rodeos were held in here.

It took two of us to get him to walk inside the building—he didn't like the change of light, or maybe it was the dank smell. The sound of people walking up and down the empty bleachers made him tremble.

"I'll be lucky to complete a dressage test, let alone get a decent score, if I have to ride in here," I told Mark. The taste of panic rose in my throat.

We spent the next half hour trying to lead Kermit around the perimeter. The arena was all gussied up, a dressage letter painted on the side of each planter of dwarf palms. Kermit didn't trust the planter marked with an R painted in bold black script—the curlicue tail on that letter put him off. I felt frazzled.

That night we left Kermit at the show in his temporary stall. The trainer stabled across the aisle offered to keep an eye on him, and I felt grateful for her sportsmanship. She'd brought several young horses that were also competing at their first show and was free with advice that I sorely needed.

"A handsome beast," she said, running her man-sized hand over his shoulder. "Just look at that engine." She studied his hind end. "You got your test memorized?" I assured her that I had, but for a split second, I couldn't remember if I turned left or right after saluting the judge.

Mark and I arrived at the fairgrounds at six the next morning. Unlike the day before, the sky was overcast, the air cool. The weather was perfect for a competition, the horses' brilliance unhampered by rising temperatures. I gave Kermit some hay, and when he'd finished most of it, I haltered him and led him around the show arena. What luck—after checking the schedule posted outside the office, I found I had no classes in the coliseum. A runaway horse was a possibility, however, especially if a plane flew over us. Mark walked with Kermit and me to the covered warm-up area, an arena like ours at home, only three times the size. It was showtime, eight A.M. A bystander admired the way Kermit's dapples appeared like snowflakes spreading across his otherwise black coat. The professional stabled across from us called out words of encouragement. "Keep him in front of your leg."

A technical delegate checked that we had the correct bit in Kermit's mouth (a snaffle broken in the middle) and that my whip, which I grasped so firmly I thought it would break, was no longer than forty-eight centimeters. The next thing I knew, I was on deck, due to ride my test in five minutes. I felt faint, but after some deep breathing, my mind cleared. Mark led Kermit by the bridle to the entrance of the twenty-by-sixty-meter rectangle. The judge rang her bell, signaling that I had thirty seconds to begin. So far, Kermit behaved like a prince. I realized that though planes were taking off across the highway, they were not landing. Even better, the runway pointed the departing Cessnas to the west, away from me. When I realized that no plane would fly over us, making a shadow that would spook my horse, I squeezed my calves around Kermit's giant barrel with all the assurance I could muster. He arched his neck, his back came up to meet my seat, and his mouth accepted the contact of the bit. As he moved forward, I felt him power himself from his haunches. When we entered the arena at the letter A, he trotted straight down the center line. We made a square halt at X, I saluted the judge, and we trotted forward, heading deep into our first corner, swirling out of it like wine in a champagne glass. At the end, we turned down the center line and halted. The judge smiled and the spectators clapped. I dropped my reins and fell on Kermit's neck in relief. Reaching my arms down over his shoulders, I slapped him with my white-gloved hands, now black on the palms. "What a good boy!"

As it turned out, Kermit—that frightened, worm-infested baby horse on the high-desert range who had cowered in the shadow of his mother, who had quivered and lain as if dead on his stall floor when brought home, and who at first I couldn't get within ten feet of—won his first class and was noticed by nearly everyone.

A vast regimen of drugs is necessary to breed a horse via artificial insemination. We began with a series of injections to bring Vera into heat, another to make the follicle mature, an injection to induce ovulation, then one to make her go out of heat. There were serious side effects: The tall white mare cramped violently, her hindquarters trembling and then buckling under her before she broke into a copious sweat. After insemination, progestin helps a mare hold on to a pregnancy. I injected ten cc's into Vera's mouth daily. If I got only a drop of the medication on my bare skin, the drug brought on electrifying night sweats, bleeding, and migraines. Granted, it would have been easier to pasture-breed Vera to Kells—the two seemed inordinately fond of each other—but I was still hopeful of breeding my elegant white mare to an Olympic dressage horse.

Daily I paraded Vera in front of Kells's stall. As her optimum breeding date neared, the long-stemmed rose stopped of her own accord in front of Kelly's door. The two horses chewed on each other and nuzzled; she squatted, squirting urine. The next day they were even more amorous. Their mouthy kissing noises could have been used as the sound effects for a French movie. On day two, I ordered the semen. When it arrived twenty-four hours later by air express in a refrigerated container the size of a guitar case, Mark studied the contents of one of the straws under his microscope. Only 40 percent motility, better than last year but probably not good enough, according to our new practitioner, Dr. O'Leary, an athletic redhead who specialized in equine reproduction. He had recently joined Doc Short's practice.

In order to inseminate Vera, we had to tranquilize her. Just before her head dropped and she went to sleep standing up, Dr. O'Leary asked me to position her so that she stood in the open doorway of her stall, her tail facing the aisle.

Dr. O'Leary uncovered the ultrasound machine and placed it carefully on an upturned muck bucket, then plugged it in with the use of an extension cord. I watched as he swabbed the hot dog–shaped sensor with K-Y jelly. Pulling a clear plastic sleeve over his hand, he rolled it up his arm to his shoulder. He swabbed the sleeve with lubricant, took hold of the sensor, and inserted his arm in Vera's rectum. Her right ovary appeared on the ultrasound's computer screen.

How had the technicians at Twin Tamaracks managed all this with the nearly feral True Colors? T.C.'s stall stood opposite Vera's. A mute witness, she stared, motionless.

Mark motioned toward True Colors. "We pasture-bred our Thoroughbred mare to our new stallion," he proudly told the vet.

Dr. O'Leary raised an eyebrow. "Your jittery mare? I'm glad to hear it." He smiled with relief. It's not uncommon for a vet to be injured, sometimes seriously, by a cranky or excitable broodmare.

"Actually," said Mark, "when she has a foal, she's imperturbable. And when she doesn't, she's just . . . hyper-suspicious. Some days she's not bashful at all and lets me put a halter on her," he added, pleased with himself.

As Dr. O manipulated the sensor, his deputized helper, Mark, studied the ultrasound, looking for breedable follicles. "Whoa!" he exclaimed.

There it was in black and white: a fat fifty-millimeter follicle, inside of which was an egg.

Dr. O injected one straw of serum through Vera's cervix. He would return tomorrow morning to inject the second straw. We hopped for the best. I dreamed of having two foals again, so they could grow up playing together. Electron clearly needed someone other than his mother to chase across the pasture.

Twice a day for three weeks, morning and evening, I paraded T.C. and Vera up and down the aisle in front of Kells's stall, measuring each mare's interest in the stallion. I kept a daily log of their reactions. *No interest* meant that the mare had stopped cycling, meaning she was probably in foal. In sixteen days, Dr. O'Leary would ultrasound Vera to look for a beating heart. True Colors, on the other hand, I would have to check the old-fashioned way: wait and see.

Vera was a tall mare, and when she puffed up in excitement over our stallion, she looked doubled in size. I was beginning to suspect that she wasn't pregnant, even before Dr. O'Leary returned to confirm it. Oh, words of one syllable! Another year without a foal from Vera. My spirits sank under the weight of having expended so much on something so futile, if not foolish. That night I awoke to my temples being jackhammered by a migraine. Somehow I must have gotten progestin on my skin.

I continued to tease True Colors daily, walking her up the aisle to Kells's stall. She seemed docile. When she glanced in my direction, I saw the shadows of the desert sage fires that bled into the white of her sclera recede. Each day she looked uninterestedly at Kells, shying away from him as if he were a wolf. I took her into the arena. Lunging her at the walk—that is, making her circle around me at the end of a long rope—I asked her kindly, "Are you lying to me?" She dropped her eyes. "Are you not showing to him because you don't want me to turn you out with Wild Boy again?" What flawless feet she had, black horn and perfectly formed; luckily, she had passed this quality on to all her foals. "Good journey," I whispered to her.

She was in foal after only one live cover.

SEVENTEEN

As True Colors's belly spread like a pumpkin and her late-spring due date neared, I began to fret: One of her foals would have to be sold. Our farm was organized as an agricultural business; unless we showed a profit this year or next, we would owe the government a great deal of money. But how could I part with any of them?

I went through the list: Kermit, Colette, Daybreak, Ms. Piggy, Electron, even True Colors's unborn foal (whose name would begin with F), prefacing each horse's name with "I couldn't possibly part with." I had a rationale for not selling each: Kermit would fetch a good price, but how could I replace him? Daybreak had grown into a handsome bay and showed a lot of promise; I planned for Monte to break her next spring. How could I sell her before I knew what kind of a riding horse she would be? Selling this year's foal out of True Colors, our first baby by Kells, was out of the question. I needed to see what kind of an offspring they were going to create. At night I lay in bed; rain lashing the windows in the Winter Palace kept me from sleep. As I breathed in the pungent aroma of hop vines that grew on the trellis below the upstairs deck, no clear answer swam to the surface.

It had been a hard winter filled with something we usually had very little of: ice. New Year's Day, when we finally got Electron weaned, temperatures dived below freezing during the night. Oddly enough, when we woke up, our house felt cozy.

"Finally," Mark exclaimed as he crawled out of bed, "I've stuffed enough insulation into the attic." We didn't have an attic, just a crawl space, but never mind.

Alas, this was not the case. As Mark ground the beans for coffee, I glanced out the kitchen window. When I saw a silver sheen of ice glazing the wooden siding, I knew that we were experiencing the igloo effect. How insulating ice could be: when it plugged every crack, no wind eked through. We felt like we were back in California—as long as we stayed indoors. Outside, ice encrusted the bare limbs of trees, and when the relentless wind gusted, I heard the noise of artillery fire. Broken branches were strewn everywhere, including across our fences—I couldn't count the rails that had come down. At the barn, snow blew in the crevices. All but T.C. were heavily blanketed. It was a dry snow, and they seemed not to mind the cold.

There's a saying in the Northwest: If you don't like the weather, just wait a minute. The next day dawned calm and warm but overcast. It snowed in the late morning, dry cottony flakes that covered the rosemary bush and bay tree outside the kitchen window. In the afternoon, a gale blew up, the wind pummeling our house so hard that it drove snow like grains of sand under the doors.

Spring came early. Temperatures rose and the dark gray days of February paled into the light gray days of March. True Colors and the other horses began to shed their winter coats. When Vera lay down to roll on the new grass, she left piles of white fur that I mistook for frost until True Colors lay down in a spot nearby and left wads of blush. When Kells was turned out in the early evening after the mares were locked in the barn, he sought out these nests of mare fur and wallowed in them.

In April, Monte came back to the farm to break Kells before the testosterone that would course through his veins during breeding season took over his brain. The little bay had filled out over winter and now had a well-muscled neck. Monte suggested that we hold off using Kells for breeding this year and wait until next, so the colt could keep his mind on his training. "And," Monte said, "you'll wanna see what kinda foal Shylotte throws before you breed him again."

I cleaved to his advice. All of our stalls were full, and we expected another foal any day. Plus, the idea of being the handler when breeding two hard-hoofed half-ton out-of-control creatures terrified me. "I second that motion," I told Monte as he tightened the saddle girth while Kells stood quietly cross-tied in the grooming stall. Mark was on the fence about whether to hold off on breeding Kells, but when Monte agreed to help us with the mechanics of breeding next spring, Mark readily acquiesced.

A few weeks later, I got to sit on Kells as Monte led the three-year-old around the perimeter of our riding arena, a lead rope clipped to the bit ring of the brand-new (thanks to Jewel) snaffle bridle. Today the lesson was to go forward. Astride, I squeezed him lightly with my calves while Monte encouraged the young horse along with a slight tug on the rope. Kells had a great brain and might have a dressage future—as if I didn't already have a barn full of prospects.

"Which horse are we going to sell?" Mark asked that night at dinner. I'd just dribbled radium-green sorrel soup on my white polo shirt and was dabbing at it with a napkin. Though few edibles grow year-round, we always had a hardy sorrel that kept us supplied with pungent leaves. Luckily, our bay tree and rosemary bush (Mediterranean plants brought to us from California by Kolika) had survived the winter ice.

"I don't know." I pursed my lips. "This soup tastes yummy. You didn't use real cream, did you?" Fat migrated to my soft bits and made unsightly bulges in my riding breeches.

"You can't make cream soup without real cream," Mark said dismissively. His Indiana grandfather had owned a dairy, and his Minnesota grandfather had been a dairy veterinarian. Mark subscribed to the culinary tenet that there is no substitute for cream. "Which one are you going to sell?" he asked again. "Pretty soon we'll have so many you'll have to start keeping two horses in the same stall."

"That's a thought," I said, though I knew he made this statement as a reprimand. I recalled that when we hauled our horses here from New Jersey, we'd spent a night at a horse farm in Wisconsin. There they'd kept two horses to a stall, something I'd never seen done. It looked dangerous; if one horse kicked, the other wouldn't be able to get out of the way. The owner told me that never happened, because the only horses he put together were a mare and her grown foal. "That *is* a thought," I said again. I bet I could put T.C. and one of her weaned foals in the same stall for the night. "Just until I get one sold."

"Which?" Mark pressed me.

"Let's decide after T.C.'s foal is born," I said. "Are there seconds on soup?"

The days got longer and warmer. The weeping birches budded out, and the pink and white dogwoods came into flower just as the deep purple lilacs finished. There is nothing like the smell of the wind in May when it blows off the melting glaciers. True Colors's spring coat glistened. Though her belly looked enormous, she streaked across the pasture ahead of Vera as if she were a two-year-old. As usual, she hid every sign of parturition.

This year Mark was hell-bent on making our own hay. He'd purchased a used baler but still needed to buy several tractor attachments: a rake that gathered the cut grass into windrows and a tedder that fluffed the hay to hasten drying and curing. Used haying equipment littered the roadside, because all our local dairies were going out of business—a sad situation, since their clover-filled pastures were well suited to cows. Some of this river-bottom land would go fallow, and some was slated to be turned into subdivisions. The only thing we didn't have and couldn't buy to make hay was the weather: endless sunny days. If put up wet, hay ferments, causing the bales to spontaneously combust and explode. If you put uncured hay in your loft, you'd probably lose your barn and its contents, including the livestock.

But Mark was mad for taking advantage of our fields of grass. The stars in his eyes shone so brightly that I tried to look excited about producing our own timothy. And I would be excited about it if it worked. The prime haymaking day was the Fourth of July, when the grass reached its height, after which the stems thickened and it went to seed. But it always rains on the Fourth of July, the kind of rain that flattens the grass in the field.

This time when T.C. foaled, I happened to be walking through the barn on my way to opening the south-facing door. I'd had it closed during the late afternoon to discourage flies, and I opened it for a few hours once dusk came on. Striding purposefully down the aisle, I looked in on Kells, who was dunking his hay in his water bucket. Colette stuck her dish face over the door, hoping for a treat. Turning in the other direction, I glanced in at T.C.'s stall. Because I knew the exact date of conception, I had counted 340 days ahead to calculate her due date. Only maiden mares tended to foal early. When I noticed that T.C. wasn't standing in her stall, I almost didn't look in.

Taking a gulp of air, I went into panic mode. Not only was she down, but a white bubble protruded from her vulva! I hadn't laid out the foaling kit, and the contents were scattered. White lab coats, sterile gloves: Where were they? Where was Mark?

Running up the gravel drive and through the gate, I rapped on the living room window. Mark was watching a Mariners baseball game on TV.

"Hurry," I screamed.

"Yeah, yeah," I heard him say through the glass. He was enraptured, his eyes glued to our new wide-screen. The game had gone into extra innings.

"She's foaling now!"

By the time we had everything ready, the foal was out. Once again, T.C. hadn't needed our help. Sometimes older mares—T.C. was in her teens—rupture the artery that runs through the ligament suspending the uterus, and the mare hemorrhages. Nothing can be done for her, but the foal can be saved. In such cases, the fetus usually has to be pulled out. I kept my fingers crossed that we wouldn't lose True Colors, or any mare, this way.

Baby had broken the sack, and the little bobblehead was taking stock of her surroundings. Mark put on sterile gloves and his lab coat and darted in to make sure the foal's air passages were unobstructed. He always took charge at this stage, for which I was thankful—my knees felt like they were made of water. T.C. sat up on her shoulders. Alert, she glanced back at her offspring and nickered. She seemed glad that Mark was there. The foal answered in a high-pitched squawk. Another prehistoric bird had appeared in our barn. At the baby's noise, the other horses went berserk in their stalls, kicking and squealing.

T.C. always did all the work. She didn't stop pushing, like Ms. Piggy had with Electron. How could I be so lucky to be this horse's human? Old-timers have a saying: *A good broodmare is a pearl without price.* True Colors's foals were healthy, always possessing a strong willingness to thrive. When she first came to our ranch, I had not known what I would do with this horse; she'd felt like an albatross around my neck. Now I wondered what I'd do without her.

The foal was an absolutely gorgeous bay filly: Fionula, Fifi for short. We couldn't have asked for better. Postpartum, True Colors showed no sign of discomfort, as she had after Daybreak was born. On mare and foal's first day of turnout, flocks of crows descended on our fields, probably because Mark had just hayed our pond pasture. Way early for making good hay, but we had to seize the few dry days that came to us.

Crows gathered to eat whatever rodents had been laid bare by the tractor blades. Some of these vocal birds were the size of chickens. They seemed fascinated by the foal and she by them. The birds had a large vocabulary of trills and whistles. When a resident bald eagle flew over, several crows dogged him, trying to drive away the huge bird of prey. Mostly, they perched on fence posts nearest Fi, and I wondered if they admired her handsome conformation and long thin legs, as I did. She had Kells's head and delicate ears and T.C.'s long arched neck with a narrow throatlatch.

Fionula went wild when two birds jousted above her in midair. Strutting across the grass, the crows fluffed their ebony ruffs and made gurgling noises. As Mom grazed in knee-deep grass, Fi bucked and kicked like Tinker Bell. What a prize. I couldn't sell this one. This was the *one* I had been waiting for.

When I called Jewel to share my excitement, she'd have none of it. "Well, I'm glad something's going right," she barked.

"What's the matter?" I asked, taken aback.

"Monte went off the wagon and overdosed." She sounded exhausted and betrayed and angry all at once. "This is it. I don't want him back. When he gets out of the hospital, he's not coming here."

"So which one?" Mark asked, tired and sweaty from a day of haying. He wasn't in the best mood; the baler had broken repeatedly. It was a delicate piece of machinery, and getting it to perform properly with just the right tension on the twine that bound the bales together was an art. As an inky cloud bank approached, Mark gave up on the baler and forked the loose hay into the bed of the manure spreader, transporting it load by load to one of the turnout sheds. Then he forked it in, floor to ceiling. After hours of work, he managed to save most of our crop from the on-again, off-again rain. It looked like good hay, and I couldn't imagine why local timothy was so disparaged: Most people used it as mulch or fed it to cows.

"Which horse do we sell?" he implored. His face and hair were speckled with grit. Clearly, he felt overwhelmed by the hassles of farm life; I needed to give him an answer.

"There's nothing like the smell of new-mown grass," I told him. He smiled. We both leaned into what looked like one of Monet's haystacks, covered by a sheep shed. Inhaling hay perfume, we rehashed Monte Gee's situation.

"Jewel says he's in detox. She's adamant about not wanting him back, and who could blame her?" Without Jewel's support, both of us feared Monte might never come right.

"I don't think he'll be on his feet soon enough to break Daisy to saddle in September," I said, stating the obvious. "So if we sell her, we'll save ourselves the price of sending her away to be trained."

"Where would we send her?" asked Mark.

"I have no idea," I said, chewing on a stalk of hay. It tasted as sweet as one of our pears. "Monkey Gee breaks everyone's homebreds." I had my fingers crossed that he would straighten himself out by next spring, in time to help us breed Kells.

I put photo ads in all the horse-trading publications. Daybreak, at age three, was an attractive bay filly with a wide chest and the cresty neck of a stallion. One buyer thought she was too big. The next said she wasn't big enough. The first buyer came back but decided the filly was too marish, pinning her ears too often. The next person who called had to have a mare and came out immediately. This person couldn't take her eyes off Fifi. "I want that one," she said.

"Make me an offer," I told her, though no amount would convince me to part with Fi. The buyer's interest only reaffirmed my judgment about what a good nick T.C. and Kells were.

Daybreak sold in a flash to another newcomer to riding. The woman arrived with her trainer, a classy blonde with an athletic frame and a short swimmer's haircut; she coached at a hunt club in the south Puget Sound. As long as Daybreak remained in this trainer's hands, she'd have a good home. The vetting, however, didn't go well.

The tiny wartlike tumor near her udders, which Monte had told me not to worry about, proved a problem. I'd completely forgotten it, but the vet, an old-timer, after looking into Daybreak's eyes and listening to her lungs, glanced at her hindquarters and caught sight of the sarcoid.

"I'll have to flunk this horse," he said without apology. According to him, the tumor might grow and take over Daybreak's udders, rendering her useless for breeding.

This, I knew, was a worst-case scenario, and the trainer was of the same opinion. She and I dickered. I agreed to have Doc Short remove the benign tumor; it was a simple process. In two months, if it hadn't grown back, we had a deal.

The buyer had a plump face and straight crimson hair with bangs cut at eye level. Excitedly, she told me about her plans for Daybreak: Get her broken and trained so the filly could be ridden to the hounds with the hunt club next fall. At the same time, she told me with a gleam in her eyes, she was going to put herself on a diet so that she'd look good in the riding habit her new husband had bought for her when he promised her a horse. "And I'm going to be taking a lot of riding lessons so I can improve my seat and hands," she said with a nod to her trainer.

Two months later, when the prospective buyer brought me a check, I asked, "Do you want your vet to see her move around a little?" It struck me that he hadn't even seen Daybreak trot.

"I guess not," the young woman said with a shrug.

The buyer's trainer loaded Daybreak into her new trailer, painted the same electric blue as her truck. "Do you have any hay we could take with us? She doesn't seem to want to eat ours," the new owner said.

Proudly, I brought them an armful of our homemade timothy. The trainer looked at it, barely concealing her disdain. "Is that local hay?" she asked as if I were offering her barbed wire. "Local hay is usually fed only to goats." Opening the trailer's escape door, she offered Daybreak a handful. The bay filly almost took the trainer's hand off, she was so eager.

"Bye, Daisy." I turned away so that no one would see my eyes start to leak. My heart felt so heavy that it rooted me where I stood, hypnotized by the vanishing point where they disappeared in the road. For years afterward, every time I found myself in the south Puget Sound, a bell jar descended over me. I thought I could hear Daybreak calling: *Come get me. Come take me home.* I didn't act on impulse to find her. To this day I wonder if I should have.

EIGHTEEN

When the next breeding season rolled around, it was up to Mark and me to breed our own horses. Monte was we-knew-not-where. Up until now we'd had a lot of what is called good horse luck. Sometimes there is no accounting for what happens to you and your horse, except to say that the fates are with you or against you. Horse luck dates back to when the world was powered by muscle and wind. I crossed my fingers that our good horse luck would hold.

True Colors, Ms. Piggy, and Vera didn't cycle all year around but began in February, when the days started getting longer—that's the veterinary theory, anyway. But horses don't read medical books, so they don't always follow the rules. Because it was so dark in the Northwest, I left the overhead fluorescent bulbs on until eight at night. Light stimulates a mare's pituitary gland, which regulates the equine reproductive calendar. I could usually tell when Vera and Ms. Piggy were coming into heat by their mood swings, called *horsing* by old-timers.

I couldn't read True Colors's heat cycle at all this year. When I paraded her past Kells's stall, she showed no interest, except to try to get away from him as quickly as possible. He, on the other hand, was ravenous for her, no matter how cool her mood. I began to wonder if Kells had any sense of self-preservation whatsoever. At the same time, I feared that maybe True Colors had grown cysts on her ovaries, causing her heat cycle to go silent.

When Ms. Piggy started to show to Kells at the end of April, I took copious notes. *Appearing to enjoy him chewing on her neck,* I wrote in my spiral notebook. When Ms. P squealed delightedly, then squatted, squirting urine, I thought: *Time to pasture-breed, if that's what we're going to do.* I felt confident on this warm, cloudy morning. First we turned Ms. Piggy out in a paddock, and when she settled down to grazing, Mark haltered Kells.

Even before we got out of the paddock and locked the gate behind us, things started to go wrong. Kells ardently trotted up to Missy P. Fixated on a patch of new clover, she turned her butt to him. When he tried to chew on her shoulder, she wheeled around with her ears pinned. He didn't read her anger; instead, he seized the opportunity to mount her. Ms. Piggy's eyes flashed. Incensed, she began using her weapons and walloped him with her left hind. Blood gushed, and I screamed, which startled both horses out of whatever either of them planned to do next. Mark ran for a lunge whip. Rushing toward Ms. Piggy, I grabbed her by the halter. Undaunted by his injury, Kells began to dog the big gray mare, biting whatever part of her he could get hold of. I could easily read her expression, even if Kells couldn't: She was pumped on anger. Scarlet pulsed from a wound on Kelly's leg; it looked like an open mouth. He was so energized that I feared he'd bite me on the face.

Mark stood at the gate, long black whip in hand, wondering what to do next. I let go of Ms. Piggy's halter and went after Kells. I had to get him away from her. Crooking my arm to shield my face, I finally attached the lead rope to his halter. An angry Ms. Piggy sprang at him. Mark stepped in, waving the whip in her face. When we got Kells in the barn, his knee was already swollen; we feared the joint was involved.

While I ran to telephone the vet, Mark fastened a compression bandage around the stallion's leg. In his stall, Kells seemed unperturbed. He dunked his hay in his water bucket and then sniffed at his leg bandage. Grabbing it with his teeth, he shredded it.

As it turned out, we'd been fortunate. Kells needed only a few stitches, the X-rays were clean, and the anti-inflammatory made the swelling disappear. I vowed to be more cautious next time. Not only did I need to take careful notes on my mare's bad-hair days, I needed to discover the secrets of the breeding shed.

We decided to use our arena as the breeding paddock. Instead of trying to breed Ms. Piggy again, we thought we'd try Vera, who weighed slightly less, adored Kells, and was easy to manage. If ever there was a horse sick with love, it was Kells for Vera. They spent countless minutes chewing on each other's necks over his stall door, he with his head extended as far over the top of the door as he could, and she with her white swan neck reaching into his stall as far as her anatomy permitted. They spooned and slobbered. The wooden door creaked. Meanwhile,

True Colors, who was in the stall next to Kells, stood quietly in a corner, looking uninterested. It was nearly impossible to get Vera's head out of Kells's stall or to unhinge his teeth from her flesh. When at last we got her away from him and turned her around, True Colors rushed to the front of her stall and thrust her head out. Mark started shouting. I couldn't see what was happening; Vera's body obstructed my vision.

"No!" Mark yelled in a stern, deeply disturbing voice. True Colors flew back, her shoulder hitting the wall before she cowered in the corner.

"What—" My question was drowned in an explosion of cracking wood, a noise that reminded me of last winter, when ice-heavy limbs snapped off of trees, crashing to the ground. Kells's expression said it all: He was bored by unrequited love and angered by endless rehearsals. Hooves thundered as he launched himself over his stall door. A clattering rang out as the door and the stall wall splintered beneath him. Kells staggered, then rose to his feet. Vera's eyes glazed over—I was still at her head, holding her lead—and she squatted. Kells reared up. My heart raced. All I could see was a wide expanse of his russet belly as he mounted her, breeding her right there in the aisle.

I felt winded, even though I hadn't run a foot. Mark was ready to halter Kells the minute he climbed off of Vera. My husband's expression was blank, his face almost as pale as when we had the trailer accident with Kermit. Kells collapsed on top of Vera, his forelegs on either side of her barrel, like arms embracing her. When he slid off her back, he looked as if he melted down her long white tail onto the floor. Vera moved forward, and I locked her stall door behind her. Even though I could see only the top of True Colors's head, I knew that she was quaking as she huddled against the back wall of her stall. Kells stood in the aisle, looking hangdog, then shook himself. Mark had no trouble catching the stallion. But where would we put him? His stall door was in pieces, heavy planks split, nails pulled out, the bent industrial-strength hinges torn apart.

"In the arena," I suggested.

Mark led Kells out of the barn. We were wordless, relieved, and in a state of shock for hours. It took Mark most of the day and a trip to the lumber yard to repair the door.

That was day three of Vera's heat cycle. According to accepted procedure, we needed to breed her again on day five. This time we didn't go in for so much teasing. On day five I walked Vera in front of Kells's stall and paused for a moment so that the horses could get interested but not overly excited. Then I led Vera into the arena. I'd attached a chain to her halter, running it down to her mouth, over the pink gums of her upper jaw, out of her mouth on the left side, where I'd attached her lead rope to the chain. Gripping the rope with both hands, I pulled until the chain was tight. Mark and I had talked about wearing riding helmets but had decided that the football helmets we'd found at a garage sale would be safer.

As Vera stood quietly, Mark led Kelly to the arena gate. He had a chain attached to Kells's halter and ran it through the mouth. The stallion reared, flailing his steel-shod hooves. When he saw Vera, he lost control, and we feared he would go over the metal gate. I'd positioned black lunge whips and red plastic baseball bats so they'd be close at hand. If this sounds like Dungeons & Dragons, it's a lot scarier—especially with an inexperienced stallion who hadn't the remotest idea of what to do.

Vera let out a low sonorous nicker, then squatted to pee. From inside the barn, True Colors called to her pasture mate. Mark had barely gotten the gate open when Kells barged ahead, grunting like a boar. Vera pricked her ears. Bracing herself, she held her ground and looked undaunted. We had hoped that Kells would chew on her neck, slowly work his way back to her hind end, and nibble her hocks before mounting. When he reared up on top of her head, right next to where I was holding her, I shrieked. Vera froze. Kells didn't give a fig. Slowly, Mark was able to pull Kells back toward Vera's rump. It felt as if we were trying to reason with two one-ton dogs in heat. When Kells finally stood directly behind Vera, she broke down and squatted, and he mounted her. I hadn't given Vera any tranquilizers, but I did consider taking some myself. Breeding horses the old-fashioned way is hard on the heart.

Getting Ms. Piggy bred was more complicated. She would tease positive in front of Kells; walking past his stall, she looked eager for his attention. But when we took her in the arena and brought Kells in, she wanted no part of him. Ears pinned, she snaked her neck, baring her teeth like a viper. What on earth could have gone wrong in those few minutes? I wasn't taking any chances this time. In addition to all the whips and chains, I hobbled Ms. Piggy's front hooves together, then tied one of her forelegs to the opposite hind leg with a stout cotton rope, securing it with the king of knots, the bowline—several loops and curls doubling back with more loops. I said a prayer that it would hold. Though I'd given Ms. P a good dose of ace, it didn't vanquish the murder in her eye. Afraid to try to breed her, Mark lead an excited but confused Kelly back to his stall.

We decided to try it again in the late afternoon. It was a warm, sunny day with only a smudge of clouds in the east. Mark offered me a jigger of some of his homemade brandy distilled from last year's apple crop. We gave Ms. Piggy a little more wine—ace—and waited for it to take effect, then reattached all the ropes and hobbles and chains. This time, God love her, Ms. Piggy was perfectly agreeable. And this time Kells seemed to have figured out what he was doing. When he started to rear up on her head, he thought better of it and worked his way around to her hocks. She squatted, he jumped. In the end, what made the difference was the daylight. We realized that Ms. Piggy needed at least ten hours of daylight before she was in the mood. When we bred her again on day five, I heaved a huge sigh of relief. Hopefully, she'd taken and would settle, as is said of mares newly in foal, because I didn't think I had the courage to go through it again.

I hoped that breeding True Colors would be less of a trial. I had discovered an interesting factoid: Kells's great-grandsire and True Colors's great-grandsire were born in the same year on the same farm in Paris, Kentucky, and played together as weanlings. Surely this mating was fated.

Daily I entered T.C.'s stall, talking to her in a soft voice. She cast her gaze to the floor, then turned her head away from me. Quietly, I walked her past Kells's door. Finally, True Colors started showing interest: She squatted and gushed urine in front of Kells and was almost (dare I say it) putty in my hands. On day three, I put on my football helmet, ran a chain through her mouth, and took her into the arena. Mark brought in Kells. When she saw him walking eagerly toward her while making unholy noises, all interest vanished. She would not break down. When Ms. Piggy had refused to break down for Kells, her expression had been one of puffed-up anger. T.C.'s expression was terrified.

"What if we wait until the end of the day and try again?" suggested Mark.

But no amount of daylight improved True Colors's attitude, and we had arrived at day four. I knew what I had to do. In horse-breeding circles, they call it *jumping* a mare. In the afternoon—allowing T.C. as much daylight as possible, still hoping that would have an effect on her—we teased her in front of Kells, to the great excitement of both. I gave her as much ace as I dared and took her into the arena before the drug took full effect. We positioned her near the rail, and I adjusted the chain across the inside of her upper lip before hobbling her front legs. Mark tied her right foreleg to her left hind with the cotton rope. She began to sway from the drug; I stood close to her while Mark went to get Kells. We had our red plastic baseball bats and long black whips ready. Mark approached with Kelly in hand, moving as slowly as possible, considering he was leading more than half a ton of testosterone. The sun caught in T.C.'s lustrous coat and ebony mane. I kissed her nose. She seemed unaware of Kells's presence.

"Shit," I whispered to Mark. "I forgot to wrap the top of her tail." With a 3M warp, it was easier to manipulate her tail so that Kells could, as they say, get the job done.

Kells stood behind T.C., grunting, erect. I could see his heart pounding in his chest. T.C. stood firm and didn't even begin to squat.

"See if you can get him to chew on her," I told Mark, my voice harsh because I was so nervous. T.C.'s eyes winced.

Mark tried to guide Kells toward T.C.'s shoulder. Suddenly, the stallion exploded. Rearing up on his hind legs, he leaped off the ground, landing with his front legs over T.C.'s back, his hind legs together at her side.

"No!" I started hyperventilating. Mark swore. T.C. swung back and forth but didn't fall. Without conferring, Mark and I quickly saw what we had to do: move Kells's back around T.C.'s haunches and onto her hind end. Reaching down, I picked up a handful of sand and threw it at the stallion's neck to startle him. Mark raised the lead line, jangling the chain, trying to encourage him to move backward. Kells stayed on his hind legs, stepping awkwardly to her rear. True Colors didn't move or kick; it looked as if her feet had put down roots. Was his weight causing her to sink into the ground? Finally, Kells was in position and completely erect. Mark pulled True Colors's tail aside, and Kells entered her with Mark's help, pumped, collapsed on her back, and then slowly melted off of her onto the ground in a state of euphoria.

Somehow we found the courage to repeat the performance on day six. When we'd finished, I unhobbled True Colors, took the chain out of her mouth, and untied her, letting the white cotton rope fall to the ground. I stayed with her in the arena until the tranquilizer started to wear off, about half an hour. Her head drooped; her red furred lids fell halfway down her eyes like window shades.

"Will you ever forgive me?" I whispered. Stroking her neck, I promised, "I'll never make you go through this again." Too dangerous and too much like assisted rape. I felt overcome with the sense that my cup of good horse luck had just run dry.

NINETEEN

August: We had three mares in foal. I steeled myself; another of True Colors's offspring had to be sold. This time I couldn't wait to see how the unborn would shape up.

Daily, Kells waited for the mares to be paraded past his stall, but none was presented to him. At dusk, when I turned him out, he roamed the front pasture alone. When he found a spot where one of the mares had peed, he began to dig furiously, as if possessed. Soon the front field and paddocks were pocked with craters, some of which remain today. When Kells wasn't digging, or running Canada geese and coyotes off the premises, he stood outside the barn next to True Colors's stall, trying to get her to talk to him through the plank wall. She had nothing to say; none of the mares did. A befuddled expression crossed his pretty-boy face: *Don't you like me anymore?*

"Which one should we sell?" I asked Mark. He sat at the kitchen table, scanning the farm-equipment section of the *Herald* classifieds.

"Whichever one you want," he said, circling an ad with a ballpoint pen.

I didn't want to sell any of them, but we needed a new tractor. Our present Mitsubishi must have been manufactured in occupied Japan. After lunch, I went through my list: Fifi was too elegant; Electron had the strength to do the upper levels; Colette; I couldn't sell one of my mares; Kermit? Handsome had grown even larger. He was nine. If I were going to sell him, I'd better do it this year. Though it would break my heart to part with him, two things pointed in his direction: the trailer accident with Mark and the fact that I wasn't strong enough to train him up the levels. We could do the basic walk, trot, and canter with freedom, but I couldn't seem to get him to carry his weight on his hind end rather than his shoulders and forelegs. If I couldn't do that, I'd never be able to do the more advanced movements that make a horse look as if he's dancing on air.

That night I composed an ad. I made color Xeroxes of Kermit's photos, taken by a professional photographer at a horse show, and copies of his dressage tests. Kermit was the kind of horse who spread goodwill. Selling or buying a horse is a little like selling or buying a used car, in that the buyer looks at the sale item and thinks: *There must be something not right here.* To erase any doubts, I showed prospective buyers Kermit's dam and sisters. No skeletons in his closet; clearly, we had too many horses.

Peggy, a six-foot-three blonde who weighed about a hundred pounds, wanted a horse with more jumper training, but years afterward, whenever I saw her at a horse show, she would ask after him.

I spoke to Lana's trainer on the phone but never to Lana herself. The first call explained that she was engaged to a man so famous, he couldn't be mentioned. The second call established that if Lana bought Kermit, I would pay a finder's fee. I wasn't used to dealing with equine agents; this woman made me uncomfortable. During the next call, Geri, the trainer-agent, told me the name of Lana's famous fiancé. When I drew a blank, she said, "You know, the astronaut." She sounded disappointed that I hadn't heard of him.

"Maybe I should talk to Lana in person," I told Geri.

"Oh, she's so busy." Geri had a southwestern drawl. "Lana demonstrates technology at trade shows, so she travels. But she has next weekend free. If you can show Kermit to us then, I'll get Lana to book us a flight."

Lana wasn't at all what I expected, petite, extremely well turned out, with mink-colored hair and a good complexion; she looked barely out of college. Geri was about my age, tough, scrawny, with thinning brown hair kept at bay under a baseball hat. Both women rode Kermit, who was well behaved, though I couldn't see that either would advance his training. Lana's ride was interrupted by several cell phone calls—cell phones weren't so ubiquitous then—which she *just had to* take.

"We'll go with the mushroom color and the raw silk texture," she told one caller after pressing the phone to her ear for what seemed like half an hour. She sat atop Kermit, who stood quiet as a throne.

As I led Kermit back to his stall, I introduced the two women to our other horses.

"What happened to that one's face?" Lana asked.

"That's Kermit's mother," I said proudly. "She was in a fire." True Colors stood in the back of her stall but pricked her ears forward. "Hi, Mom," I called to her.

"That's what I like about owning a mare," Geri told Lana. "If they get damaged, you can always use them for breeding."

I didn't say anything.

"I like him," Lana told me as Geri ushered her to their rental car. "I'll be in touch. Gotta fly." Lana took another call from a decorator as Geri opened the car door for her.

"Thanks for coming all the way here," I said. The trainer and I stood face-to-face, our jackets zipped up against the autumn wind, hoods pulled over our heads. "Kermit's a little big for her." I smiled. An understatement, hyperbole even, Kermit was way too big for either of them. I'm a slight person, and I was larger than either woman.

"Oh, he's not for her," Geri said, dropping her voice. "He's for the fiancé."

That night Lana telephoned from Colorado. "Look, I know Kermit's your precious baby, but I'd like to make you an offer."

Her tone put me off. "I'm not willing to bargain," I told her.

"I don't think I could go much higher." Her line clicked with call-waiting signals.

When I reminded Lana that I would have to pay Geri an agent's fee, there was silence on the other end of the line. She seemed not to know anything about Geri's commission. "Could I call you back? I have to take this call," she said breathlessly.

"All fixed," she told me when she telephoned two nights later. "Can I have him for the price I quoted?"

"And Geri's fee?" I asked. Now it was my turn to be breathless. Good thing I was already sitting down at my desk in the Winter Palace.

"I said, 'All fixed,'" she replied. "Taken care of."

The phone filled with silence. "Okay," I said with disbelief.

"Do you think she's serious?" I asked Mark when he got home. He had been stuck in traffic for hours. Thousands of people were moving to the Seattle area to work in the high-tech industry. Themed neighborhoods, gated communities, bedroom estates located on man-made lakes sprouted everywhere. No new roads were planned to connect these homes to the outside world, however. No one even thought of widening the present two-lane highways. Traffic had become a travel consideration like the weather.

Mark smiled encouragingly. "We'll see," he said. "Not bad, considering that at one time you would have traded Kermit for a year's worth of hay. Now he's worth ten years' worth, maybe twenty. True Colors is the best investment we ever made."

"Can I get that on tape?" I asked.

When I heard nothing from my buyer after a week, I wasn't crestfallen. I didn't want to sell Kermit. One afternoon while I was at my desk banging on my keyboard, I heard a truck pull into our driveway. I looked out at a Ford 350 pulling a long aluminum stock trailer. A young woman wearing a straw cowboy hat sat at the wheel. "I've come to pick up Kermit," she informed me in a Texas accent.

"What?" I said. "I don't know anything about this."

The driver, who reminded me of Loretta Lynn, looked puzzled. "Lana sent me," she said, waving a work order.

"I don't know what to say," I told her. The low slate clouds hid the mountains, and a bite in the air made me shiver. "Lana hasn't had the horse vetted or paid for him. So Kermit can't go anywhere today." I glanced at the rig, which looked as if it had been made to transport cattle. "Anyway, this horse is too big for your trailer."

"You haven't paid for him," I told Lana when she called that night. "I can't let him go until you pay for him. Certified check," I added. Actually, I wasn't sure I could let Kermit go even if she did pay for him.

"I wanted to have him vetted here in Colorado," she said. "But I understand."

Had Lana intended to ship Kermit to Denver and, if she couldn't live with the veterinary report, call me to come and get him? "Let me know what you want to do next," I said. *Maybe I'll never hear from you again,* I thought, then realized that I had to stop kidding myself. I couldn't keep all of them; the workload was killing. Up every morning before six, never time to sleep in, never a day off. After hours of chores, I didn't always have the energy to ride. And the situation was only going to intensify. I'd had a lot of good horse luck in buying True Colors. She was coming to the end of her reproductive usefulness, and other mares weren't going to be so easy to foal out.

A week of granite skies went by. Everything in this part of the country looked drained of color. Our cars were gray, our house was painted gray, the metal roof on the barn was a steely gray. My beautiful Kermit was the brightest gray of all.

When the phone rang just before seven in the morning, I ran to pick it up before the answering machine clicked on. Lana's voice chimed in my ear.

The long and the short of it was that Lana's little brother was driving from Denver to pick up Kermit and would arrive tomorrow. Was he a horse person, was he bringing a handler? The answer was no on both counts.

"But you haven't had Kermit vetted," I pointed out incredulously.

"It's not necessary," Lana said. "I'm running out of time."

"Your brother's bringing shipping boots in Kermit's size, a halter with a head bumper, a size-eighty-seven blanket?" I asked.

"That's something you could help him with." It wasn't a question.

The brother was a sweet kid who knew nothing about horses. All the same, he hoped to show Kermit if Lana's fiancé wasn't interested in pursuing dressage. Bro was dressed in suburban clothes: cords and an argyle sweater beneath a cowboy hat. It took us hours to load Kermit into the trailer; the huge horse barely fit. As Bro headed out, he got stuck turning his rig around. After another hour, he sped out of our driveway, a two-day drive in front of him. Inside, Kermit stood patiently, decked out in my custom-made shipping boots, monogrammed show sheet, and halter.

I didn't have the heart to take Lana's certified check to the bank for days. Instead of a shiny new tractor, we bought a used one, as neither of us could bear to spend what we came to call "the Kermit money." A week later, I got a phone message saying that Lana's brother had driven straight through, arriving safely. I called repeatedly to learn how Kermit was doing but never reached her.

It wasn't a bad winter, no ice or snow, just endless days of low-hanging, grizzled skies. The black-green fir trees dripped constantly even when it wasn't raining; the temperature never moved above 36 degrees. "Do you miss your baby?" I asked True Colors. She didn't seem to. She still shared a stall with Colette even though, now that Kermit was gone, there was room for each mare to have a stall of her own. Fifi lived in the stall next to Mom and Colette, with Vera in the stall on the other side, next to the south-facing wall. Ms. Piggy's stall was across the aisle, with Electron next to her on the north side and Kells next to E. Kermit's stall remained empty for a long while, like a vacant chair at the dinner table after someone has died.

The bellies of our three broodmares reminded me of the holds of old ships, the wooden ribs spreading. I'd given up on riding Ms. Piggy and wouldn't be able to ride Vera much longer. In the meantime, I rode Colette and was busy with Electron's and Fifi's training. Was it the comfortless pewter sky, or was it me? Colette started to look like she was traveling irregularly behind. The gorgeous Fifi had grown taller than either of her parents. She had perfect conformation and pure dressage gaits. But as the days darkened and the weather chilled, so did her mood. One morning when I walked into her stall, the bay filly lunged at me in fury. The next day the same thing happened, only this time it was as if all three furies came at me. "Why can't you be more like your mother?" I said. Pinning her ears at me, she narrowed her eyes to slits. I never knew where I stood with her.

Electron had grown to a stout 16.2 hands and was filled with so much piss and vinegar that I had to ask a trainer who lived nearby to come help me ride him. When one of us (usually the trainer) was able to mount him, he kicked the arena fence down before moving off at the walk. Miraculously, once one of us was astride, Electron's attitude turned rosy. He preferred his person to be positioned above his head, not fiddling around on the ground. Something about his handler trying to control him from below violated his sense of order. Even better, he wanted to please his rider and didn't seem to harbor any thoughts of trying to get rid of her. Meanwhile, Kells started rearing and often got me off within minutes. I sent him to the trainer who had helped me with Electron, a tiny woman who was fearless and used to riding stallions. How I missed my sweet, uncomplicated Kermit.

No vet seemed able to figure out what was wrong with Colette, but she was lame. Dr. Vogel shook his head. Dr. Short shrugged, saying, "Wait and see." Dr. O'Leary suggested sending her to the veterinary college on the other side of the mountains. When Vera's former owner had sent her there, she'd gotten injured on the way and, in the end, received no diagnosis. The problem with my pretty Colette, it was feared, was somewhere in her hip or stifle, joints that are hard to X-ray. When a horse goes lame, it's often difficult to pinpoint the pain, and when the limp is in the hind, it's even more difficult, sometimes impossible. Bone, joint, or soft-tissue damage? The possibilities were endless. If the owner had good horse luck, the problem healed itself.

It was the coldest April in memory; all the same, True Colors and the other mares started shedding fistfuls of fur. The high sugar content of the grass prompted Ms. Piggy's milk bag to start filling early. Saturday morning, I turned out all the mares except her in the back pasture; Ms. Piggy, I turned out in a paddock next to Electron, so he'd have companionship—I couldn't turn him out with any of my other horses, as he was too ornery. Today all the broodmares looked like Shamu. As I led Ms. Piggy out of the barn, I saw her sides jump, as if the foal were doing leaps out of water like the whales at Sea World. I stared at her vast barrel. She was the size and color of a battleship, her barrel undulating like the artic sea.

Before I went back to the house, I tried to imagine the back pasture filled with our mares and their offspring. True Colors's baby would be a bay, just like her. Vera's foal I saw as a large chestnut—before she grayed to white, Vera had been a sorrel. Ms. Piggy's offspring would look like my much missed Kermit.

"Pigster's foal is going to be born running," I told Mark that afternoon, describing how I'd seen the mare's sides rumble.

Kolika and her husband were due to arrive for a special dinner celebrating our house. We weren't ready to be featured in *Sunset*, but our home's interior looked less shabby seventies. Mark busied himself making onion soup from garden onions. Just before they were due to arrive, I dashed down to the barn. All seemed well and warm inside.

Kolika had painted the bedrooms muted colors, and wallpapered the entry vestibule in nautical stripes and the back bathroom in a floral pattern. Mark had knocked out a wall in the smallest bedroom to enlarge the master bath, and tiled the floor in the kitchen and dining room. Tonight was our private housewarming.

"No more winters like this one," Kolika said as we clicked glasses of the champagne she'd brought. She wore a floor-length gored skirt made out of vintage head scarves. Raf, her husband, had on an white Mexican wedding shirt and John Lennon spectacles.

After we ate, I excused myself, jogging to the barn before Mark got dessert on the table: deep-dish rhubarb cobbler.

When I pushed open the sliding door, the horse-warm air tickled my cold ears. The horses all whinnied. No doubt they were hungry because of the chill. Electron jutted his head over the door. In the stall next to him, Ms. Piggy charged forward, then disappeared. Vera and Colette hung their heads over their doors. I looked in at T.C., who glanced up at me contemplatively, then returned to her thoughts. Ms. Piggy whinnied, pushed her nose over the door, and ran to the back of her stall.

"Whatsa matter, girl?" I looked in at her. Her eyes were wide, and she repeatedly shook her head, her thick gray mane slapping her neck. Something looked odd about her barrel. Pulling open the door, I stared in. Ms. Piggy put her muzzle to the floor, licking . . . what? A foal! The dark placenta lay next to it. The foal didn't move. I went inside with the mare and noticed that her nipples were spraying milk. She stepped next to me and then pressed her shoulder into my hip. Her body felt hot, her coat sweaty. I bent down and touched the foal. Still warm but obviously not alive.

My heart sank. I had no idea what to do, though something had to be done. Slipping a halter on Ms. Piggy, I led her from her stall, but she reared, striking the door and almost breaking it.

"Okay, I won't take you away from your baby," I told her quickly, leading her back in.

As I ran up to the house, I heard Ms. Piggy call forlornly after me, then all the others; the loudest was True Colors, who bleated again and again.

Dr. O'Leary arrived carrying a long black satchel filled with stainless-steel autopsy knives—saberlike blades, the sight of which filled my mouth with ashes. Ms. Piggy trumpeted like an elephant when Mark and Dr. O carried the dead foal from the stall; she reared up, pulled away from me, and ran after it. The two men carried the dead baby—a sleek black colt, perfectly formed—back into her stall, where Dr. O'Leary tranquilized her with a stiff opiate. She didn't notice but continued to bawl after they carried the foal to the front of the barn.

"You won't want to look at this," Dr. O told me as he and Mark set about their grim business. I went back to Ms. Piggy, trying to console her. Could horses cry? Across the aisle, True Colors began to whinny and pace the perimeter of her stall. The other horses went silent. Electron hung back in a dark corner of his box.

"How many days has it been?" Dr. L called to me.

"Three hundred," I told him.

Horses born before 321 days of gestation usually don't survive. In the end, Dr. O'Leary ruled that the foal had never breathed. He found lesions in its lungs indicating that Ms. Piggy had gotten a uterine infection that had caused her foal to die. "Lucky she aborted it," he said.

It was nearly midnight when Raf and Mark lifted the foal into a wheelbarrow, pushed it to the garden, and buried it. The next morning Kolika found a black river stone and carved *Baby G* into it. "That foal reminded me a little of Kermit when you first got him," she said. "You ever hear how he's doing?"

"No," I said sadly. In fact, I never saw or heard about Kermit again.

For the next week, I felt tired by noon. If I didn't have horses to care for, I might not have gotten out of bed at all. Ms. Piggy bellowed for days. We thought Electron would be a comfort to her, but when we put him in her paddock, she ran him off. Dr. O'Leary had come out more than once to tranquilize her. Every time she called to her dead foal, all the horses lifted their heads. Only True Colors nickered back.

TWENTY

I would not soon forget the mournful sound of Ms. Piggy's bawling. Sometimes in my dreams, I still hear her. We thought spring would never come, but finally, the back pasture filled with lavender bell towers of foxglove and long-stemmed dandelions. Winters here may be long and dark, but there is nothing like June's evening sun.

Vera was due to foal before True Colors, so we prepared the double foaling box for her. T.C. would foal about two weeks later; she was bedded with shavings and stalled in a single box. As Vera's due date came and went, I grew antsy. Daily I consulted my list of names that began with H. I hoped for a filly, but as parturition neared, I concentrated on healthy. Annabelle, Vera's former owner, waited by the phone. Vera was nearly seventeen, a little old for a mare to be having a foal.

T.C. was a year younger. "This will be your last baby," I vowed. Standing next to True Colors in her stall, I brushed her long black tail. She didn't like the noise of the spray bottle, so I was careful how I spritzed her with detangler. Her tail hung like a waterfall.

She pushed her hay around with her whiskery mouth, always happier to have me nearer her hind end than her front. Her milk bag had started to enlarge, but I'd seen no sign of wax. Vera was at the same stage. The two mares did everything in pairs. Ms. Piggy concentrated on her eating and disciplined Electron whenever he played too rough or tried to encroach on her hay. He was the apple of my eye, and his natural athleticism helped us progress in his training. Dr. O'Leary had made several farm visits to flush Ms. Piggy's uterus, prescribing an endless regimen of antibiotics.

When the phone rang, I thought it was Kolika calling about our rescheduled housewarming dinner, but I heard a voice I couldn't quite place—it was the woman who had purchased Daybreak. My spine straightened like a ramrod.

"Horses," she said tearfully, "take all my time. I love Daisy but can't take care of her and myself. My house is a mess. My husband pressures me to stay home. Then Daybreak gets sick; I have to be there for the vet . . ." She sounded at the end of her rope.

"Horses *are* a lot of trouble," I sympathized; on a bad day, I felt the same way.

"I'm willing to sell her back to you for what I paid for her," the woman told me.

"What's she like to ride?" I was eager to know.

"Oh, I don't ride her. After paying for her training and board, I don't have money for lessons. I just lead her around on a halter and rope and graze her."

That night I asked Mark if we could take Daybreak back. I thought it a great opportunity. Mark's forehead crinkled; he thought buying Daybreak back was a terrible idea. "Where would you put her?" I felt profoundly disappointed but knew that he had a point.

Kolika and her husband were due any minute. Mark planned to cook a bass he'd caught in our pond. We'd stocked it with trout, and when they'd flourished, Mark had specialized in trout bleu, made from fish dead less than thirty minutes—the delicate white meat turned an incredible robin's-egg blue when seared over an open flame. Then a well-meaning neighbor released some bass into our pond, and the bass ate all the trout. Now the bass were large and hungry and easy to catch.

Kolika brought a home movie of her latest art project, an installation of swinging doors; she'd painted a portrait on one side of the door, and when it swung open, it revealed the portrait's alter ego on the other side. We decided to watch it after Mark's and my favorite public TV program, a dramatization of the book *All Creatures Great and Small.* A few minutes beforehand, I jogged down to the barn to check on Vera. The huge white mare stood amid heaps of straw, the setting sun filling the barn with popcorn-colored light. When she saw me, Vera turned her long face in my direction and then went back to her hay. I looked in at T.C., who hadn't touched her dinner and was standing, per usual, with her butt against the back wall, dozing.

"When will they foal?" Raf asked when I got back to the house.

"No one knows," I told him. "Some mares hold out for a year."

The four of us sat on the couch in front of the TV. I can't remember the episode's plot, but Kolika's pear tart was fabulous. "I forgot," she said, jumping up, crumbs flying. "I meant to light the pears on fire. That's why I made hard sauce."

During a pledge break, I ran down to check the mares. The blazing fuchsia sun sank into the hills, the evening air warm on my bare arms. Inside, Vera swished her tail—a sign of discomfort. The first hint of labor?

I glanced at T.C. She stood exactly where she'd been thirty minutes ago. Grabbing hold of the metal bars of her stall, I looked in. She turned her head, I thought to look at her hindquarters, but no: She looked to the floor. And there it was: a bright sorrel foal in the exact spot where Ms. Piggy had borne her baby! This one was alive and sitting up on its shoulders, still in its white sack. It bobbed its head, and True Colors began to lick the space between its ears.

"Ohmygod!" Luckily, the foal kit was spread out on a bale in front of Vera's stall.

When True Colors nickered softly to her baby, it let out a tiny bird peep, then stretched its stiletto legs. Fifi and Colette began braying. Ms. Piggy's eyes went wide as she thrust her head enthusiastically over her door. Vera came to the front of her stall.

I ran for Mark, and he came in an instant. Our guests weren't far behind. The foal was a huge chestnut colt, exactly the foal that I'd imagined Vera would have. He was up and nursing without help. T.C. seemed utterly calm, not at all flighty or skittish, and not excited. She stood as close to Baby as possible, her huge body sheltering him. I don't remember how, but we got Vera out of the straw-filled foaling box and into a single stall and then put T.C. and baby Hemish into the mare-and-foal quarters. The colt could barely walk but was a little sweetheart and very correct-looking. The movie *Babe* had recently come out; Hemmy looked just like its piglet star, his skin the same color pink. He looked nothing like T.C. or Kells. Where had he come from?

Kolika and Raf returned to the house and cleared dinner, washed the dishes, then wandered back to the barn. They stood in the aisle watching T.C.'s foal nurse. Our guests shook their heads. "It's feast or famine around here," said Kolika.

"The agony and the ecstasy," added Raf.

The next morning I took True Colors a handful of carrots with their green tops attached. For the first time, she took a carrot from my hand without my having to turn my head away. Amazing. I'd though this would never happen. It seemed like such a small thing, but it had taken years for her to trust me enough for us to carry on like a normal horse and human.

A week later, Vera waxed up and then started to drip milk; I moved True Colors and Hem to a single stall and put Vera into the foaling box. Vera foaled out by the book—my first experience with that. After she spent an hour looking uncomfortable and showing signs of colic, her water broke. She lay down and stretched out stiff, as if rigor mortis had set in. Soon the caul protruded from under her long white tail. Her foal turned out to be a tiny bay filly that looked exactly like Kells—about half the size of Hemish when he was born. The name Ikon just fit her. We'd cleaned her off, doctored her umbilical, and gotten her up before we hit a roadblock. Vera, the most placid mare in the world, would not let the foal nurse. She was engorged, her belly cramping. For what seemed like hours, we tried to get the foal near her udders, but Vera was too nervous. The foal began to tire. She was such a frail mite that I was really worried. It was eleven at night when I called the vet.

"By the time I get there, everyone's usually got it figured out, and I've made the trip for nothing," moaned Dr. O. But when he arrived, we still hadn't gotten Ikon to nurse. Vera paced her stall, her abdomen clenched. Dr. O'Leary injected painkillers. Within minutes Vera relaxed. The vet squirted out a little milk from her large black udders, then Mark guided the tired foal toward the food source. Baby latched on and started to suck, dancing on her two white hind legs, which wobbled to and fro as she swallowed. Her belly full, Ikon paused, licked her chops, and collapsed on the floor of the stall. I knew just how she felt. Mark and I headed up to bed.

No sooner had we gotten our foals on the ground and turned out with their dams than I had to teach in a summer writers' workshop in Kentucky. I'd timed my departure so that the foals would be well established before I left, but (blame it on the frigid spring) the mares had held out for so long that the youngest, Ikon, was only a week old when I had to leave.

This wasn't just any job; for me, it was the chance of a lifetime. The

project was the brainchild of the poet Karl Garson, who had offered
me a two-week position teaching journalism majors and others how
to write about horses. I had been so looking forward to it, but now I
waffled. Hemmy, True Colors's adorable piglet of a foal, had developed
a weepy navel, a symptom that could portend disaster: joint ill, septice-
mia, pneumonia. How could I leave? We'd already lost one foal; I'd be
bereft if we lost another. And I could not bear to hear True Colors bawl
for him. I would feel my flesh tear if I left.

The vet thought that Hemish's wet navel was isolated at the umbilical
stump and would be fine if we treated it daily with iodine. "That's what
we've been doing," I told him. Hemish was prescribed an antibiotic. But
without help, how would Mark cope?

Most farms are at least a two-person operation. The trouble with
farming is that you can never leave together, and if you leave separately,
you can't stay away long because of the heavy workload left to the one
who remains. The problem of taking even one day off was always a stumbling block: We needed reliable help.

Fortunately, we found Millie, a strong young woman who'd worked at
several breeding farms. She liked to tell people that her mother named
her for her favorite mare. She could medicate a foal by herself and handle Kells without turning a hair; handling a stallion is beyond most
horse people. In some ways, True Colors was even more difficult to manage. Millie, however, didn't think it at all odd that she might have to
herd T.C. and her foal out to pasture if it was one of those days when
True Colors wouldn't allow her halter to be put on by a stranger. "You
have to work with 'em, not against them. You're the captain, they're the
team," Millie lectured, taking command. " 'My way or no way' just ain't
gonna work."

I called Millie "the godsend."

Still, it was with much trepidation that I flew off to Louisville. The
spires of Churchill Downs gleamed in the southern sun, and the ornate
Victorian grandstands looked like a wedding cake. My students and I
sat in the humid early morning at a picnic table under a giant chestnut
on the track's backside, near D. Wayne Lucas's training barn. Some class
members were acquainted with the language of horses—one turned
out to be the poet Norah Pollard Christianson, whose father, Red Pollard, had ridden Seabiscuit. On that first morning, our eyes fixed on the

famous track, notebooks open; we watched apprentices from Ireland exercise the Aga Khan's horses. "The canter has three beats, like an anapestic foot of poetry," I began. A large chestnut colt caught my eye. He looked just like Hemmy. I called Mark twice a day to check on the foals and their navels.

When I got home, Hemish had almost doubled in size. He didn't look like a Thoroughbred; he had too much bone. It was a comforting sight, watching the mares with their foals orbiting around them in the back pasture. I marveled at how each had borne the other's foal. Ikon was fine-boned and as hot-tempered as a firecracker; she'd jet off at top speed, twirling on her hind legs, then charge back to Mom's udder. Hemish was pensive, always hiding in the cool of True Colors's shadow.

Millie pointed something out: "Look," she said, gesturing at T.C.'s hind legs. She was half my age and about twice my size. "True Colors has this one white anklet with some little onyx jewels on it down by her hoof. Can you see that?"

"Yes," I said.

Vera and True Colors in the back pasture
with Ikon and Hemish. *Marj Dente*

"Ikon has the same marking, only she has it on both hind legs. Are you sure you didn't mix these foals up when they were born?"

The foals would soon need to be weaned, and in order to accomplish this, each needed a stall. I would have to sell either sweet Colette or devilish Fifi. For a while I solved the problem by sending Fi to a race trainer across the river. I hoped that he could stop her from rearing; he was fearless, sometimes getting on a horse bareback and without a bridle. I didn't want to sell Colette, as she was so easy to manage, though she was lame much of the time. A breeder in Oregon wanted her as a broodmare. I pondered it.

One morning as I was on my way over to Hidden Valley Stables to watch Fifi be worked on their track, I noticed something odd about the way Colette grazed. She hadn't moved in over an hour. It dawned on me that maybe she couldn't move. I'd heard of "tying up" syndrome in racehorses. When they were worked during the week and left in their stalls unexercised over the weekend while being fed buckets of grain, these horses' muscles had accumulated so much lactic acid by Monday that they were paralyzed. Could a horse tie up from eating grass?

I called Dr. Short and was astounded to learn that horses with efficient metabolisms could tie up from eating most anything. The vet came as soon as he could and injected Colette with muscle relaxers. She was put on stall rest, and I was told to keep her off grass. Colette had to be sold, but I cried to see True Colors's pretty girl go down the road. From before the day she was born, we had all worked so hard to get the filly to come right. It depressed me to think all my diligence, all my lobbying for her, was for naught. I took solace in the fact that she got a caring home.

Meanwhile, this year's foals grew exponentially. Ikon ran around so recklessly that we feared she'd hurt herself. Hemish was still the slow shy one. Kells's foals all seemed to inherit his head—even today, as I look at his grandbabies, I see Kells's pretty face. One morning a few weeks after I returned from Kentucky, I stood on the deck of the Winter Palace watching as the little ones circled their dams, then homed in on a tug at the udder. I wondered when they would stop peeping out from under their mothers and actually walk up to each other. Sun filled the narrow river valley. In our garden, pink cosmos and orange nasturtiums pulsed like fiesta lights. Suddenly, the foals walked toward each other and sniffed noses. Their dams raised their heads to watch. In that moment, the bubble that encapsulated each mare and foal broke. As the foals played together for the first time, True Colors and Vera walked toward each other and began grazing side by side. A small thing, but I felt I'd witnessed a natural wonder.

Fifi stopped rearing, but before I could get her home, she caught pneumonia and was marooned at the training stables for months. Soon she went back to her old tricks; never wanting to go forward when standing on her hind legs seemed easier. She felt very confident rearing, while most horses don't. Rearing is considered a serious vice in a horse; the rider has no control of a mount that might topple sideways or go over backward—a good way to break your spine. If I'd learned anything in my brief stint as a horse trader, I'd learned that pretty sells. A photo ad was a must. The text stated: *professional riders only*.

The first serious buyer, a young woman with a blond ponytail, asked her price and then, after working with the filly for ten minutes, made me an offer: If I paid her that amount, she'd take the horse off my hands.

I eventually sold Fionula for a pittance to a glamour girl with the world's most elegant brake-light-red fingernails. Glam didn't trust conventional medicine, so she had Fi vetted by calling her psychic. The psychic directed that the horse's name be changed to Reba McEntire, whom the new buyer greatly resembled. The deal almost fell through in the eleventh hour and not because Fi wouldn't go in the new owner's trailer. While we were trying to devise ways to get the lovely but spiteful mare to step up into the rig (Fi had been hauled only in trailers with ramps, never a step-up), I offered to send along all of Fi's vaccination and worming records kept since birth. I used conventional wormers? she asked incredulously. Didn't I know that those chemicals were dangerous?

Yes. But worm infestations were more dangerous. The prospective owner looked stricken. Just then Fi hopped on the trailer. I took a personal check, and they were off to Idaho. We heard back from the new owner only once. Fi, now Reba, had a new spirit guide—her owner had switched psychics. The new practitioner wanted Fi's conception and birth hour so that she had adequate astrological information to help the mare. *Help her with what?* I wondered.

We were down to seven horses, counting foals. To wean, I had in mind putting Hemish and Ikon in the same stall at night and then turning T.C.'s foal out with Vera and Vera's foal out with T.C. in separate paddocks during the day. It was January, and there was a powdering of snow on the frozen ground. Grazing was difficult. Ikon, a matchstick, found it easier to nurse from T.C. than to forage for food. Only one mare in a thousand suckles another mare's foal. A placid Madonna-like expression fixed in True Colors's brown eyes as Ikon nursed. The next day, I had to pair foal with foal and mare with mare. T.C. forged a bond with Ikon that lasted long after the foals were weaned.

Electron was doing exceedingly well, though difficult to handle from the ground. Kells was even more recalcitrant. A false spring was in the air; the clean smell of melting snow wafted down off the glaciers. For reasons unknown to us, on Washington's birthday, Kells took offense at being turned out in his stallion pen and kicked the five-rail fence inside the turnout shed, breaking all two-by-six planks as if they were pencils.

The next question we had to answer was: Should we castrate or sell?

Our only plan for breeding in the New Year was for Ms. Piggy. We booked her to a stallion owned by the farm where Millie worked. True Colors would be our babysitter, as every farm needs one: a cornerstone retired broodmare who puts the nervous or stressed horse at ease, a mare who won't threaten or harm an overly playful youngster or steal all of its food. This was the year I hoped to show Vera at the higher levels and to start campaigning Electron.

The week before I was due to take Vera to Annabelle's new farm for lessons, I wondered why there were all these white patches of fur in her paddock. When I went to feed lunch, I noticed her lying in an odd position, her body downhill from her feet. Alazan had done this when his hooves were trimmed too short; lying down with his feet uphill relieved the pain. Vera hadn't been shod recently. I watched her get up, paw, circle like a dog, and lie down. Clearly, she was in pain.

Dr. O'Leary arrived within an hour; Vera was one of his favorite horses. "You'll be riding her in a couple of days," he enthused. He injected painkillers and pumped electrolytes dissolved in water into her stomach.

When I left the farm to teach a night class at the university, she looked markedly improved. Just as a student nervously stood to read what he called a heart-wrenching story, my cell phone rang. It was Mark; he'd had to rush Vera to the veterinary hospital. I drove directly there. The

situation looked grim: surgery or euthanasia. Surgery brought no promise of survival, and if she lived, it would take Vera a year to recover. She'd
be nineteen. At ten P.M. I called Annabelle. "Would you hate me forever
if I put this horse down?" I asked her tearfully. Just before midnight,
Annabelle arrived at the surgery to say good-bye. As Mark drove our
rig home, I followed, watching the empty trailer sway and bump over
the road. I missed Vera at every turn. In the morning the surgeon called
to say that we'd made the right decision; Vera had had colic surgery six
years before and had burst a two-foot internal scar left by that operation.
"A nearly impossible repair," she said.

When I went down to the barn to feed, True Colors had her head over
the stall door. She looked anxious, her expression imploring: *Where's my
friend, my white shadow?* I turned True Colors out alone in Vera's paddock. When I checked on her a few hours later, she was lying in one of
Vera's nests of white fir. When I brought her into the barn that afternoon, she was covered in white hair. By the next morning, she hadn't
shaken it off and wore it like a shroud.

TWENTY-ONE

Everyone, equine and human, felt sad about losing our elegant dressage mare, and the endless succession of overcast days didn't help. Mercifully, the organizing principle sent us rainbows. Over time, I've become attuned to these Dutch skies: at dawn, a Vermeer ceiling of towering clouds looking as if they were painted on with gobs of blue-gray monochromatic pigment, followed by showers and the most magnificent rainbows arching over our pastures. Here, the skyscape can be galvanizing.

While True Colors wallowed in the patches of white hair that Vera had left, Kells dug craters. When spring came and no mares were presented to him, I sensed that he felt abandoned. Maybe that was why he came down with hives that had to be treated with steroids. Time to castrate.

Veterinarians call this a minor procedure, but it felt like major surgery to me. Anesthetizing a horse and laying it flat on the ground—called *laying a horse down*—is tricky; if it's not done properly, permanent injury can result. If scrotal tissue is left behind, the horse retains a stallion's aggression. We think that this is what happened to Electron. Ms. Piggy's first foal, now weighing thirteen hundred pounds, was the devil's own. But never mind; without Vera to ride, I concentrated my energies on him, and his dressage career took off. Though he had terrible ground manners, when I mounted him, he took care of me as if he were a Knight Templar.

To keep the swelling to a minimum after the surgery, I chased Kells around his paddock, careful that he didn't kick dirt into the wound. The procedure had an immediate benefit: He ceased rearing—it hurt too much to climb up on his hind legs. Because surgery had momentarily hobbled him, I was able to turn True Colors out in the next field so he'd have company. She kept her distance. According to the surgeon, it would take at least thirty days for the testosterone to exit Kells's system.

Ms. Piggy came home in foal to a Kentucky Thoroughbred. T.C. managed the yearlings, Hemish and Ikon. When people saw a bay mare and two youngsters grazing in the field, no one asked which one was True Colors's foal—they assumed it was Ikon, the little bay with pipe-cleaner-thin legs. Everyone had a job but Kells. We decided to sell.

Studying the classical arch of Kells's neck while he stood under the giant fir tree next to the fence, I pondered the relationship between horse and master. Ever since purchasing True Colors, I'd thought about what exactly it meant to *own* a horse.

When I first put Mr. K on the market in April, he was difficult to spur out of a walk, unless it was to try to rub his rider off on the arena fence or to spin like a rodeo horse. He liked children and inexperienced riders, anyone who let him be the boss.

"I'm calling you about a horse," said a woman's voice on the phone.

"The bay gelding?" I asked.

"No, sorry, I don't want to buy a horse. I just bought one." I wondered what this woman was selling. "Jewel at the tack shop told me you bred her. I bought Daisy, and I wanted to get her registered."

"You made my day!" Readily, I agreed to send her a copy of T.C.'s papers, plus a notarized statement as to the date of Daybreak's birth. "Let me know when you show her so I can come watch." I breathed a sigh of relief that Daisy had found a good home. In November, I almost sold Kells to a real estate agent/pony-club mom. She was an expert in hammering out a deal and had her chops down to a science. But when her husband lost his job at Boeing, the deal unraveled. Many ads later, I almost sold Kells to another pony-club mom for her daughter. She was purchasing without her husband's knowledge, so negotiations took place in secret, but when her daughter suffered a head injury in a car accident, a CAT scan nixed the sale.

Meanwhile, Ms. Piggy was getting ready to foal, and my new super-star, Electron, was entered in his first recognized show. Pigster was due on the exact day we planned to return from the horse show, held at a facility seventy miles south of us. Hours of travel time required us to be away from the farm for two nights, but we couldn't leave Ms. Piggy unattended. If I hadn't found the perfect person, I wouldn't have left her. Heidi—she even looked like the storybook character—my new black-smith's wife (Nils, my old blacksmith, had disappeared). Heidi was also the daughter of the family who owned the stallion we'd bred to Ms. Piggy, and she had foaled out countless mares.

The show was held at another of Washington's state fairgrounds, this one on an island between two interstate highways. Like Kermit before him, E caught people's attention. Immediately after his class, we loaded him up and headed for home. When we returned to the farm that afternoon, Heidi had her red Trooper parked in the barn aisle in front of Ms. Piggy's stall, ready to spend another night in her car.

"Let's unpack and unhitch the trailer later," I told Mark. "You look exhausted."

Right after Heidi left at about five-thirty P.M., Ms. Piggy foaled. Baby looked like a giant red spider. Our newest filly was a chestnut, like her sire. She could barely make a squawking noise—that should have been my first red flag. My second should have been the way True Colors called to our newest addition with the frantic neigh of a new mom who had lost sight of her offspring. By the time Baby was eight hours old, it dawned on me that something wasn't right: Her ears flopped uncontrollably, and her lower lip hung. Such foals are called *dummies*. Either she'd been deprived of oxygen at birth or, though she'd gestated long enough, she wasn't fully developed.

Fourteen hours after she was born, we loaded our very sick foal and Ms. Piggy into the horse trailer. The foal gushed fetid yellow diarrhea and would die without medical attention. I didn't want to think this was really happening: Dr. O'Leary sent us back to the emergency clinic that had euthanized Vera. I hadn't forgotten its low ceilings, serious voices, and formaldehyde smell. My feet felt as if I were wearing cement shoes; I'd hoped never to see the place again. The foal could barely walk, so there was much concern as to whether she would be able to balance herself for forty minutes in a trailer. Mark volunteered to ride in back to help keep Baby upright, which was both dangerous and illegal.

What an agreeable foal she was—she was just like one of True Colors's foals in that respect. I couldn't bear for something to happen to her or for Ms. Piggy to lose another newborn. The huge gray mare continually licked Baby's neck and back. I took the wheel of the truck, but I was so tired and hysterical that I made a wrong turn and ended up at Heidi's parents' farm up on the hill, instead of down in valley at the vet hospital. When we finally arrived at the hospital, a technician led Ms. Piggy to a stall, and

Mark cha-cha'ed Jalaan (Malaysian for *run fast*) alongside her mother. A medical team immediately took Jalaan's vital signs, then stuck an IV into her neck, securing it with miles of red 3M sticky tape. "To match her rose color," the technician said with a smile. Blood samples were rushed to the lab, after which the foal was embalmed with antibiotics.

"That's all we can do for now," the chief surgeon told me. She was the same woman who had attended to Vera: a tall, sturdy brunette with a no-nonsense manner. In private life, she adopted foster kids. I breathed a very short sigh of relief; if the foal could be saved, she was the person to do it. Still, I felt as if I'd been knocked down by a tidal wave. My shoulders hunched. I didn't remember ever being so exhausted. I wondered if it was time to give up on horses and find another life. How much good horse luck could be left in my account?

The next day, Jalaan looked full of energy; Ms. Piggy looked horribly bored by living in a windowless stall. We brought a muck bucket of grass that Pigster devoured while a clinician fed Jalaan yogurt through a syringe. The clinic was short-staffed, so Mark and I walked mare and foal in the marshy grass in back of the facility, carefully avoiding the dead-animal pile and the shed rows housing horses in post-op care with drool buckets affixed to their muzzles. Some would be on the dead-animal pile tomorrow.

Jalaan improved, despite the fact that she developed rodavirus, which kills thousands of children each year in Third World countries. Our foal's tender pink butt was so scalded by diarrhea that she scarred. After two weeks, Ms. Piggy and Jalaan were discharged; the amount due was indescribable.

I was so busy with Electron's training and the kerfuffle concerning our latest foal that I decided to give the sale of Kells a rest and spend my time worrying about Jalaan: Would her ears ever stand up? Would her lower lip always hang open? If she were human, she'd have been a cerebral palsy baby, but since she was a horse, the damage wasn't permanent. Day by day, she gained teensy amounts of muscle development. If I'd had a spare moment, I might have used it to blame Mark for the Kelly Crisis, since he had threatened to divorce me if I didn't buy a stallion. Kells had indeed saved us money in stud fees, as Mark had hoped; at the same time, he had seriously added to our workload and further curtailed our ability to travel. I put in a new ad with a serious price reduction.

The day before the ad was to appear was the day when Jalaan was finally well enough to be turned out for the first time. I called Heidi to help us; I had to be at work that day, there was no getting out of it. The hoofed orca Ms. Piggy was beyond frustrated at being cooped up, allowed outside for only a few brief minutes while she was hand-walked, with Mark at the ready to waltz Jalaan back to the nursing stall. Jalaan wasn't the problem; she was at once the world's largest and the most cooperative baby beast. She stood still while I pushed huge amounts of ulcer medication into her mouth, horse Tagamet tablets, which looked exactly like pale yellow Easter eggs.

Mark and Heidi developed a strategy: Heidi would lead the mare to grass, then let her loose. Mark would clutch Jalaan in the ballroom-dancing position until Ms. Piggy ran and bucked and got the beans out of her system. When there was no danger of the mare kicking her foal, Mark would let go of Jalaan. The pair would be allowed to graze, during which time they would be constantly supervised. Then Heidi would lead Ms. Piggy back to her stall, and Mark would waltz the foal. The plan sounded foolproof, so with a light heart, I got into my old red Miata convertible and sped off through the summer air to the university. *If only all mares could be like True Colors, able to birth and raise healthy foals without help*, I thought as I drove across the bridge over Lake Washington.

During a break in my summer school schedule, I called Heidi from my cell phone.

"How did turnout go?" I asked anxiously.

"Fine," she told me. I waited for some embellishing, but none was forthcoming. "How'd Jalaan do?" I asked.

"Fine." She clipped that word even shorter than her first one.

"So everything's okay?" I asked.

"Fine," she said. I chalked the conversation up to a bad connection.

On my way home, as I turned off the state highway, I thought I saw Doc Short coming in the other direction. I told myself: *There are millions of red Japanese trucks.*

When I pulled into the drive, both Heidi and Mark were there to meet me. They looked tired but relieved and told me what had happened: Everything had gone perfectly during turnout. Then, just as Heidi was about to attach the lead to Ms. Piggy and bring her back to the barn, the mare went berserk, bucking and kicking with abandon.

Panicked by Mom's actions, Jalaan raced around trying to keep up. That was when Ms. Piggy whacked her foal squarely in the jaw with a hind hoof, stunning her.

Heidi combed her wavy blond hair with her fingers. "I asked Mark, 'Didn't you think that foal was dead?'"

Mark covered his face with his hands.

The memory of Byron flashed before me. I recalled how his jaws had been surgically wired together after his mother had kicked him. Dr. Short was the vet on call and diagnosed Jalaan's jaw as badly bruised, not broken. I decided right then: I didn't have the courage to breed Ms. Piggy again. True Colors, my pearl-without-price broodmare, always guarded her foals with her life. She'd never have done such a thing. I recalled fretting that T.C. would try to steal Ms. Piggy's first foal. Perhaps I should have stolen this foal and given it to her. I turned it over in my mind: Did I ever want to breed another horse?

True Colors seemed content to stare wistfully at Jalaan through the paddock rails. Ms. Piggy's new foal's ears soon came right, as did her lower lip, and I could direct my full attention to selling Kells. More phone calls, more beginner riders whom, surprisingly, Kells took good care of. *There's hope for this horse,* I thought. Sadly, when every potential buyer got home and watched the videotape of her ride, Kells was never the horse of her dreams. After one woman complained that he made her look fat, I despaired and could barely be civil to potential clients when they telephoned.

By the end of July, I felt exhausted by horses, teaching, project deadlines, the garden, my spiderweb-ridden house (Joan Crawford had been yelling a lot lately). Not riding Kells would be a load off my mind.

"Please, could you ride him?" I begged Mark. But it took an equal amount of energy—nagging, threatening, and any other kind of mental torture I could come up with—to get my husband to exercise Kells. Mr. K required riding five days a week, and we could barely ride him twice. But Mark and Kells got along famously, galloping around the arena in whatever pattern Kells chose.

Another price markdown. What I needed was a snappy ad, and so after much thought, I called one in to the local paper: *MUST SELL. Husband never rides . . .* When it came out, the ad read, *MUST SELL HUSBAND . . .*

"It's wishful thinking, isn't it?" Mark said flatly.

That afternoon, as I led True Colors down the aisle to the front pasture, she stopped abruptly in front of Kells's stall, planted her feet, then craned her shiny mahogany neck in his direction. "I'm not teasing you," I told her. "No more foals for you." But it wasn't that kind of attention she was paying him. He jutted his head out, and they touched noses for a very long second, then she put her head in front of her and moved on. As we walked out the door, it struck me: It was as if she knew he was leaving and wanted to say good-bye.

The first weekend in August, I had several buyers scheduled for visits and prayed Kells wouldn't take offense at being asked to canter a twenty-meter circle more than once in a two-day period. Marlena called and asked Kells's height. She was from Germany and had done a little dressage. *This will never fly,* I thought; *he's a hot-blooded Jockey Club* Thoroughbred, not a Rhineland warmblood. I told Marlena that I was booked up for the weekend but that Tuesday was a possibility; I'd call her.

Because Kells didn't get ridden during the week, I never scheduled anyone to try him out on a Saturday. On Saturday Mark rode him to take the edge off his temper. Kelly would have gone fine for nearly anyone if he could have been turned out twenty-four hours a day and fed only hay. But there was enough clover in our pasture to kill a horse that grazed on it longer than four hours at a stretch. I turned him out in the evenings, when True Colors and the other mares were safely locked in the barn, then got up in the middle of the night to bring him in before he colicked on clover. Pouches grew under my eyes from lack of sleep. The "boyfriend," as owners sometimes called their stallions, was controlling my life.

The family who came to try Kells out on Sunday didn't arrive until eight P.M., and considering it was well past his "riding time," Kellikins performed exceedingly well.

On Monday I gave him the day off: Beginner riders (my ad read "advanced riders only") bouncing around on his back three days in a row might further sour his mood. The woman who was supposed to call on Monday evening to confirm for Tuesday never rang me up, so I tried to phone Marlena but must have had the wrong number. Pat called, asking how much jumping experience he'd had. Kells could jump the moon, but he'd rather do it riderless.

The next morning Marlena called again. I made an appointment with her for Tuesday afternoon at three. It was a very humid 90 degrees, and even Kells swooned from the heat. Up the driveway came a cranberry SUV with Eddie Bauer's signature inscribed in gold on the door. A Marlene Dietrich look-alike stepped out. She wore Hawaiian-print short shorts, white tennis shoes without socks, a tiny white tank top, and a purple satin Wonderbra. Scraping my jaw off the porch, I said, "You're not dressed for riding." She smiled shyly.

We haltered Kelly, took him out of his stall, and I chased him around the arena. He galloped down the long side, spun around, galloped back, and stopped next to us. "He's not sixteen hands," she said, standing at his shoulder. Though Kells was a quarter inch short of that magic dressage mount's height, I was surprised that she'd noticed. If a blacksmith nailed on a thicker shoe, everything would be copacetic in that department. Or so I reasoned.

"Let's put him on the lunge line and see if he puffs up and looks larger," she suggested. Obviously, Marlena knew horses. Not only could she judge height by sight, but she knew Kells might expand his lungs when trotting and thus raise his withers a fraction of an inch. Gladly, I put the bay gelding on a long line.

"Wow." Marlena beamed, her accent sounding more French than German. "He has *presence*!" Her perfect white teeth gleamed like jewelry.

I agreed—puffing up like a dragon was something Kelly did exceedingly well. Then she made me an offer and I nearly passed out. Was I hearing correctly? She hadn't ridden him, nor was she interested in seeing anyone else ride him.

"Does he have any bad habits?" she asked. She ran her honey-skinned hand down Kelly's fine unblemished leg. "Could you deliver him tonight?"

She told me that she'd just had her old wooden paddocks removed and installed in their place white four-rail vinyl fencing. This evening she was throwing a party for the young man who'd done the construction work, and she wanted Kells in the pasture when her guests arrived. In fact, she was in a rush to get to the caterer's and pick up the buffet.

"Can you pay me cash?" I asked. Why not go for broke? It appeared that Marlena wasn't even going to have a veterinarian examine Mr. K. Since the purchase of a horse carried only a "buyer beware" warrantee, vetting an equine was practically mandated by the laws of common sense.

"Right now?" Marlena asked, looking vulnerable.

"N-n-no," I stammered. "If I trailer him up to your place tonight, can you pay me in cash?"

"No problem." She appeared relieved. "He'll look beautiful in front of my new fence." Marlena acted as if she'd won a Caribbean cruise at a charity benefit.

My voiced cracked, and I felt heartsore. "I've always liked the way he looked in my front field." *You will not cry,* I told myself; *try to think of something funny.*

Landscaping with horses—had I missed that issue of *Martha Stewart Living*? A special edition sent to the ten thousand new high-tech multimillionaires in the Seattle area.

"I take very good care of my horses," she said, and I believed her. Kells stood patiently as she stroked his velvety ear. Marlena stared at the mahogany gelding, dreamy-eyed. "The photographers will love him."

A photo session for her new fence? I gave Kells a long good-bye pet, then sighed. Instead of feeling elated that I'd finally sold this horse, I felt glum to see him go. It marked the end of an era. Selling him felt like breaking up with a bad boyfriend; even though the relationship wasn't working, there were a lot of strong feelings. Though I'd been driven to exhaustion by my slavish devotion, I knew that when I let go of him, a part of me would die.

After dumping the contents of several filing cabinets on the floor of my office/bedroom in the Winter Palace, I located Kelly's registration papers and signed over my seven years of ownership. Several hours later, after delivering him to Marlena, I detected a melancholy ping in the engine of our blue and gray Silverado. As I turned the empty rig into the driveway, I tried consoling myself with the fact that I'd found Kells a gorgeous new romantic interest. Automatically, I scanned the front pasture for the bay gelding's neck, which had arced for so many summers like a flame in the grassy field outside my window. How imperfect the landscape felt without him. Taking immediate advantage of the situation, a raucous flock of Canada geese—the Gang of Ten had multiplied to fifty—staked out the road to the barn, leaving an array of slimy green sculptures for me to trip over.

Noting that True Colors and the mares were secured inside the stable, I automatically proceeded to do what I normally did at this hour of the evening: turn Kells out. Flicking on the barn light, I found his stall door ajar, his dinner hay half eaten. Standing in his empty box, I breathed his special smell and stared at the water bucket where he dunked his hay before eating it. I was gripped by existential depression. What was *ownership*, anyway? My name was inked permanently on all of their registration papers: True Colors, Fifi, Hemish, Kells. Although you could own a horse the way you owned a piece of real estate, my ownership of any horse was not something that I could simply sign away or trade for money. In my heart, Kells would always be mine, from the heart-stopping moment when I'd bought him at auction as he was about to be snatched away by another buyer, to today, when I see his features in his grandchildren. In my mind, he would be forever two years old, racing through the rain-glittered grass of our back pasture, the craggy white mountains in the background. A stallion is youth and power and freedom personified, and now he was gone.

Teary-eyed, I walked into True Colors's stall and buried my face in the ruby fur on her flank while combing my fingers through her tail. I felt guilty for not paying more attention to her, though there was no need: She was totally self-reliant. When she lifted her head from her hay, regarding me as she would a foal, I could not imagine my life without her.

TWENTY-TWO

Suddenly, we had a pink horse! When she was a year old, Jalaan started to roan before turning gray. She'd grown to a monstrous size but was sweet-tempered. We pastured her with True Colors and Ikon. We turned out the others—Hemish, Electron, and Ms. Piggy—in the smaller paddocks so they wouldn't overeat. True Colors was the only horse I ever knew who could be trusted to stop grazing when her stomach was full. Looking out the window, I felt my spirits lift to see T.C. shepherding the next generation. A pink horse was the icing on the cake, a happy relief amid midwinter's dark skies, mud, and bare branches.

Jalaan's unique coloring made me think of one of our earlier Christmases at the farm, when Ms. Piggy and Kermit were three-year-olds. Though their coats looked black, their tails had turned nearly white and hung to the ground. It snowed just before the twenty-fifth; the storm knocked out our power. Mark and I were in dour moods due to shivering temperatures. I dyed Ms. Piggy's tail red and Kermit's green using the food coloring I'd bought to make Christmas cookies. Ms. Piggy's tail came out fuchsia, Kermit's the color of lime Jell-O. On Christmas morning, I turned the pair out in the snow-covered front field; a Christmas art installation with animals. Cars stopped. Neighbors walked over to our fence and stared in disbelief. So did the other horses, especially T.C., who flared her nostrils and snorted.

Now I stared dotingly at my herd, the sky above them a hopeful shade of chrome. True Colors kept lifting her head; she arched her neck and pricked her ears as if listening to faraway music. Hard to believe that she was over twenty years old: She had the body of a young mare, though the scars on her ears and face had whitened as if dusted with frost. Ikon, whom she still regarded as her foal, was never out of her sight. I went outside on the deck but heard only the whistle of the Burlington Northern. True Colors stared transfixed, gazing into the southwestern horizon as if she saw a ghost—not in itself unusual. But this time she called out in a low sonorous whinny.

During the next week, I often caught True Colors staring at the horizon and calling to ghosts. At the feed store, I ran into Cornelia, the person to whom I had sold Willie, and heard miraculous news. True Colors's old pasture mate now lived only a quarter of a mile away. Cory, who looked just the same—sand-colored pageboy and dancing hazel eyes—brought me up to date. Willie had developed Cushing's, a disease of the pituitary gland (there's an analogous condition in humans) common in older horses. Cornelia needed to retire him, so she and her husband bought a farm.

At long last, a horsey neighbor! At first he'd been alone at Cornelia's; that was when he'd called out and True Colors had answered. Now that Cory had a new riding horse, Willie had companionship. "He's one of the great loves of my life." She beamed. What luck to have a friend to fill the void that Kolika had left when she moved to Hawaii.

Cornelia was dedicated to the care of geriatric horses and knew how to navigate the Web's minefield of misinformation. Every time True Colors, my cornerstone mare, wasn't looking 100 percent, I was on the phone to Cory, who seemed to be more knowledgeable about older horses than most veterinarians. She put me on to the possibility that T.C. might also suffer from Cushing's. An excessively long coat year-around was "a dead giveaway"; the treatment was easy to administer. Our aim was to make our older horses' last days enjoyable.

Soon we bonded over matters other than equines, including personal safety. Up until now the only time I had need of the sheriff was when I feared that an intoxicated neighbor was shooting at my property; a stray bullet can travel up to two miles. To tell the truth, I feared more for the welfare of my horses than for myself. Even so, I'd estimate that a police car sped past our house once a year, if that.

The Patriot Militia Party, as I heard they called themselves, kept the peace in our part of the county. Since Mark and I owned no guns, the Militiamen helped enforce our no-trespassing signs by making citizens' arrests of anyone they caught deer hunting on our farm. Because they owned horses, they found it necessary at times to ask Cornelia or me for help with them.

Just after the turn of the new century, it felt as if things had started to run amok. Developers discovered the loveliness of these foothills, and property values skyrocketed. The Patriot Militia Party saw their chance, sold out to the developers, and decamped for Idaho. No sooner had they sold their fifty-acre plots to Wildridge Estates than our neighborhood suffered an influx of methamphetamine cooks who set up kitchens in abandoned cars, hollow trees, and derelict outbuildings. This was well before the middle class had heard of ice or believed that anyone would risk life and limb stewing battery acid, Sudafed, livestock-strength iodine, and household ammonia into a powdery mood booster to sell on the street. With the meth cooks came hordes of unneutered pit bulls. Before I moved to the farm, I had never been bitten by a dog. Now I can't count the bites I've suffered. Pit bulls make good pets, I've been told, but there is something hardwired into their nature that compels them to sink their teeth into human flesh and never let go.

In addition to a nation of tweakers living in their vans in the state woodlands above our farms, or almost next door in the abandoned barns that weekend watercolorists used to commit to canvas, we had unbridled development threatening our way of life. Acres of evergreens and big-leaf maples were clear-cut overnight; rows of houses mushroomed in what yesterday had been a tranquil horse pasture. As with melanoma, once the developers took root, nothing could get rid of them, not anything that we or any citizens' action committee or the lawyers said or did could turn the tide. Worse, no new roads were considered, and traffic became hopelessly clogged. One night it took Mark seven hours to drive thirty-five miles.

Over tea made from the mint that grew everywhere, Cornelia and I compared notes on Willie and True Colors, bemoaned the state of our neighborhood, and kvetched about the price of hay—Mark and I still made our own, but it was never enough; we used many tons of hay a year. True Colors had to be fed timothy, as any other hay gave her diarrhea. Willie had to have timothy soaked in water to reduce the sugar content. Every year the price of timothy went up. Most hay is grown in the desert part of the state, yet the excuse for the price hike each year was that the crop got rained on. Every so often we heard a variation: The price of gasoline to haul the hay over the mountains went up; the Arabs bought all the hay and shipped it to Dubai; hay farmers planted crops for biofuel. What I used to pay for half a year's hay, I now paid per truckload. We're not even talking good hay—bleached, moldy, stemmy, and cut too late. A lot of it ended up on my manure pile. When the price of gasoline went down, the price of hay did not. When we ran out of horse problems to discuss, Cory and I looked for silver linings: Since all the trees had been cut down to build sub-divisions, the power seldom went out, and when it did, all the people living in those new tract houses a mile down the road complained en masse. I'm not convinced that there is safety in numbers, but there are results. I would never again have to endure a wintry two weeks without power.

Mark and I had to sell Ms. Piggy, once the apple of my eye, my stuffed toy of a baby horse. She was as large as a battleship and, with the spring grass coming up, on the verge of eating herself into oblivion. We tried muzzles. When attached to her halter, she looked like a horse with an eraser nose. She banged and rubbed and chewed until the muzzle fell off or tattered into uselessness. We feared she would founder.

Without much trouble, I sold her to a woman with an ample figure and a long gray ponytail the same color as Ms. Piggy's mane. The new buyer let me know in plain language that she took offense at the name we had given our horse and changed the name back to beDazzled—more dignified. The buyer brought her equine chiropractor to the vetting because she knew how "we full-figured gals can suffer back pain." Ms. Piggy went off to a life free of grass near Reno, where her new owner hoped to join a hunt club that chased coyotes through the sage.

I did miss her and her heart-shaped upper lip and silver lily-shaped ears. So did Electron. When I led him in from his paddock to the barn the day his mother left, he began to bray piteously until we moved True Colors into the box next to him. In the pasture, T.C. avoided Electron and his pushy nature. But without Ms. Piggy, Electron was inconsolable, a shadow of his tiger self. True Colors softened her heart and played mouthy games with E over the stall divider, something I'd never seen her do. Her companionship was the tonic that restored his spirit, for which I was grateful. Electron was, after all, my dressage dance partner, my Fred Astaire.

After Monte had vanished, we started sending our horses for training to an establishment about fifteen minutes away as the crow flies. Deer Creek Training Stables looked as if it had been airlifted in from Virginia: acres of well-fenced green pastures framing a racing oval. The manager and head trainer, Brian, could have passed for Brian Wilson of the Beach Boys. His motto was engraved over his office door: *Equine legs are my life.* Brian was a genius at lameness in horses.

Shortly after I started riding Ikon and Hemish, Mark dropped a bombshell. He was very late getting home one night, which I attributed to traffic. "I've had a job offer," he told me as he gulped down his dinner—some unnamed casserole I'd concocted from the weekend's leftovers, anchored by an array of heritage potatoes. Mark grew fifty-odd varieties, some purported to be extinct.

He'd gotten job offers before. "Where this time?" I asked distractedly. It was the end of the quarter, and I was sitting at the kitchen table tallying final grades.

"Southern California," he said, pouring himself a second glass of wine. "They want you, too. They've invited us for interviews. This would be a good career move for me. And being there wouldn't hurt your career, either."

I was thunderstruck. "I suppose you're right."

"We'd take the horses, of course," he hastened to add.

Something inside me clicked to automatic pilot. "I'll see if Millie can horse-sit for three days next week," I told him, trying to grasp the finality of the situation. *Think of it as a surprise vacation,* I told myself.

The university was well endowed, the jobs challenging, the weather to die for. But the city looked as if a dust storm had settled over it. A real estate agent found a few hours to show us some equestrian properties. I'd forgotten how arid California was. Endless brown hills blackened by fires unfurled into the eastern horizon. The place would disturb True Colors's fragile psyche, I thought, recalling the oozing burn sores on her face when she was first delivered to our farm.

In addition to being gated, all the homes we were shown had security systems. We weren't used to locking our doors. The water was chlorinated, expensive, and rationed; at home we paid only for the electricity to pump water out of our gushing spring in the ground. Even a small ranchette without a shade tree was priced at a million plus. Our real estate agent, who looked like Clark Gable, assured us we'd have no trouble getting what he called a bridge loan, but the payments felt staggering, as did the taxes. California had no farm assessments or grass paddocks. As near as I could tell, there was no grazing land anywhere. The commute looked even longer than our present one. Homes closer in were priced a little lower and had more security but no possibility of keeping a horse. Tattered plastic bags flew from eucalyptus and live oak trees.

"Whattya think?" asked Mark when we got back to Washington State. We were drinking white wine in our backyard, sitting next to the outdoor bread oven Mark had built out of stones we'd picked up from our paddocks. People mistook it for a kid's playhouse, so we called it the Hansel and Gretel Memorial Oven.

"I don't know what to think," I told him. Give up my dream of a horse farm in exchange for endlessly sunny (albeit smoggy) days and the possibility of a better (albeit different) life? I wasn't getting any younger; I should count myself lucky that I had choices.

"I could concentrate on research and wouldn't have to teach as much," Mark said. He looked sorrowful and wouldn't meet my eye.

I poured myself another glass of fumé blanc. I wasn't a drinker; perhaps it was time to start. "Then I guess we'd better accept." The moment felt unreal. Though I found the possibility of again living among writers appealing, I'd stumbled on to a good life that was a lot to give up.

Mark was silent. Then it dawned on me that he was just as tied to this place as I was—maybe more so. I watched as he stared at an imperfection in the stem of his wineglass. "A good move careerwise, but financially, we'd have to take on a whole lot more debt," he said, twisting his lips.

"I don't know what I'd do with True Colors," I told him. "How long do we have to think about it?"

"The offer'll be on the table for a while," he answered.

We agreed not to decide anything for the moment.

A month later, Cornelia and I were talking about the scandalous price of hay when I looked out my kitchen window into the back pasture. Why was True Colors just standing there in the hot sun and not eating?

"You won't believe their excuse this year," Cornelia told me. She was more worked up than usual. The problem with hay is also a problem with the equine digestive system. A horse cannot vomit. What goes in the mouth has to come out the other end. A horse's intestines often get crimped or twisted—the same problem exists in some large dogs, like German shepherds—which is why colic is so scary. If a horse gets a twist, it's either surgery or euthanasia. Timothy hay causes the least digestive problems; all equine hospitals use it. Diarrhea can cause gas pain; a horse rolling from pain can twist its gut. Timothy hay saves in the long run.

According to Cory, the rumor this year was that all the timothy blew away in a windstorm, hence the price hike.

After she left, I pulled on my worn paddock boots and headed out to bring the horses in from the field before they started running from flies. Ikon and Jalaan trotted to the gate of the back pasture, harassed by B-52 botflies. True Colors remained in the field, facing south. I grabbed her blue lead rope from the hook by her stall door and walked out to get her. Picking up one front hoof, she put it down in the same place. In the next minute, I realized that she wasn't stomping flies but trying to walk. Maybe she'd been stung by an insect, as Ms. Piggy had been the time that her mouth got paralyzed, or maybe she had tied up, like Colette had done.

When I clipped the lead to her halter, T.C. didn't move. Her eyes looked normal, not dazed or full of pain, as when a horse has colic. I dropped the rope, and she didn't take a step, except to try to pick up one front hoof and then another, as if trotting in place in slow motion. I walked around her. Her coat gleamed like red cedar. She had a good weight on her; older horses had trouble keeping on pounds. Willie was so thin I didn't recognize him. No blood, she wasn't injured. Then I noticed that the top of her right hind leg was a little swollen inside the stifle, and a pinprick of blood had clotted, forming a small pearl at the top of the swelling. Spears of dead grass clung in her mane, as if she'd lain down. Nearby, I saw the grass flattened where she'd either rolled or napped in the sun, as was her habit—in all the years that I owned her, I rarely saw her lie down in her stall.

Gently, I pulled her head to one side, trying to move her off balance. When she finally took a step, she sounded like an old oak bed creaking. When I got her turned around and facing the barn, I had to tow her along; each step took tremendous effort. It felt as if she were drugged. My heart pounded with fear. Horses start dying in their late teens.

It must have taken us an hour to get as far as the gate, and by this time I was sweating and the other horses were whinnying. At first they called in a concerned manner and then frantically. Their cries hurt my ears. I noticed that T.C. dragged a hind leg, wearing the toe on the gravel path so that it looked squared off. This was the leg with the white anklet and the two onyx jewels down by her hoof. What could the matter be? Whirling the lead like a jump rope normally would have caused her to bolt away, but it didn't make her move any faster.

It must have taken me the better part of another hour to get her into the barn. When I took off her halter, her head drooped like a wilted flower. She looked tranquilized. I went outside her stall and watched

261

from the aisle. Slowly, she maneuvered herself to her water bucket and took a long drink. A good sign: If a horse gets dehydrated, it is a slippery slope. As a horseman once commented about an injured Derby winner: *A horse is a house of cards.*

Very slowly, True Colors chewed her hay. How to describe her attitude to the vet—limp and deflated? I went into the feed room and grabbed the thermometer, surprised that her temperature was only slightly above normal. Her pulse was a little fast and her breathing shallow. It was hard to watch one of the most steadfast and true things in my life start to slip away right in front of me on an otherwise brilliant day. I counted the years we'd been together: seventeen.

I was trying a new vet, one who lived in my neighborhood and, in theory, would be minutes away in an emergency. Dr. Starlene Rhodes was a tall auburn-headed lovely who, if she hadn't gone to veterinary school, might have been a model for country-western *Vogue*. Every time she testified at a state senate subcommittee on animal abuse, she made a distinct impression. I got Starlene on her cell phone and explained the symptoms.

"Wow!" Starlene said through a barrage of static. "Doesn't sound like a stroke. Clearly not an aneurysm. Can I call you back in fifteen? I've gotta stitch up this horse."

True Colors had endeared herself to me in so many ways over the years: the gifts of her precious foals, all except one of which had been an untroubled birth. Five healthy foals was a lot from any mare, and she'd borne six. True Colors was stoic, neither cuddly nor demonstrative, but she had a quiet grace. She never wrinkled her lip, like other mares—the prelude to a snarky reaction of some kind.

"Are you sitting down?" Starlene asked when she called back. "Brown recluse spider bite. Can be deadly to humans unless they're put on life support. Causes organ failure."

"Will she die?" It felt as if I were another person, a calm, rational woman, talking.

"Probably not. The poison will have to work itself out. Keep her warm and dry, and let me know if she stops eating or drinking. Could take a while."

"Are you sure?" I asked in disbelief. "I mean about the spider bite?"

"It's a bad year for them. I just lost a dog to a brown recluse. They don't bite unless their nest has been disturbed. Your mare might have rolled over on one. That's what the blood bead and the swelling on her hind leg is probably about."

A spider no bigger than the nail on my thumb might bring down my twelve-hundred-pound horse?

Daily, I led her to pasture; it took us half an hour to walk to the gate. She dragged her hind leg, and beneath her belly, on her midline, fluid began to accumulate. After four days, so much fluid accumulated that the swelling started to sag. I called Starlene.

"Can't come today. I've got a trailer wreck."

"Shouldn't True Colors be seen?" I asked, annoyed.

"Nothing I can do," she said. "Did I tell you I'm breaking up with my boyfriend?"

I demanded that Starlene come look at her.

"We just have to wait it out," she told me as we watched T.C. manage to bend her head to eat a little grass.

When the vet left, I asked myself fearfully, *If she dies, would Mark and I feel better about selling this farm and finding a new life, maybe one free of animal care?* If she dies, she would free us. That made me feel not one degree better.

"Do you think I'm crazy?" I asked Cornelia, who'd stopped in to see how T.C. was doing. "Letting a horse determine my life?" Cory had brought a list of procedures from the Web that might help True Colors.

"Not at all," she said. She wore a striped sweater, blue jeans, and clogs. "I'm staying here until Willie dies. No vacations, even. What if he died while I was gone?"

True Colors continued to operate in a narcotic haze. Positioning her in the aisle of the barn, I let the end of the blue lead rope attached to her halter dangle down by her front feet. No need to worry about her bolting out into the day. The north-facing sliding door was open for ventilation; the south-facing door closed against flies and the heat of the caramel sun. The other horses munched hay in their stalls. Brushing her, I stood back and admired the shine, like taffeta. When I squirted her with a bottle of coat polisher, she didn't react to the hissing noise. There's a saying in the horse world: *Ride the horse you're on.* Why not take advantage of the horse T.C. had become? I threw my arms around her well-muscled neck, then kissed her floppy, whiskery lips. Even her eyes blinked at a snail's pace. She stood with her neck at half-mast;

every so often she cocked her head as if to ask: *What's come over you?*

The swelling on her stomach, caused by toxins accumulating too quickly for her lymphatic system to bear away, began to hang down even more. Was I granted this extra time with her so I could say good-bye or so I could long for the day when her flightiness would vex me once again?

She'd never needed an owner, but if this turn of events didn't sit well with her, she didn't let on. For twenty minutes twice a day, until my hand ached from fatigue, I held an ice pack to the puffiness on the inside of her left thigh. After sponging her leg with cool water, I dried her with a towel before massaging her all over. Manipulating her afflicted leg, I drew it back, then brought it around to the side, rotating it like a giant stirring stick. Her muscles had no tone. As I stared at her unmoving head, I tried to memorize her, beginning with her ears: almost black at the tips, lighter at the base.

Her survival instincts amazed me. In her stall, she no longer stood with her tail resting against the back wall but with her head positioned between her water buckets and her hay. She turned toward the blue plastic bucket hanging nearest her, bent down until her lips touched the meniscus, sipped, swallowed, raised her head, took a chew, lowered her neck, put her mouth around a stem of hay, chewed ever so slowly, swallowed. Back to the water bucket. Mark and I took turns checking on her. Sometimes we sat together on a hay bale in front of her stall. During one such watch, Mark remarked, "It's amazing. She knows that drinking will help her body flush away the poisons."

Early in the morning, when I led her to pasture, she walked slowly through the gate, then plodded toward an area that in winter was marsh. There she spent her turnout hours, head bent in the posture of a very old horse. When I went to check on her later, she was licking marsh dirt like a salt block, trying to relieve her acid stomach. I worried about kidney failure. Slowly, the edema on her midline started to diminish.

Occasionally, Ikon galloped up to her and tried to wither. Standing tail to head with her adopted mother, Ikon gnawed on the crest of T.C.'s neck. *Grooming*, old horsemen called this. True Colors was unable to raise her head high enough to return the favor, and eventually, Ikon wandered away. But no matter how dull True Colors appeared, the horses had to have her out in the field with them. She belonged to the herd as much as she belonged to me.

TWENTY-THREE

illie started to fail. It was a cloudy morning weeks down the road, and a white fog covered the valley like bedsheets laid out to dry. I walked into True Colors's stall and, thinking of Willie, threw my arms around her. Recovered from the spider bite, she glanced at first at me as if on the brink of good cheer, then spun away in fright. I almost missed her sick self. Never again would she allow such liberties, hugs or picking up her hind legs and moving them like stirring sticks.

True Colors had achieved the small miracle of surviving a deadly spider bite at the age of twenty-five. While she was ill, Mark and I could not bring ourselves to accept or reject the job offer from California; finally, the university hired someone else, and my attention returned to riding.

It's a good idea to work with two horses in case something happens to one—lameness, colic, lost shoe. Electron seldom took an off step, but his large rear end inhibited his flexibility. He got fat on air, and soon I would have to start muzzling him, like we'd had to do with his mother. At first I had hoped that the tall, stately Hemish would be my spare dance partner, but he lacked willingness. He showed talent as a jumper, so, sadly, we sold him—T.C.'s last offspring. That left me with Ikon, Vera's foal, and Jalaan, Ms. Piggy's baby, as potential dance partners.

In Ikon I had a wealth of hope, for she'd inherited Vera's fabulous gaits; she was slight, wiry, and athletic, but hot-tempered—often when she came to the end of her very short fuse, she'd start rearing. Jalaan, whose pink coat faded to the light gray of a winter sky, grew to mastodon size, with long ears that reminded me of a rabbit's, and she had a wiggly, rabbit nose. I loved riding her bareback; on cold days, she felt like a heated car seat. Unlike the tempo of most unschooled horses at the trot, hers never varied: one-two, metronome-perfect. But at the canter, Jalaan dropped her giraffe neck, and I lacked the strength to get her to rock back on her hind legs. We sold her to a company of vaulting cham-

265

pions who balanced on her back like circus riders. Never again would I own such a large horse; I gave them Jalaan's silver-edged bridle.

When True Colors achieved a full recovery, I began to feel that other extraordinary equine accomplishments must surely be at hand. I sent Electron to Elspeth, a German trainer temporarily working in this country, hoping to polish his flying changes of lead at the canter. When I sent Ikon, my prize peach, to the same woman, True Colors turned even more stoic and withdrawn, occasionally nickering for her lost pasture pal. At dressage school, Electron languished without me, and Ikon's stifles started locking up. A locking stifle is similar to a bad knee in a human athlete—the stifle is that huge joint just below the horse's hip at the top of its hind leg. We tried fancy wedged shoes, but she always pulled them off. True Colors's eyes nearly popped out the afternoon Ikon returned. All the next day, T.C. stood with her neck protectively over her adopted daughter, shielding Ikon from the murder of crows that circled their pasture.

I decided to get a new horse. Elspeth found me an elegant warmblood pinto with black and brown splashes of color swirling across his mostly white body; he moved like Vera and looked as if Picasso had used him as a canvas. According to his trainer, he had never been lame. His owners were desperate to get rid of him, so they let me take Joselito home on trial. He fell in love with Ikon and jumped the fence to be with her. True Colors took extreme offense at this Gila monster–colored creature encroaching on her baby. As Joselito approached Ikon, True Colors circled the younger mare, gesturing threateningly at the interloper. The dance of the mares looked as if it had been choreographed. True Colors, who almost never called out, bleated loudly, and I came running to save Joselito from harm.

"But how could I buy a horse that True Colors doesn't like?" I asked Mark. It was just before Thanksgiving, and the sky was glacier blue.

"She doesn't dislike him," Mark told me. My husband was looking for a hammer so he could repair the fence. "She just doesn't want him anywhere near Ikon."

In the end, Joselito flunked the prepurchase exam. A slight surgical scar inside his right front leg above the knee tipped off the vet. Two years before, when Joselito had tried to jump a metal gate, he'd gotten caught in it and broken his leg.

"A broken leg isn't a lameness?" both Elspeth and I asked his trainer.

"You Americans," Elspeth told me. "We do not do business like this in Germany, selling a horse that has had a broken leg as a horse that has nothing wrong with him."

Mark and I decided to retire Ikon and breed her in the spring. We brought her into heat and, after a lot of work by Starlene, got her pregnant. At this point, Starlene broke out in a fertility dance in Ikon's stall. "No charge," she assured me as she whipped her auburn hair around like a pole dancer. At sixteen days, we ultrasounded, looking for a beating heart; at twenty-five days, we ultrasounded to make sure there weren't twins. There were, and the vet pinched off one of them. Multiple births are disastrous in equines.

Again I started thinking about a new horse, though by now I was suspicious of every mount I came across. After Memorial Day, Elspeth telephoned from Germany. "I found your dream horse," she said. "He goes on the market next week, so if you're interested, you should make a move."

On Thursday, I took all the money we'd made selling True Colors's foals—feeling too sentimental about them, we hadn't spent any of it—plus some money I'd inherited from an aunt I'd never met, and boarded a flight to Frankfurt. It was a chilly, overcast day at the beginning of June, I was severely jet-lagged, the airline lost my luggage, and I spoke not one word of German. Somehow I found the train to Köln. After Elspeth picked me up, we sped down the autobahn. When I saw a sign for the exit to the road to Poland, I recalled that my father's grandfather, a tailor, had emigrated from there. I always wondered what his surname had been before he changed it along with his history. In the horse world, old-timers say that it's bad luck to change a horse's name.

The old-timers also say: *New owner, new life.* Don Leon was sired by a world-famous stallion. The handsome seven-year-old chestnut stood seventeen hands, with matching white hind stockings and a long white face. Walking over to me, he put his copper head in my arms and purred like a cat. I had wanted to never again own a chestnut horse with white legs or blond horned hooves, but those criteria flew out his stall window. What stood in front of me amid the strawberry fields of Westphalia was, even more than True Colors, Whistlejacket in the flesh, a live version of the painting at the British National Gallery, all nine feet of it rearing up on hind legs and staring out at me. Like True Colors, Don Leon was mine the minute I laid eyes on him. He had extravagant gaits, automatically extending his trot at the push of a button, while it had taken me ten years to get Electron to achieve only a slight lengthen to his trot.

D.L. (as I called him) had a passport, making it easier to arrange for his transportation to the United States: A truck hauled him to Amsterdam, where he was tranquilized, led into a crate shared with two other horses, lifted into the fuselage of a KLM jet, and flown at thirty-five thousand feet for fifteen hours to Los Angeles. At LAX, he was taken to the quarantine facility; after three days, an equine transportation company picked him up and hauled him to Seattle.

Later, I learned that not all horses survive this journey. Physically, Don Leon was buzzard-tough; psychologically, he was a china figurine. I had him delivered to Deer Creek Training Stables, where he spent his first two weeks in the country away from our farm; we didn't want him bringing home any viruses that would cause Ikon to abort. No one told me that German horses have only one third the immunity of an American racehorse and that it was Don Leon who should have been quarantined.

When he arrived, I didn't recognize him: He'd lost a hundred and fifty pounds. He didn't know me, either. He was too distracted to eat, uninterested in grass, and so jumpy he seemed to have been fed amphetamines. He did, however, drink buckets of water, which was a godsend. After Brian delivered him to our farm, he remained in a constant state of unease. No food or equine friend pacified him. True Colors was so busy guarding Ikon that she had no use for him. First D.L. threw a shoe, then he ran a temperature; a swelling the size of baseball developed under his chin. Dr. O'Leary prescribed a hundred daily antibiotic pills that I had to grind up, dissolve in molasses water, and inject into D.L.'s mouth. Here I found his silver lining: He loved being a patient.

No sooner had he recovered from his mysterious infection than he started to look odd at the trot. In November he had to be hauled back to Deer Creek for a protracted layup—months of stall rest. Electric shock treatments to the afflicted ligament followed, and stem cell therapy was considered; the only exercise allowed was a twenty-minute walk twice a day. While packed in cotton, he pulled a shoe, straining the tendon on his injured leg. There's an old racetrack quip: *That horse didn't hurt himself standing in a box stall.* Yet Don Leon had managed exactly that. I was starting to hate this horse.

In February, Brian moved D.L. to his brand-new fifty-million-dollar facility with a view of Mount Rainier. This farm rivaled Versailles and was equipped with an equine swimming pool, an outdoor quarter-mile track with all-weather footing made of mattress fibers, and a hyperbaric chamber to speed healing. When I received their brochure, D.L. was featured in all the photographs—demonstrating the dog paddle while submerged in Caribbean-blue water; posing in front of the diving bell–shaped hyperbaric chamber with a leggy blond model holding his lead rope. *He's good for something,* I thought; *he's the stable pet.* He looked spectacular. I took Cornelia with me when I went to watch him ridden around the track as I carefully monitored his exercise program, from ten steps of trot to ten minutes of trot, then from eight steps of canter to eight furlongs.

I didn't bring Don Leon home until after Ikon had her foal and after Mark and I built three small pens where Don Leon couldn't hurt himself, or so we hoped. He had turned into such a different horse from the one I'd bought—perhaps the airplane ride had damaged his brain. The blacksmith's forge and grinder, and other loud but ordinary noises, brought him to the edge of panic. He cried incessantly and walked in endless circles. He became phobic about small spaces: shoeing rooms, shower stalls, trailers.

He did, however, love Ikon's foal Kabaret, Kabby for short, which distressed Ikon beyond measure—she didn't eat for two weeks after he was born. True Colors was the only horse Ikon would let near her handsome black bay colt.

"He has Kells's head," I told Mark as we admired Kabaret on his first day of turnout. T.C. stood on the other side of the fence, her doe eyes watching Baby's every move. Within months Kabby grew almost as large as his mother and increasingly demanding. True Colors often gave him a little nip on the butt to keep him in line.

After I put D.L. back to work, I hit a stumbling block: He either didn't have as much training as I'd thought, or I didn't know how to get him to do the maneuvers. One cold February day, Mark and I trailered him to Annabelle's new stable, Over the Rainbow Farm, located just down the road from the Versailles-like facility where Don Leon had recuperated. I attended dressage school at the Rainbow with my new horse five days a week, like a job, getting up at four-thirty in the morning in order to get my farm chores done before leaving. Don Leon loved it there. He had a roomy night stall, a double day stall, a private grooming stall, and a shower stall of which he was suspicious, though he enjoyed the warm water. It seemed that he liked it everywhere but our farm. He especially liked to be grazed on the lawn by the gazebo. We competed in a few horse shows and even won a class. During the three and a half years he lived there, I think I averaged four hours of sleep a night.

After Ikon had a second colt, Ludwig, she immediately turned her first foal, Kabby, now a rammy two-year-old, over to True Colors in order to put her full attention to devouring grass and producing milk.

Poor Kabby was bereft. I can still see his stunned expression when, on the way to his paddock the morning after Ludwig was born, he stopped at Ikon's stall to play mouthy games with his mom, and instead of greeting him with an enthusiastic nicker, she lunged over the door with the expression of a harpy. In the pasture with True Colors, Kabaret chewed on the old mare's neck, chased her, smashing into her in what looked like a college-football offensive tackle. T.C. passively allowed him to use her as a punching bag, which seemed to frustrate him: He wanted her to play hard. We wouldn't have blamed True Colors if she'd pulled out her weapons and pummeled him, but she never did. Finally, I put Kabby in a paddock by himself.

I'd worried about replacing True Colors ever since the spider bite and lately had been searching for another horse like her—as if that were possible. Something lovely, something that didn't bite or kick no matter what. One overcast spring day, when I meant to check weather conditions but accidentally called up the website of an online equine classified, I saw a photo of a horse that looked a lot like T.C.—Topaz.

She reminded me of a Chinese terra-cotta statue of a horse like those found in Han Dynasty tombs: wide shoulders, spherical butt, enormous widely spaced eyes. Our newest equine marched into her stall as if she belonged there. The first horse she gravitated to was True Colors, though it was Kabby who needed a friend. In no uncertain terms, Topaz let the two-year-old know who was boss; she could be an acre away, but if she started backing up in his direction, he flew to the far end of his field. Topaz was a true alpha mare. "She'll teach him some boundaries," I told Mark as we watched the pair.

A no-nonsense horse with perfectly shaped hooves, Topaz didn't need shoes and never stumbled: the perfect horse for Mark. And she didn't mind being Kabby's chew toy, within limits. T.C. much preferred Ikon and the new foal, Ludwig, who at two months stood as tall as my head. What good fortune to have so many prospects! Kabby, Ludwig, Don Leon. But if your chickens are horses, it's never wise to count them even after they've hatched.

One summer morning about a week after Topaz arrived, when the perfume of clover hung in the air, I had Kabby and Topaz in the back field, Electron in his own paddock, and True Colors in the front field with Ikon and Ludwig. Walking back to the house after cleaning stalls, I stopped to unlatch the gate. Glancing over my shoulder, I was surprised to see Topaz standing in the drive between me and the barn. When True Colors had taken refuge from flies under the hundred-year-old fir, she'd drifted out of Topaz's sight, and our new mare had jumped the four-foot-high gate to be with her new best friend.

"T.C. hasn't lost her charisma," I told Mark when he got home from work that night. "Topaz ferreted out the lowest point in the fence to be with her." We had started to replace our old fences, installing tall no-climb stable mesh with a rail across the top of each section—the safest horse fence possible, according to the experts.

Though Don Leon was progressing in his training at Rainbow Farm, it was clear that I couldn't keep him at the high-end stable forever; I felt run ragged getting up before first light to take care of the horses at home, driving to dressage school on the Ridge, then working at my teaching job, which had been converted to online instruction. D.L.'s tuition cost as much as sending a kid to a private school, and oh, what luxury: The footing in the indoor area spread out as smooth as frosting on a chocolate cake. D.L. was one of six horses in a fifty-stall barn. We had elbow room.

Ludwig's first winter was the first time that True Colors finally let me put a turnout rug on her. One damp November morning when Ludwig was about six months old, he and his mother were grazing in the back pasture. All the grass had dried, and the trees were leafless. True Colors (wearing one of Kells's winter rugs), Topaz, and Kabby were in the front pasture, nosing around under the old fir, where the grass was still green. It was about seven-thirty—mornings felt brighter now that we'd set the

271

clocks back to standard time. Everything seemed calm with all horses in sight of one another. I looked out my window and saw Kabby pawing the ground and went out to investigate—was he colicking? Sometimes horses stop drinking in cold weather, which can bring on an impaction. Cornelia had just called to say that her riding horse was ill with colic symptoms. Outside, I heard a sharp cracking noise from the southwest corner of our property—a gunshot? I didn't think so. I continued walking toward Kabby, who was happily rooting up new shoots, then headed over to see what had caused the noise in the southwest—a tree falling on the fence?

When the back pasture came into view and I saw Ludwig, I felt as if someone had put an ice-cold hand on the back of my neck. Ikon paced the new no-climb fence, nickering to Ludwig, who had somehow gotten on the other side of it. As I ran to him, my rubber steel-toed boots felt like lead weights. At first Ludwig was simply stunned, his back humped like a dromedary's. But other than a skinned patch at the base of his neck, I saw no marks of an injury. I walked the foal slowly to the gate and returned him to Ikon, then watched him: His neck seemed all right, and he could bend down to nurse—that was the first thing he did, take a long tug on Mom's udder.

What we think happened was that he reared up and somehow landed on the new fence, went over, and did a somersault, landing on his neck. The top rail had been pulled down, and a stout pressure-treated post had broken in half—that was probably what made the cracking noise. Long afterward, we couldn't but wonder: If only Ludwig had gone over the old fence, he might have come out unscathed.

That afternoon he was worse, walking sideways like a crab. I called Cornelia to help me give him an anti-inflammatory. The clouds were low, the sky a dull pewter. True Colors watched Ludwig maneuver in his crazy sideways locomotion as if he didn't know where his legs were. She walked up to him and started to lick the top of his head where it joined his neck, as she would a newborn who was trying to get up for the first time and couldn't figure out how to do it. Ludwig bent into her touch like a kitten to a mother cat, as a new foal would do. Cornelia and I looked at each other. His condition was frightening.

The vet injected Ludwig with steroids. "It might take him a month to recover," he told me. I wondered if he would ever come right. Where could I find expert advice? Brian had left Deer Creek Training Stables and gotten out of horses completely. I hadn't heard from Kath in years. I felt marooned.

It was a terrible winter. Temperatures crashed into the teens, one snowstorm followed another; houses in this part of the world aren't built for midwestern weather. True Colors wouldn't let me put a blanket on her unless she was going outside. I didn't try to wean Ludwig, leaving him with his mother for warmth. Though he showed some improvement, the vet suggested that we donate him to the state veterinary school in exchange for a tax credit. There is little one can do to help a horse with an injured neck, and I didn't want him to be experimented on; in my view, it's tantamount to torture.

Ludwig grew more unstable, like a table with wobbly legs. There are surgeries for his condition, but they are experimental, and I have never known them to be successful. On his own, Ludwig might improve enough to be a pasture pet, but he would never be ridable. "He needs a friend," I told Mark one windy, comfortless day at the end of February when the sun had just set between the naked branches of the alder grove. In the top of every tree perched a crow, like a black bobble. Mark agreed.

We bought Raven sight unseen off the Internet; supposedly a dressage prospect, part draft horse, a filly the same age as Ludwig but half his size. In the photo, she was marked like our rescued dog, a black-and-white border collie. When Raven was delivered on the ides of March, a dirt ball backed off the trailer. She was smart, came like a dog when we called her, and let Ludwig chew on her like a licorice drop.

A few months later, we had to euthanize. Ludwig, our brightest promise, had injured his spine up where it joined his head, the very spot where True Colors had spent an afternoon licking him. When he started falling down, we knew his condition was hopeless. First I led T.C. up to his lifeless body, which lay on a pile of soft shavings and looked as if a Pegasus had dropped out of the heavens. When True Colors saw her fallen swan, she balked wildly, refusing to go near him. Mark brought Ikon next; she nickered to her baby. I followed, leading Raven. When Ikon saw Ludwig, she jigged excitedly up to him and bit his neck, pulling the skin away from his body, as a person does when checking to see if a horse is dehydrated. When Ludwig's head didn't move, she walked away and never called to him again. Raven stepped in, playing kissy-face with Ludwig's lower lip. When he didn't kiss her back, she stomped her front foot in temper, then turned away. Only True Colors remained rattled for the rest of that very dark day. Sadness spread over our farm like fog. From the very beginning of his life, we'd done everything we could think of to ensure Ludwig's safety, and still he'd perished; the very definition of bad horse luck. For a very long time, losing our baby horse tainted all our hope with cynicism.

We brought Don Leon home; I couldn't bear Ludwig's empty stall. D.L. had calmed. It was as if his overseas flight had tied his brain in knots, and after five years, the tangles had worked themselves free. He decided that he liked it here. I turned him out in a little pen next to True Colors, whom he had to have right next to him, not in the larger grass paddock, where she could wander out of reach. Clearly, she enjoyed having a job; I hadn't seen such a spring in her stride in years. T.C. and D.L. ate their morning hay nose-to-nose through the wire mesh fence. When he reared and plunged, then threw himself on the ground because Ikon drifted too far into the back pasture for his liking, True Colors stood steadfast, a faithful comfort mare.

Willie died. Cornelia buried him in her back pasture and planted yellow roses on the mound. The blackberries took over, and black bears, displaced by the subdivisions, stripped the fruit. During the summer, her riding horse died suddenly of colic. Old-timers have a saying: *Fine in the morning, dead in the afternoon.* In September, much to my shock and dismay, Cornelia filed for divorce, put her farm up for sale, and moved back to New Mexico.

Today True Colors looks like a raggedy teddy bear. She continues to be Mark's on-again, off-again girlfriend. Though her lungs healed, the burn scars on her face never faded. She never gave up her weapons. Long ago I stopped trying to put a leather halter on her. She still regards commercially grown apples with suspicion and never begs for treats, never thrusts her head over her door looking anxious or wanting, even when I've forgotten to feed her or to take her out to her paddock with the others. She has never jumped a fence or broken a rail or injured herself. She's never menaced another horse. When I neglect to bring her in from the field, she never calls to me or runs in panic. It's the braying of the other horses that reminds me I've forgotten her: She continues to anchor the herd. Despite the pummeling wind, horizontal rain, and record cold temperatures, True Colors wouldn't let me put a stable blanket on her until this winter. She still regards Ikon as her foal, and Ikon regards T.C. as her soulmate. On January 1, 2011, True Colors turned thirty-three.

We soldier on. The fences need mending. All the renovations on our house, the interior and exterior paint, Kolika's wallpapering, and the bridge to the island in the pond need to be made new again. Mark gave up growing rare varieties of potatoes and now grows heritage tomatoes. The developers who cut down all the trees at the bottom of our road to build subdivisions went bankrupt. The meth kitchens moved elsewhere. Joan Crawford seems to have given up on me. Mark and I don't have a moment's regret about not moving to California.

By mid-January, I thought that Colors wouldn't live to see Ikon's spring foal; she was fading. I left Kells's heavy Gore-Tex blanket on her 24/7 and periodically medicated her with bute, aka horse aspirin, hoping to mitigate her arthritis. She hung on through February. In March, in preparation for the foaling, I moved True Colors into Kells's old stall, where I'd been storing hay. Though it is low-ceilinged and dark, she walked in without complaint—perhaps it reminded her of a cave in the high desert of the Okanogan where she took shelter from the driving snow. I can't explain it, but as Ikon neared her due date, True Colors began to thrive. It felt magical. For the first time in years, she started shedding her buffalo-length winter coat in fistfuls. From beneath her teddy-bear fur emerged a sleeker coat; in the clear light of day, I swear I see dapples. She's gained weight and, for the first time, gobbles grain as well as all the hay I put before her. She isn't shy about eating in front of me. Her joint stiffness has abated, and she streaks across the back pasture just like old times. A few years ago, she developed what the vet thought was a sarcoid tumor in the corner of her eye. Now it has all but disappeared. It's as if she reimagined herself a younger horse.

Ikon's bay filly, Madrigal, was born on a snowy night at the beginning of the coldest April in Northwest history. On Baby's first day of turnout, True Colors stood patiently on the other side of the foal paddock fence, waiting to be allowed in.

Though I continue to look for True Colors's replacement, I'm starting to wonder if that old adage is true: *You're lucky to find even one horse in a lifetime who is a pearl without price.*

Every day is a gift.

Ikon's filly, Madrigal, twelve hours old; True Colors stands guard in the next stall. *Mark Bothwell*

True Colors today. *Mark Bothwell*

ACKNOWLEDGMENTS

Brief portions of this memoir previously appeared in slightly different forms in *Horsepeople: Writers and Artists on the Horses They Love*, edited by Michael J. Rosen (Artisan/Workman: New York, 1998); and in *Karamu*, Spring 2005, edited by Olga Abella. My eternal thanks to these editors.

Thanks also to the following people for their input and support: my agent, Robin Straus, and my editor, Leslie Meredith; my riding buddies, Susan Reichlin, Jeni Bolen, MD, Susan Hunter, Barbara Bloxom, Linda Remington, and Mary Nell Harris; and to Thomas Hansen DVM, Ruben Davalos, Jennifer Oliver, Kathryn Ellingson, and Karl Garson. Special thanks to my husband, Mark Bothwell.

ABOUT THE AUTHOR

A poet, novelist, short-story writer, and essayist, **Jana Harris** has been a Washington State Governor's Writers Award winner and a PEN West Center Award finalist. Born in San Francisco and raised in the Pacific Northwest, she worked for six years as the director of Writers in Performance at the Manhattan Theatre Club in New York. She now lives with her husband in the foothills of the Cascade Mountains, where they raise horses. She studies the riding discipline of dressage and competes. Ms. Harris teaches creative writing at the University of Washington. She is the editor and founder of *Switched-on Gutenberg*, one of the first electronic poetry journals in the English-speaking world. Her seventh book of poems, *The Dust of Everyday Life*, an epic concerning the lives of forgotten Northwest pioneers (Sasquatch), won the 1998 Andres Berger Award; she was nominated for the Pulitzer Prize for *Manhattan as a Second Language*. Her poetry book *Oh How Can I Keep On Singing?* was adapted for television.